Hands-On RESTf
Patterns and Best Practices

Design, develop, and deploy highly adaptable, scalable, and
secure RESTful web APIs

Harihara Subramanian
Pethuru Raj

BIRMINGHAM - MUMBAI

Hands-On RESTful API Design Patterns and Best Practices

Commissioning Editor: Richa Tripathi
Acquisition Editor: Chaitanya Nair
Content Development Editor: Tiksha Sarang
Technical Editor: Riddesh Dawne
Copy Editor: Safis Editing
Project Coordinator: Prajakta Naik
Proofreader: Safis Editing
Indexer: Pratik Shirodkar
Graphics: Jisha Chirayil
Production Coordinator: Jyoti Chauhan

First published: January 2019

Production reference: 1310119

Published by Packt Publishing Ltd.
Livery Place
35 Livery Street
Birmingham
B3 2PB, UK.

ISBN 978-1-78899-266-4

www.packtpub.com

`mapt.io`

Mapt is an online digital library that gives you full access to over 5,000 books and videos, as well as industry leading tools to help you plan your personal development and advance your career. For more information, please visit our website.

Why subscribe?

- Spend less time learning and more time coding with practical eBooks and Videos from over 4,000 industry professionals

- Improve your learning with Skill Plans built especially for you

- Get a free eBook or video every month

- Mapt is fully searchable

- Copy and paste, print, and bookmark content

PacktPub.com

Did you know that Packt offers eBook versions of every book published, with PDF and ePub files available? You can upgrade to the eBook version at `www.PacktPub.com` and as a print book customer, you are entitled to a discount on the eBook copy. Get in touch with us at `service@packtpub.com` for more details.

At `www.PacktPub.com`, you can also read a collection of free technical articles, sign up for a range of free newsletters, and receive exclusive discounts and offers on Packt books and eBooks.

Contributors

About the authors

Harihara Subramanian works for the SABRE Corporation as a senior principal software architect. Hari has been working with software development and various software architecture concepts since 1999. He is an energetic and highly focused technology leader with a proven track record in software development, software architecture principles, and implementations. He has been an active contributor to various online and offline forums in different technologies, and focuses his time on technology consulting, software development, microservices architecture (MSA), Service-oriented architecture (SOA), and more.

Pethuru Raj (PhD) works as the chief architect at the Site Reliability Engineering Center of Excellence, Reliance Jio Infocomm Ltd. (RJIL), Bengaluru. Previously, he worked as a cloud infrastructure architect at the IBM Global Cloud Center of Excellence, IBM India, Bengaluru. He also had an extended stint as a TOGAF-certified enterprise architecture consultant in Wipro Consulting's services division and as a lead architect in the corporate research division of Robert Bosch, Bengaluru. He has more than 17 years of IT industry experience and 8 years' research experience.

I sincerely acknowledge and appreciate the moral support provided by my managers, Mr. Anish Shah and Mr. Kiran Thomas, at RJIL, and my esteemed colleagues, Mr. Senthil Arunachalam and Mrs. Vidya Hungud. I also recognize the enhanced tolerance level of my wife (Sweelin Reena) and my sons (Darren Samuel and Darresh Bernie). Above all, I give all the glory and honor to my Lord and Savior, Jesus Christ, for all the strength and knowledge granted to me.

About the reviewers

Kenneth Geisshirt is a software developer based in Copenhagen, Denmark. He is a chemist by education, and a geek by nature. Working for a small database vendor, he implements SDKs for various programming languages (including Java, JavaScript, and so on) for a variety of platforms (including Linux, Android, and macOS). He is a strong believer in open source software, and endeavors to contribute where and when he can. He has authored books on PAM, Git, Linux, and JavaScript, and he writes technical feature articles for computer magazines.

Harshad Kavathiya is a backend software developer with extensive industrial experience. He has worked for companies including Altair Engineering, Honeywell, CoWrks, and many more reputed multinational corporations. He is currently working for Accion Labs as a senior software engineer. Harshad holds an M.Tech in computer science from Manipal Institute of Technology, Manipal. His expertise lies in Python, data structures and algorithms, and MSA. He is passionate about real-time, scalable application development.

Packt is searching for authors like you

If you're interested in becoming an author for Packt, please visit `authors.packtpub.com` and apply today. We have worked with thousands of developers and tech professionals, just like you, to help them share their insight with the global tech community. You can make a general application, apply for a specific hot topic that we are recruiting an author for, or submit your own idea.

Table of Contents

Preface

This book is intended to empower you with knowledge of API design principles and best practices, such that you will be ready to design highly scalable, reusable, adaptable, and secured RESTful APIs. This book also introduces some common and some emerging patterns in the most indispensable domain of RESTful APIs.

RESTful patterns impact various layers of web services that span across multiple functions, such as CRUD operations, databases, presentation layers, applications, and infrastructure layers. Other prominent and dominant patterns in the RESTful domain include communication, integration, orchestration, security, management, software deployment, and delivery. This book will help you become familiar with the most significant patterns, such as client/server discovery, API gateways, API compositions, circuit breakers, enterprise security, content negotiation, endpoint redirection, idempotent capability, API façades, and many more essential patterns.

While this book predominantly covers medium-level to advanced-level topics about RESTful APIs, it covers a few basics of service-oriented architectures and resource-oriented web service architectures as well, to help you gain a better understanding of what's being covered more quickly.

Who this book is for

This book is for anyone who needs a comprehensive yet simple-to-understand resource to help them with their RESTful API design and development skills and expose them highly adoptable RESTful APIs that give insights into best practices and key principles, along with proven RESTful API design patterns.

What this book covers

Chapter 1, *Introduction to the Basics of RESTful Architecture*, intends to refresh your understanding of a few fundamental concepts of the web, its architecture, and the way it is evolving, hoping to lay a firm foundation for RESTful service designs and applications. We will discuss World Wide Web layers and architecture, web API development models, and REST-based service communications. You will also be introduced to service-oriented and resource-oriented architecture principles and characteristics, then move on to the foundations of REST's principles, constraints, qualifiers, and goals.

Chapter 2, *Design Strategy, Guidelines, and Best Practices*, discusses a few essential API design guidelines, such as consistency, standardization, reusability, and accessibility through REST interfaces, aiming to equip API designers with better thought processes for their API modelling. Also, this chapter intends to introduce a few practices for better REST API implementations, along with a few common, but avoidable, mistakes of API strategies.

Chapter 3, *Essential RESTful API Patterns*, provides both information about the concepts and also practical code examples to do with common and fundamental design patterns of RESTful APIs, so that you can better understand and power your RESTful API services. As part of this chapter, you will learn a few common and essential API design patterns, such as content negotiation, URI templates, pagination, Unicode, and more, along with the code implementation of those patterns. Each pattern addresses the RESTful constraints, and helps you to ensure that these essential patterns are accounted for in your API designs and implementations.

Chapter 4, *Advanced RESTful API Patterns*, is the second part of our look at API design patterns, and intends to discuss a few advanced design patterns, versioning, backend for frontend, authorization, idempotence and its importance, and how to power APIs and delight customers with bulk operations APIs.

Chapter 5, *Microservice API Gateways*, mainly talks about the crucial contributions of API gateway solutions to making microservices vital to producing enterprise-scale, mission-critical, cloud-hosted, event-driven, production-grade, and business-centric applications. We discuss popular API gateway solutions in this chapter and also look at the implementation of an aggregation service through the API gateway.

Chapter 6, *RESTful Services API Testing and Security*, intends to take you on an API testing journey, looking at types of API tests, challenges in API testing, and security in API testing. You will get a glimpse of various API testing tools, API security tools, and frameworks, and also learn how you can expose any security issues and API vulnerabilities as part of API testing, quality, and security measures.

Chapter 7, *RESTful Service Composition for Smart Applications*, is specially crafted to tell you all about the contributions of the RESTful services paradigm toward designing, developing, and deploying next-generation microservices-centric and enterprise-scale applications. It looks at how RESTful services that are capable of finding and binding with one another results in process-aware, business-critical, and people-centric composite services. You will understand the need for service composition, various compositions methods such as orchestration and choreography, and also the use of hybrid versions of orchestration and choreography for smarter applications.

Chapter 8, *RESTful API Design Tips*, discusses the design patterns and best practices needed for building competent and compatible REST APIs that can easily keep up with technological and business changes. This chapter deals with the importance of APIs; API design patterns and best practices; API security guidelines; the various tools and associated platforms of API design, development, integration, security, and management; and trends in the API-driven digital world.

Chapter 9, *A More In-depth View of the RESTful Services Paradigm*, focuses on conveying the emerging techniques and tips for producing RESTful services and their corresponding APIs. We discuss methodologies such as software-defined and driven world, and emerging application types that help in quick and easy deployments of APIs. Also, this chapter discusses topics such as the REST paradigm for application modernization and integration, RESTful services for digital transformation and intelligence, and the best practices for REST-based microservices.

Chapter 10, *Frameworks, Standard Languages, and Toolkits*, introduces you to a few prominent frameworks that can come in handy when deciding on the right framework for your API development needs. It discusses a few prominent frameworks for app developers who want to kick-start their RESTful APIs and microservices with their acquainted programming languages. This chapter is an attempt to provide you with information on a few programming language-friendly frameworks so that you can pick the most suitable framework for your RESTful API development needs. Also, this chapter has a reference table for various frameworks and their supported languages, along with their prominent features.

Chapter 11, *Legacy Modernization to Microservices-Centric Apps*, discusses how **microservices architectures (MSAs)** are the way forward for modern applications that are highly nimble, versatile, and resilient. This chapter provides the reasons for legacy application modernization, delineating why applications have to be modernized to be migrated and run in cloud environments, discussing how the combination of microservices and containers is the best way to achieve legacy modernization, and detailing legacy modernization methodologies.

To get the most out of this book

As this book presents many web services and RESTful services concepts, there are no specific requirements for you to follow; however, if you want to run and execute the code samples provided in the book (which you should), then you need a basic understanding of Java programming languages, Maven, or knowledge of any build tools.

The chapters with sample code have clear explanations of how to run and test the samples, and come with the build and run scripts as well.

Download the example code files

You can download the example code files for this book from your account at `www.packtpub.com`. If you purchased this book elsewhere, you can visit `www.packtpub.com/support` and register to have the files emailed directly to you.

You can download the code files by following these steps:

1. Log in or register at `www.packtpub.com`.
2. Select the **SUPPORT** tab.
3. Click on **Code Downloads & Errata**.
4. Enter the name of the book in the **Search** box and follow the onscreen instructions.

Once the file is downloaded, please make sure that you unzip or extract the folder using the latest version of the following software:

- WinRAR/7-Zip for Windows
- Zipeg/iZip/UnRarX for Mac
- 7-Zip/PeaZip for Linux

The code bundle for the book is also hosted on GitHub at `https://github.com/ PacktPublishing/Hands-On-RESTful-API-Design-Patterns-and-Best-Practices`. In case there's an update to the code, it will be updated on the existing GitHub repository.

We also have other code bundles from our rich catalog of books and videos available at `https://github.com/PacktPublishing/`. Check them out!

Conventions used

There are a number of text conventions used throughout this book.

CodeInText: Indicates code words in text, database table names, folder names, filenames, file extensions, pathnames, dummy URLs, user input, and Twitter handles. Here is an example: "The four basic HTTP operations: GET, POST, PUT, and DELETE."

A block of code is set as follows:

```
@GetMapping({"/v1/investors","/v1.1/investors","/v2/investors"})
    public List<Investor> fetchAllInvestors()
    {
        return investorService.fetchAllInvestors();
    }
```

When we wish to draw your attention to a particular part of a code block, the relevant lines or items are set in bold:

```
public interface DeleteServiceFacade {
    boolean deleteAStock(String investorId, String stockTobeDeletedSymbol);
    boolean deleteStocksInBulk(String investorId, List<String>
stocksSymbolsList);
}
```

Any command-line input or output is written as follows:

```
$ mkdir css
$ cd css
```

Bold: Indicates a new term, an important word, or words that you see onscreen. For example, words in menus or dialog boxes appear in the text like this. Here is an example: "The **Pipeline** entity is entirely responsible for orchestrating control and data flows"

Warnings or important notes appear like this.

Tips and tricks appear like this.

Get in touch

Feedback from our readers is always welcome.

General feedback: Email `feedback@packtpub.com` and mention the book title in the subject of your message. If you have questions about any aspect of this book, please email us at `questions@packtpub.com`.

Errata: Although we have taken every care to ensure the accuracy of our content, mistakes do happen. If you have found a mistake in this book, we would be grateful if you would report this to us. Please visit `www.packtpub.com/submit-errata`, selecting your book, clicking on the Errata Submission Form link, and entering the details.

Piracy: If you come across any illegal copies of our works in any form on the Internet, we would be grateful if you would provide us with the location address or website name. Please contact us at `copyright@packtpub.com` with a link to the material.

If you are interested in becoming an author: If there is a topic that you have expertise in and you are interested in either writing or contributing to a book, please visit `authors.packtpub.com`.

Reviews

Please leave a review. Once you have read and used this book, why not leave a review on the site that you purchased it from? Potential readers can then see and use your unbiased opinion to make purchase decisions, we at Packt can understand what you think about our products, and our authors can see your feedback on their book. Thank you!

For more information about Packt, please visit `packtpub.com`.

Introduction to the Basics of RESTful Architecture

A web service is a software service or a software functionality provided by one set of computing devices to another set of computing devices. These devices communicate using established or standardized communication protocols through the **World Wide Web (WWW)**.

This chapter intends to refresh your understanding of a few fundamental concepts of the web and its architecture, and the way it is evolving, hoping to lay a firm foundation for RESTful service designs and applications. The following topics are covered in this chapter:

- A brief history of the WWW and its evolution
- WWW layers and architecture
- Web API development models and REST-based service communication
- A brief introduction to service-oriented architecture
- Resource-oriented architecture principles and characteristics
- Introduction to REST
- REST constraints
- RESTful qualifiers
- REST architecture goals

Technical requirements

As this book deals with intermediate to advanced topics of RESTful design patterns, we expect you to have a good understanding of web service concepts and their unique functions. As mentioned earlier, this chapter is an attempt to refresh your understanding of various fundamental concepts of the WWW, its evolution, and the types of web services it offers, so there are no formal technical requirements for this chapter.

Evolution of web technologies

Generally, the aim of this book is to provide more elaborate RESTful patterns; however, this section intends to give you a quick introduction to web services and their evolution since the early 1990s, giving you exciting facts about Web 1.0 through to Web 3.0, and then moving on to details about **service-oriented architecture (SOA)** and **resource-oriented architecture (ROA)**.

As you are aware, today's web is a universe in itself, with a massive amount of interlinked web-based apps, images, videos, photos, and various interactive content. Which web technologies have made this possible, where did it start, how has it evolved over time, and how does it enable web app developers to develop amazing and interactive web experiences?

The following diagram provides a brief overview of the **WWW** and its evolution over time. Please note that each web version has its enabling technologies mentioned in the corresponding box:

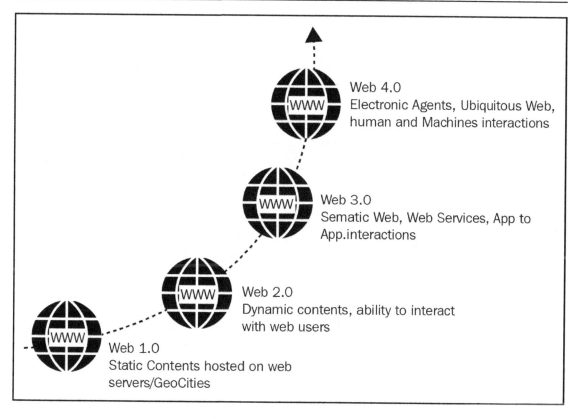

Let's discuss **Web 3.0** more and focus on web services and their evolution as part of the third generation.

Learning about Web 3.0

The following sections focus on Web 3.0 and the evolution and history of web services.

Web 3.0 is generally referred to as executing semantic web, or read-write-execute web. Web 3.0 decentralizes services such as search, social media, and chat applications that are dependent on a single organization to function. Semantic and web services are the primary constituents of Web 3.0.

The following diagram depicts layers of typical Web 3.0 constructs. The semantic web layers are **Static Web**, **Translations**, and **Rich Internet Applications (RIA)** or **Rich Web** built on top of the internet:

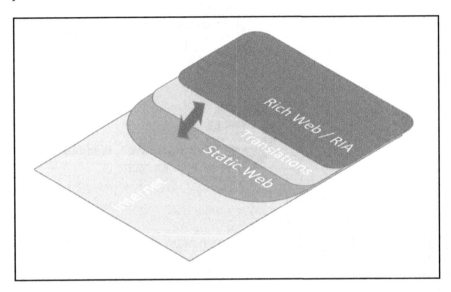

The layered structure of Web 3.0

This data-driven web adjusts according to the user's searches, for instance, if a user searches for architecture patterns, the advertisements shown are more relevant to architecture and patterns; it even remembers your last search and combines the last searched queries as well. Interesting isn't it?

What you see in the following diagram is a Web 3.0 stack, with various building blocks as URI, Unicode representations, syntax (XML/JSON), RDFS taxonomies, and so on; they constitute a Web 3.0 stack:

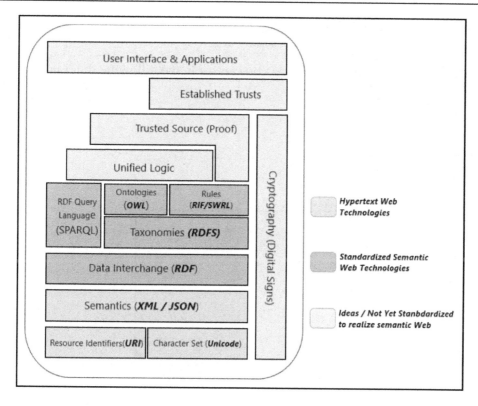

Web 3.0 stack (Ref: https://www.w3.org/DesignIssues/w3.org)

Let's move on to the web service architecture, the specifications, and the communication protocols, as they are the fundamentals before we move to ROA, SOA, and **Representational State Transfer (REST)** or RESTful services.

Learning about web service architecture

Web services are a method of communication between two computing devices over a network, and the communication happens in standardized ways (and specifications) for the integration of heterogeneous web applications using XML/JSON, SOAP, WSDL, and UDDI. XML/JSON is the data format that provides metadata for the data that it contains; SOAP is used to transfer data; WSDL is used for defining available services to be consumed, and UDDI will have the list of services available.

Web services architecture (WSA) mandates the presence of certain characteristics, and suggests a few optional ones, when developing any web service.

WSA consists of three significant roles, as you can see in the following diagram, and they are as follow:

- **Service Provider**
- **Service Consumer**
- **Service Broker**

This is shown in the following diagram:

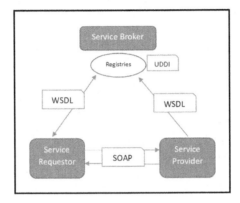

The **Service Requestor** finds the **Service Provider** through **UDDI**, and contacts the provider using the **Simple Object Access Protocol (SOAP)**. The **Service Provider** then validates the service request and responds to the requestor with XML/JSON as a service response.

Discussing the web API

So far, we have discussed the fundamentals of the client-server/web services paradigm, and the way they communicate with standard protocols; however, we are yet to touch upon REST-based communication and after all, that's what this book is about. This section will cover the introduction of web APIs, and how a web API is a development model for web services. The communication between the devices is REST-based. RESTful APIs do not use/require XML- based web service protocols, such as SOAP or WSDL, to support their interfaces, but they use simplified representations instead.

The following diagram depicts the web **API** and their simplified representations as the client side and the server side are exposed to each other through high-level interfaces:

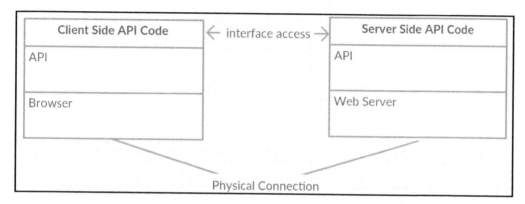

So the web **API,** as shown in the preceding diagram, is available on both the client side and the server side. The client-side interfaces are generally exposed as JavaScript or browser plugins, and the server-side interfaces are generally exposed through the web as JSON/XML. Some of the key terminologies that we will come across concerning web APIs are endpoint, **uniform resource identifier** (URI), and resources.

The web API is an **application programming interface** (API) for *either* a web server or for a web browser. So, Web API is a concept or methodology for accessing any API (available over the web) through the HTTP protocol. There are many categories of APIs, SOAP, XML-RPC, JSON-RPC, REST, and so on. APIs can be developed with any programming language such as Java, .NET, and many more.

So now you have got an idea of what is a Web API is and where REST API development fits into the Web API landscape, let's move on and see more details of SOA, ROA, REST, RESTful APIs, and their key constituents in the following sections.

Learning about service-oriented architecture

Service-oriented architecture is an architectural style of web services. It defines some standards and lays down best approaches to design and develop a web service. Any web service is the logical representation of repeatable business activities that have a specified outcome, such as retrieving a weather report for a particular city, accessing stock prices for a given stock, updating a record to an inventory service, and so on. SOA is self-contained, and also provides guidelines to combine a service with other services as well. Another fact about SOA is that it is a black box (or abstract) to the service consumer who consumes it.

In short, SOA is essentially a collection of services, those services communicate with each other, and a service is an operation or a function that is well defined, self-contained, and independent of other service contexts and states. Services are applications hosted on application servers and interact with other applications through interfaces.

 SOA is not a technology or a programming language; it's a set of principles, procedures, and methodologies to develop a software application.

Learning about resource-oriented architecture

Resource-oriented architecture is a foundation of the semantic web (please refer to the *Web 3.0* section of this chapter). The idea of ROA is to use basic, well-understood, and well-known web technologies (HTTP, URI, and XML) along with the core design principles.

As we all know, the primary focus of web services is to connect information systems, and ROA defines a structural design or set of guidelines to support and implement interactions within any connected resources. Any business entity can be represented as a resource, and it can be made accessible through a URI.

For example, in an organization's human resource system, each employee is an entity, and salary, employee details, and profiles are associations (descriptors) of that entity.

The following is a quick comparison table for object-oriented and resource-oriented concepts, and it gives a quick insight as to what ROA is:

Objects in object-oriented architecture	Resources in ROA
Every entity is defined as an object	Entities are services
An object has attributes and actions	A service has descriptions and contracts
Objects need to maintain state to interact	Interacts over the network with a defined location or address

Resource-oriented design

The resource-oriented design section intends to walk you through the ROA design guidelines, design principles, and characteristics, along with its properties as well. Having introduced ROA properties, we will look at REST architecture in subsequent sections.

ROA-based web services describe a self-discoverable entity, and modeling is based on its logical form (unlike services, as they are based on the technical form).

Let's look at the basic blocks of ROA such as resources, representations, and so on in the following diagram:

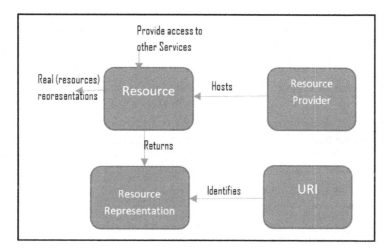

The blocks in the preceding diagram represent the typical structure of ROA and give an idea of how resources are consumed by the service consumers.

Let's briefly consider the concepts and properties of ROA, as follows:

- **Resource providers**: Resource providers expose the resources for the service consumers to invoke the services with HTTP methods. Microsoft Azure and Amazon AWS are simple examples of resource providers.
- **Resource**: A resource is an explicit reference to an entity that can be identified and assigned and, most importantly, referenced as a resource. Some examples of resources could be servers, devices, web pages, JavaScript, or the latest version of software, the latest defect in software, a directory or list of information about an organization, and so on.
- **Resource name**: The resource name is the unique name or identification for the resource. So, no two resources can point to the same data. For instance, the latest version of software is 2.0.9.
- **Resource representation**: Resource representation is the useful information about the current state of a resource, specified with a specific format, in a specific language.

- **Resource link and connectedness**: Represents (linkage) another resource or the resource itself. Connectedness is all about how reliable and relevant the resource's links are.
- **Resource interface**: The resource interface is an interface for accessing the resource and handling its state.
- **Addressability**: Addressability is exposing datasets or functionalities as a resource, and the addressability of a resource happens through URIs.
- **Statelessness**: Statelessness is maintaining the isolation and independence of client and server states. Every request from the client should be self-contained.
- **The uniform interface**: Every service needs to use the HTTP interface the same way, such as GET, POST, PUT, DELETE, and so on. The uniform interface simply means using some common nomenclature that is interpreted the same way across the web. For example, GET does mean get (read) something.

The following table summarizes the HTTP operations that can be used to implement an ROA-based web service:

HTTP operation	Description
GET	Read the resource representations
PUT	Create a new resource
DELETE	Delete the resource (optionally linked resource as well)
POST	Modify the resource
HEAD	Meta information of the resource

The preceding table shows the HTTP methods to implement ROA.

The benefits of ROA

The following are the benefits of ROA:

- **Independent of client contracts**: Free from interface agreements/contract formulations, that is, no need to formulate the contact as the entire web is based on HTTP operations.
- **Explicit state**: As the resource itself represents states, servers won't receive unknown application specific payloads; the server does not have to keep track of the client who called the server, and also the client doesn't need to know which server it has talked to.

- **Scalability and performance**: Scalability with ROA is shown by characteristics such as no contract boundaries, explicit states, and freeing up the clients from the server's stickiness(session). The performance improvement regarding response time for the ROA caching, load-balancing, indexing, and searching play a significant role in improving performance.

> A process of creating an affinity between a client and a specific server by a load balancer is called **session stickiness**.
>
> A contract or agreement is fundamentally a collection of metadata that defines many aspects of an underlying software program.

Beginning with REST

So far, we have looked at ROA and a set of guidelines, such as statelessness, resources, addressability, uniform resources, and so on. Those guidelines are the fundamental implementation of REST architecture. As this book is all about RESTful patterns, we are going to explore more about the REST architectural style in this section.

The REST concepts were submitted as a PhD dissertation by Roy Fielding. The fundamental principle of REST is to use the **HTTP** protocol for data communication (between distributed hypermedia systems), and it revolves around the concept of resources where each and every component considered as a resource, and those resources are accessed by the common interfaces using **HTTP** methods:

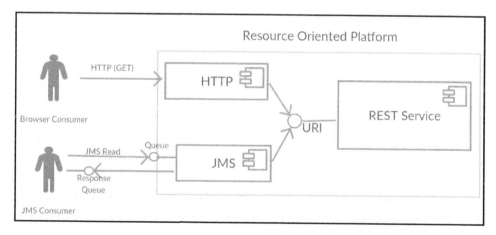

An example implementation of an ROA/REST service

The preceding diagram shows you where REST stands in the ROA architecture and how it can be accessed by different consumers.

REST is an architectural style and not a programming language or technology. It provides guidelines for distributed systems to communicate directly using the existing principles and protocols of the web to create web services and APIs, without the need for SOAP or any other sophisticated protocols.

The REST architecture is simple and provides access to resources so that the REST client accesses and renders the resources on the client side. In REST style, URI or Global IDs helps to identify each resource. As you know REST uses several resources representations to represent its type such as XML, JSON, Text, images and so on.

REST architecture style constraints

There are design rules that are applied to establish the different characteristics of the REST architectural style, which are referred to as REST constraints:

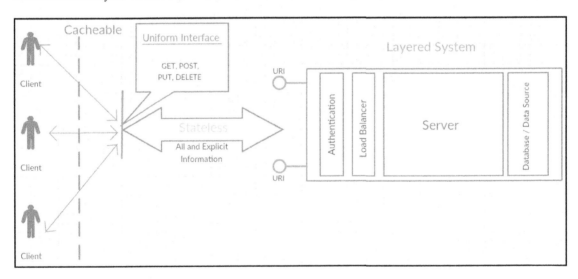

REST architectural style constraints

The preceding diagram depicts REST constraints in a typical web/internet-based application. The following are the REST constraints:

- Client-server
- Statelessness

- Cacheable
- Uniform interface
- Layered systems
- Code on demand

Beginning with client-server

The client-server architecture or model helps in the separation of concerns between the user interface and data storage:

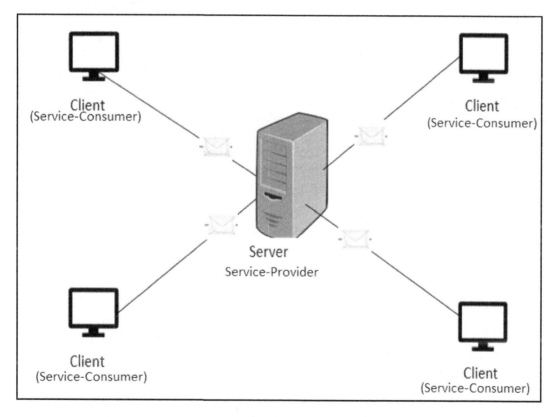

The client and server

Let's discuss the client and server in the context of ROA as follows:

- **Client**: It is the component that is the requestor of a service and sends requests for various types of services to the server

- **Server**: It is the component that is the service provider and continuously provides services to the client as per the requests

Clients and servers typically comprise distributed systems that communicate over a network.

The client in client-server architecture

There is no upper bound on the number of clients that can be serviced by a single server. It is also not mandatory that the client and server should reside in separate systems. Both client and server can reside in the same system, based on the hardware configuration of the system and the type of functionality or service provided by the server. The communication between client and server happens through the exchange of messages using a request-response pattern. The client basically sends a request for a service, and the server returns a response. This request-response pattern of communication is an excellent example of inter-process communication. For this communication to happen efficiently, it is necessary to have a well-defined communication protocol that lays down the rules of communication, such as the format of request messages, response messages, error handling, and so on. All communication protocols that are used for client-server communication work in the application layer of the protocol stack. To further streamline the process of client-server communication, the server sometimes implements a specific API that can be used by the client for accessing any specific service from the server.

The service in client-server architecture

The term service used in the context of client-server architecture refers to the abstraction of a resource. The resource could be of any type and based on the one provided by the server (service); the server is named accordingly. For example, if the server provides web pages, it is called a **web server**, and if the server provides files, it is called a **file server**, and so on. A server can receive requests from any number of clients at a specific point in time. But any server will have its own limitations about its processing capabilities. Often, it becomes necessary for a server to prioritize the incoming requests and service them as per their priority. The scheduling system present in the server helps the server with the assignment of priorities.

Client-server benefits are in addition to separation of concerns and help with the following:

- Improving the portability of the user interface
- Improving scalability by simplifying server implementations
- Developing with standalone, independent testable components

Understanding statelessness

The statelessness constraint helps services to be more scalable and reliable. Statelessness, in the REST context, means that all the client requests to the server carry all the information as explicit (stated), so that the server understands the requests, treats them as independent, and those client requests keep the server independent of any stored contexts. Keeping the session state within the client is important to manage this constraint in the services.

The following diagram shows the **Service Consumer** (client) and the **Service States** are independent and managed within the client and server respectively:

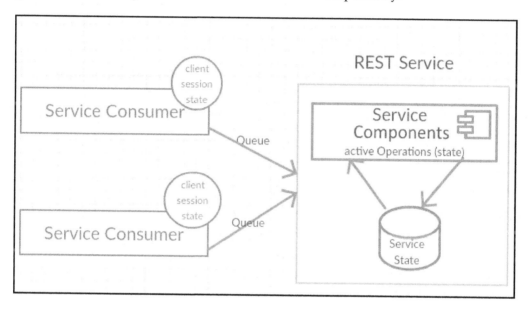

Statelessness (managing states independently)

The statelessness constraint imposes significant restrictions on the kind of communications allowed between services and consumers, to achieves its design goals. The following are the restrictions to achieve statelessness:

- It is the complete responsibility of the client to store and handle all the application states and the related information on the client side.
- The client is responsible for sending any state information to the server whenever it's needed.
- No session stickiness or session affinity on the server for the calling request (client).

- The server also needs to include any necessary information that the client may need to create a state on its side.
- HTTP interactions involve two kinds of states, application state and resource state, and statelessness applies to both. Let's see how the statelessness constraint is handled in each state:
    - **Application state:** The data that is stored on the server side and helps to identify the incoming client request, using the previous interaction details with current context information
    - **Resource state:** This is referred to as a resource representation, and it is independent of the client (the client doesn't need to know this state unless it is available as response is needed), and this is the current state of the server at any given point in time

 The statelessness constraint of REST applies to the application state, that is, being free only on the application state and nothing to do with resource state. Twitter's API is the best example of a stateless service (GET: https://api.twitter.com/1.1/direct_messages.json?since_id =xxx&count=x).

Advantages and disadvantages of statelessness

The following are some advantages of statelessness:

- As the server does not need to manage any session, deploying the services to any number of servers is possible, and so scalability will never be a problem
- No states equals less complexity; no session (state) synchronize logic to handle at the server side
- As the service calls (requests) can be cached by the underlying application, the statelessness constraint brings down the server's response time, that is, it improves performance with regard to response time
- Seamless integration/implementation with HTTP protocols is possible as HTTP is itself a stateless protocol
- Improves visibility as each request is its own resource and can be treated as an independent request
- Improves reliability as it can recover from partial failures

The following are some disadvantages of statelessness:

- Increase per-interaction overhead
- Each request of webservices needs to get additional information so that it get parsed (interpreted) so that the server understands the client state from the incoming request and takes care of the client / server sessions if needed

Caching constraint in REST

Caching is the ability to store frequently accessed data (a response in this context) to serve the client requests, and never having to generate the same response more than once until it needs to be. Well-managed caching eliminates partial or complete client-server interactions and still serves the client with the expected response. Obviously, caching brings scalability and also performance benefits with faster response times and reduced server load.

As you can see in the next diagram, the service consumer (**Client**) receives the response from the cache and not from the server itself, and a few other responses are directly from the server as well. So, caching helps with the partial or complete elimination of some interactions between the service consumers and so helps to improve efficiency and performance (reduced latency time in response):

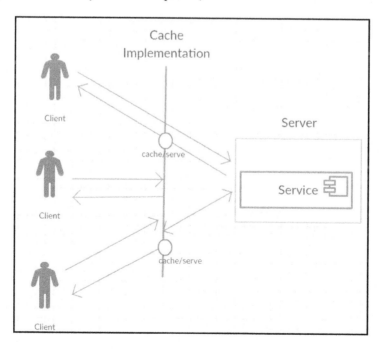

There are different caching strategies or mechanisms available, such as browser caches, proxy caches, and gateway caches (reverse-proxy), and there are several ways that we can control the cache behavior, such as through pragma, expiration tags, and so on. The following table gives a glimpse of the various cache control headers one use to can fine-tune cache behaviors:

Headers	Description	Samples
Expires	Header attribute to represent date/time after which the response is considered stale	Expires: Fri, 12 Jan 2018 18:00:09 GMT
Cache-control	A header that defines various directives (for both requests and responses) that are followed by caching mechanisms	`Max age=4500`, cache-extension
E-Tag	Unique identifier for server resource states	ETag:`uqv2309u324klm`
Last-modified	Response header helps to identify the time the response was generated	Last-modified: Fri, 12 Jan 2018 18:00:09 GMT

For more about cache-control directives. Please refer to `https://tools.ietf.org/html/rfc2616#section-14.9`.

Benefits of caching

Obviously, there are a lot of benefits to caching frequently accessed data, and the following are the significant ones:

- Reduced bandwidth
- Reduced latency (faster response time)
- Reduced load on the server
- Hide network failures and serve a client with the response

The cache constraint builds upon the client-server and stateless ones, with the requirement that responses are implicitly or explicitly labeled as cacheable or non-cacheable.

Understanding the uniform interface

As we mentioned earlier in the uniform interface section as part of ROA, REST-based services can use the HTTP interface, such as GET, POST, PUT, DELETE, and so on, to maintain uniformity across the web. The intention of a uniform interface is to retain some common vocabulary across the internet. For example, GET does mean to get (read) something from the server. The services can independently evolve as their interfaces simplify and decouple the architecture, and the uniform interface brings a uniform vocabulary to those resources as well. The following diagram depicts the combination of **HTTP Methods** and the **Resource Names** for **Uniform Interfaces**:

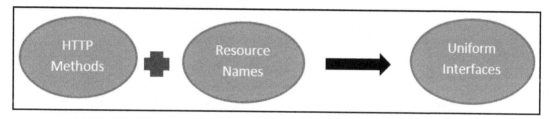

There are four guiding principles suggested by Fielding that constitute the necessary constraints to satisfy the uniform interface, and they are as follows:

- Identification of resources
- Manipulation of resources
- Self-descriptive messages
- Hypermedia as the engine of application state

We will see each constraint in detail in the following sections.

Identification of resources

As we have seen in earlier sections, a resource represents a named entity in a web application, and it is usually a **Uniform Resource Locator** (URL). So, an entity can be identified and assigned as a resource by an explicit reference to it.

A URL in a web application is usually a link, and it is in fact a URI. For example, a home page URI, https://developer.twitter.com, uniquely identifies the concept of a specific website's root resource. In REST constraints, the URIs we use are described as follows:

- The semantics of the mapping of the URI to a resource must not change. For instance, Twitter's https://api.twitter.com/1.1/statuses/retweets/:id.json as a URI may never change, and of course the contents or values will keep improving, according to the latest updates.

- Resource identification is independent of its values so two resources could point to the same data at some point, but they are not the same resource.
- For example, URI 1, `https://api.twitter.com/1.1/statuses/retweets/:id.json`, returns a collection up to 100 of the most recent retweets of a tweet (specified by the ID).
- The other URI 2, `https://api.twitter.com/1.1/statuses/retweeters/ids.json`, responds with a collection of 100 user IDs (maximum) belonging to users who have retweeted the tweet (specified by the ID parameter).

 The second method offers similar data to the first method (statuses/retweets) and may produce the same results or combinations, but both methods certainly represent a different resource.

- URIs bring benefits such as only one way to access a resource, dynamic media types for resource responses (serve the media type at the time it is requested) with the help of the **Accept** headers, and clients accessing those dynamic resources do not need to change any identifiers if any change is made in the response content type.

Manipulation of resources

Resources, once identified, can be returned by the server in a different format, such as JSON, XML, HTML, PNG, SVG, and so on. These formats are a representation of the identified resources, and the client will understand the list of possible well-defined formats or media types (also called **Multipurpose Internet Mail Extension (MIME)**) from the headers.

The resource's representation is manipulated or processed by clients. The application needs to support more than one representation of the same resource and the same URI; in other words, the same exact resource is represented by different clients in different ways.

Let's take an example; a document might be represented as JSON to an automated program, but as HTML to a web browser. The purpose of these representations is to provide a way to interact with the resource, and so the clients can indicate the intended representations they wish to receive.

The preceding conceptual distinction allows the resource to be represented in different ways without changing its identifiers. It is possible with the HTTP header (**Accept**) getting passed to the server by the clients in each request. The resources are updated or added by sending representations from the client by the RESTful application. The following diagram is a sample representation format, captured for a sample request from my Postman tool:

Text

Text (text/plain)

JSON (application/json)

Javascript (application/javascript)

XML (application/xml)

XML (text/xml)

HTML (text/html)

So, the decoupling of the resource's representation from the URI is one of the crucial aspects of REST.

The following list shows various content-type representation formats (as headers) that one can use in the request or response:

- Text/HTML, text/CSS, text/JavaScript
- Application/XML, application/JSON, application/x-www-form-urlencoded
- Image (SVG, JPG, PNG, and so on)

Postman is a tool that helps us to interact with REST APIs. It offers a very friendly user interface that can quickly test the APIs by constructing requests and reading responses. Chapter 6, *RESTful Services API Testing and Security* of this book provides more information about the Postman tool and its wider abilities to test RESTful APIs.

Self-descriptive messages

A client's request and server's response are messages; those messages should be stateless and self-descriptive. They can have a body and metadata. RESTful applications operate on the notion of constrained message types (GET, HEAD, OPTIONS, PUT, POST, and DELETE) and they are fully understood by both the server and the client.

A resource's desired state can be represented within a client's request message. A resource's current state may be embodied within the response message that comes back from a server. As an example, a wiki page editor client may use a request message to transfer a representation that suggests a page update (new state) for a server-managed web page (resource). It is up to the server to accept or deny the client's request.

Self-descriptive messages may include metadata to convey additional details regarding the resource state, the representation format and size, and even the message itself. An HTTP message provides headers for organizing the various types of metadata into uniform fields. The following diagram depicts a sample request and its headers, and the server response for the same request along with its headers:

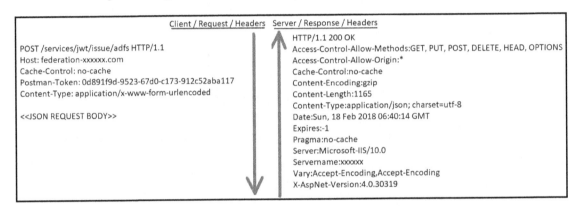

So a self-descriptive message in REST style is all about not maintaining state between client and server, and needs to carry enough information about itself or explain with explicit states. So in the following table, you can see the self-descriptive messages with examples:

Resource	GET	PUT	POST	DELETE
`booktitles.com/resources`	Get all resources belonging to the collection	Replace with another collection	Create the collection	Delete the whole collection
`booktitles.com/resources/title18`	Lookup for title 18	Modify title 18	Create new resource as title 18	Delete title 18

Hypermedia as the Engine of Application State

Hypermedia as the Engine of Application State (HATEOAS) is one of the most critical constraints; without addressing it, services cannot be termed RESTful services. However, before we get into the details of HATEOAS, let's get a brief idea about the **Richardson Maturity Model (RMM)** as it is an essential reference and serves as a guide to any RESTful services to follow the HATEOAS constraints.

The RMM is a model developed by Leonard Richardson, and it breaks down the principal elements of the REST approach to **Resources, HTTP Verbs**, and **Hypermedia Controls**. The following diagram depicts the RMM's four levels, and those levels are used to grade the APIs; that is, the better the API adheres to these constraints, the higher the scores are:

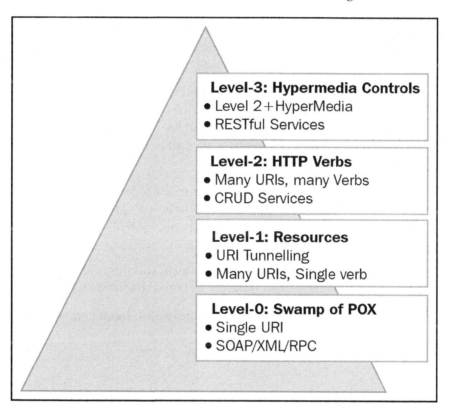

So, an API is fully qualified to be a RESTful API only when it scores **Level-3**. We will see more guidelines for how APIs can be RESTful APIs later in this chapter. However, now you know why we touched on the RMM here before we move on to HATEOAS.

Once the client gets the initial response to its resource request from the server, it should be able to move to the next application state by picking up hyperlinks from the same received response.

Let's take an example to explain the preceding statement. Say a client will POST a representation of a new TODO item to the server, then the state of the Task Manager application will change by growing the list of the TODO item and both POST and GET are accomplished via hypermedia links.

Resource representations are shared by sending self-descriptive messages to any identified resources. Then, they change the state of the application, and the client with the received hypermedia links will move to the next application state.

In an HTML browser, GET methods are accomplished by clicking on anchor tags (<a>) that have an HREF attribute, and HREF contains a resource URI. POST methods are achieved by pressing the **Submit** button within a <form> tag that has an action URI attribute. The anchor (<a>) and form (<form>) tag elements were sent to the client as part of the representation of the client requested resource.

The web contracts (sharing representations) are expressed regarding media types; a client that calls the service would know the media types and how to process the content as well. So the application enables the server to inform the client of possible ways to change its application state via hypermedia.

Some media types work well (in harmony) with the web, and they are called **hypermedia** formats. The formats that host URIs and links are hypermedia formats.

 Plain old XML is not hypermedia-friendly as it doesn't carry the links and protocols.

The following diagram depicts a sample JSON response from a server without and then
With HATEOAS (with links and HREFs):

```
Without HATEOAS:                            With HATEOAS:

1    Request:                           1    Request:
2    [Headers]                          2    [Headers]
3    user: jim                          3    user: jim
4    roles: USER                        4    roles: USER
5    GET: /items/1234                   5    GET: /items/1234
6    Response:                          6    Response:
7    HTTP 1.1 200                       7    HTTP 1.1 200
8    {                                  8    {
9        "id" : 1234,                   9        "id" : 1234,
10       "description" : "FooBar TV",    10       "description" : "FooBar TV",
11       "image" : "fooBarTv.jpg",       11       "image" : "fooBarTv.jpg",
12       "price" : 50.00,                12       "price" : 50.00,
13       "owner" : "jim"                 13       "links" : [
14   }                                   14           {
                                         15               "rel" : "modify",
                                         16               "href" : "/items/1234"
                                         17           },
                                         18           {
                                         19               "rel" : "delete",
                                         20               "href" : "/items/1234"
                                         21           }
                                         22       ]
                                         23   }
                                         24 }
```

Before we conclude this section, let's have a recap of HATEOAS:

- HATEOAS means an application state representation (resource) that includes
  links to related resources. The absence or presence of a link on a page is an
  essential part of the resource's current state and so is essential for the RESTful
  APIs.

- A URI is a differentiator of REST architectural style, and defining the URIs is
  really critical, as it will be around for a very long time. So it is crucial to evaluate
  the links (when they change), keeping their future in mind, or put it in a simpler
  way, the *URI should stay the same regardless of the many changes its representations go
  through*. There is an interesting read about this at
  `https://www.w3.org/Provider/Style/URI.html.en`; it supports this point in
  great detail, and we encourage you to have a look.

Layered systems

In general, a layered system consists of layers with different units of functionality. The essential characteristics of layered systems are that a Layer communicates by means of pre-defined interfaces and communicate only with the layer above or layer below, and the layers above rely on the layers below to it to perform its functions. Layers can be added, removed, modified, or reordered as the architecture evolves. Consider the following diagram of layers:

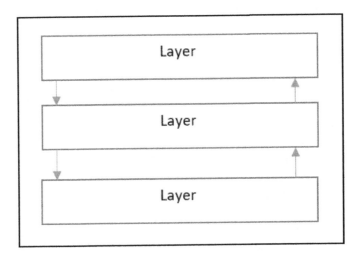

So, let's start with an example. The REST style allows services to make use of a layered system architecture where we deploy the REST APIs on server A, store data on server B, and authenticate with server C. The client calling the REST API doesn't have any knowledge of the servers the services use:

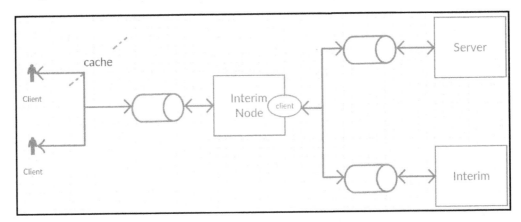

The REST architectural style suggests services can consist of multiple architectural layers. The layers will have published service contracts or intermediaries. The logic within a given layer cannot have knowledge beyond the immediate layers above or below it within the solution hierarchy.

 Intermediaries are the layers present between the client and the server and can be added or removed, more importantly, without changing the interfaces between components.

The intermediaries have the following properties:

- Intermediaries can be event-driven middleware components to establish processing layers between consumers and services
- They can be proxies (selected by the client to provide interfaces with data translation services, enhanced performance, or security protections)
- They can be gateways as well (chosen by the server or the network, and used for data translation, security enforcement, and performance enhancements)

A client may not be able to tell whether it is connected to the services directly with the server endpoint, or to an intermediary before reaching the actual server. Intermediary servers help to attain improved system scalability by having load balancers and shared caches. Layers may also enforce security policies for their calling clients.

It would be helpful for us to understand a few applications of layered systems (design), so let's look at the following points:

- Enables the service clients to invoke the services; the service that is called by the client doesn't reveal any information about other services it's using to process the client requests. In other words, the service consumer (client) only knows about the service it directly calls and doesn't know about other services consumed by the called service to process its requests.
- The messages between the client and the server are processed by intermediaries helping to free the clients from the runtime message processing logic and making them unaware of how those messages are processed in other layers as well.

- It's very critical for stability and scalability to add or remove layers in the layered system without any changes to the service consumers.
- Request and response messages won't divulge any details to the recipients about which layer the message comes from.

While layered systems bring additional latency and overhead as a drawback, there are trade-offs that are the benefits of layers and layered system designs, as follows:

- Encapsulates legacy services
- Introduces intermediaries
- Limits system complexity
- Improves scalability

Code on demand

In distributed computing, **code on demand** (COD) is any technology that enables the server to send the software code to the clients to be executed on the client computer upon request from the client's software. Some well-known examples of the COD paradigm on the web are Java applets, the Adobe ActionScript language for the Flash player, and JavaScript.

The following can also be called the advantages of COD:

- COD is the optional constraint of REST and intends to allow business logic within the client web browser, applets, JavaScript, and ActionScript (Flash). I think video on demand sites are good examples of COD, as the video data files are downloaded and played according to the client system's specifications.
- Only one optional constraint according to REST architectural style and it is COD. COD allow it clients to be flexible because the server that decides how specific items need to be handled on the client side. For instance, with COD, a client may download action scripts such as JavaScript, Applets (not widely used these days), Flex scripts to encrypt the client-server communication, so the underlying servers won't aware of any specific encryption methods used in the process.
- COD can also be applied to services and service consumers. For instance, service design can enable the servers to dynamically defer some portions of logic to the service client programs. This approach of delaying code execution to the client side is justifiable when service logic can be executed by the consumer more efficiently or effectively.

- RESTful applications may very well be able to utilize clients that support COD. For instance, web browsers can allow servers to return scripts or links that can be executed at the client side. This sort of additional code execution helps to expand the capabilities of the client, without needing the user to install new client software.
- In the COD style, a client component has access to a set of resources, but not the know-how of how to process them. It sends a request to a remote server for the code representing that know-how, receives that code, and executes it locally.

However, the down side of using COD is reduces the visibility of the underlying API, and not every API prefers these kind of flexibility.

COD is classified as optional; architectures that do not use this feature can still be considered RESTful.

RESTful service mandates

In one of the online discussion forums, Roy Fielding recorded his frustration about a service that claims to be RESTful, but that service is a mere HTTP-based interface. The service was not fulfilling all the necessary REST architecture constraints. He even said that if the Engine of Application State (and hence the API) is not being driven by hypertext, then it *cannot* be RESTful and *cannot* be a REST API.

With that said, any services that need to be termed RESTful must strictly adhere to the mandatory REST architecture constraints. Those constraints are design rules that are applied to establish the distinct characteristics of the REST architectural style.

Roy, the founder of the REST style, enforces the following REST constraints as mandatory for any web service to be qualified as RESTful. These mandatory constraints are as follows:

- Client-server
- Statelessness
- Cache
- Interface/uniform contract
- Layered system
- The optional REST constraint is COD (architectures that do not use this feature can still be considered RESTful)

Each constraint is a predetermined design decision and will have positive and negative influences on the services. However, these constraints are meant to provide a better architecture that resembles the web (perhaps positive impacts balanced with negative consequences).

There may be a need for potential trade-offs when deviating from REST constraints. Ensure those trade-offs don't weaken or eliminate the mandated constraints. If so, that architecture may no longer conform to REST, or in other words, the services (architecture) are not RESTful.

Architectural goals of REST

The REST architectural style brings a set of properties that help to establish the design goals that are embedded in the application of REST constraints. These properties are as follows:

- Performance
- Scalability
- Simplicity
- Modifiability
- Visibility
- Portability
- Reliability
- Testability

The preceding properties signify a target state of software architecture and fundamental qualities of the WWW. Adhering to REST constraints in design decisions helps to achieve the preceding listed goals, and, of course, these properties can be further improved with more design decisions that are not necessarily parts of REST. However, as quoted in the *RESTful services mandate* section, a web service, to be called a RESTful service, should adhere to the RESTful constraints.

Summary

Let's summarize what we have covered in this chapter and what we can take away in the context of the REST architectural style. We started with a brief history of the evolution of the World Wide Web, its layers, and its architecture. Then we moved on to the web API, a development model for web services, and how REST-based services communicate with existing web protocols with simplified representations.

We looked briefly at SOA and also in more detail at ROA. We covered the purpose of ROA (to use simplified, well-understood and well-known web technologies along with core design principles), its principles, and its characteristics as well. After setting the ground with ROA, we got introduced to the concept of REST; the mandatory constraints of REST architecture, such as client-server, statelessness, cacheable, uniform interface, and layered systems; and also the optional code on demand constraints.

As part of a uniform interface, we learned its four guiding principles, which are the identification of resources, manipulation of resources, self-descriptive messages, and HATEOAS, and we also touched upon the importance of the RMM to get a foundation for building RESTful services.

This chapter described in detail the five mandatory constraints and how in Roy's view they define an architectural style as RESTful. It is critical to understand what makes REST RESTful and what does not.

We concluded this chapter with a quick introduction to the software architecture properties of the WWW, and how REST constraints help to achieve the architecture goals of REST, such as performance, scalability, and simplicity.

I hope you have enjoyed this chapter. In the next chapter, we will learn about API design strategies, such as self-service enablement, resource collaboration, and how to address security and scalability concerns along with RESTful API guidelines and constituents.

Design Strategy, Guidelines, and Best Practices

2

In the today's digitalized world, the challenges are about interconnecting various heterogeneous devices with abundant software services available across the internet and intranets. The **application programmable interface (API)** is one of the most promising software paradigms to address *anything, anytime, anywhere,* and *any device,* which is the one substantial need of the digital world at the moment. This chapter discusses how APIs and API designs help to address those challenges and bridge the gaps.

This chapter discusses a few essential API design guidelines, such as consistency, standardization, reusability, and accessibility through REST interfaces, which could equip API designers with better thought processes for their API modeling.

The following are this chapter's objectives:

- Learning about REST API and its importance
- Goals of RESTful API design
- API designer roles and responsibilities
- API design principles
- RESTful API design rules

Also, this chapter intends to introduce a few traits and constituents of better REST API implementations along with a few common, but avoidable, mistakes of API strategies.

Technical requirements

This chapter is primarily intended to introduce readers to various RESTful design concepts involving design strategies and best practices; we expect that readers already have a basic understanding of software design concepts, client-server architecture, and basic data exchange formats, such as JSON and XML.

We assume readers have a basic understanding of web architecture, HTTP methods, headers, and related client-server concepts. However, we strongly encourage our readers to refresh their knowledge of design principles such as SOLID, OO designs, enterprise integration, SOA, and microservice architecture fundamentals.

Learning about REST API and its importance

In the first chapter, we learned about RESTful principles such as client-server, statelessness, cacheable, and layered, and we'll recognize and apply those principles to the low-level yet functional APIs in this chapter. Also, we will learn RESTful API design strategies and best practices that can help us to meet the challenge of *any time*, *anywhere*, and *any device*.

Let's think of an example—assume you're going to an event, where along with other activities there will be a screening of the film *Solo* (the latest in the *Star Wars* series), and you know that some of your friends joining the party aren't familiar with *Star Wars* and the earlier sequels. So being a tech geek, you wanted to help your friends with a simple mobile application that can send search results to your WhatsApp group as messages with details about *Star Wars* characters, lists of films, starships, and so on; also it sends messages when any of your friends ask for any specific information.

But how can a standalone mobile application get data about *Star Wars*, how will it use WhatsApp to reply, how can we integrate three different systems (mobile, messaging, and data) and help your friends with their *Star Wars* queries?

Do we need to create a massive dataset of *Star Wars* by ourselves? How will the mobile app leverage WhatsApp messaging abilities to send star wars information? How can the message be a search string for our app? And we don't know yet how many more unknowns that we need to solve as part of the development.

And you think it would be great if the *Star Wars* dataset was readily available and searchable, and there should be an ability within WhatsApp to programmatically send messages to your friends.

After some research say we found the following list of items that gave us the confidence to build a mobile app within a short time:

- A readily available dataset about *Star Wars* at SWAPI (`https://swapi.co/`) that the app can leverage, and, not only that, it also exposes a mechanism that we can search and get responses, so we have a solution for the dataset/data store about star wars

- WhatsApp also provides out-of-the-box messaging capabilities that your program can use to send the messages

With the preceding information, let's put the following cues in sequence to visualize the app:

1. A friend is asking about Beru on Whatsapp, and so the app picks it up.
2. The app uses `https://swapi.co/api/people/?search=beru`.
3. The SWAPI REST API sends a response to the app's request. The app creates a text with details about Beru from the received response.
4. The app builds a *click chat* API request and sends the message to the group.
5. `https://api.whatsapp.com/send?text=<"Beru Whitesun Lars, born: '47BBY', she belongs to Human Species and from Tatooine Planet">`.
6. Your friend/groups receive the message—`Beru Whitesun Lars, born: "47BBY", she belongs to "Human" Species and from "Tatooine" Planet`.

So, by having all necessary details about those REST APIs, you gain confidence to build a mobile app that helps you to send search results as a message to your WhatsApp group, and you are ready to rock the party. Interesting, isn't it?

So, now you know SWAPI and click chat (`http://api.whatsapp.com`) are REST APIs and can be consumed by any applications as your mobile app consumes those APIs. With our example, can we say that the app is an attempt to address the digitization challenge of *any time, anywhere,* and *any device* with RESTful APIs?

Google Maps and Locations, Apple iTunes, Google Books, UK police forces (`https://data.police.uk/api/forces`), sunrise and sunset timings (`https://sunrise-sunset.org/api`), and the British National Bibliography (`http://bnb.data.bl.uk`) are few examples of public APIs.

The REST API examples that we have so far are more reading operations. However, in reality, the APIs can do a lot more, and we will show how well we can design RESTful APIs that can support **create, read, update, and delete (CRUD)** operations, pagination, filtering, sorting, searching, and much more as you read through this book.

We encourage you to get to know various publicly available APIs, their purpose, response formats, and so on as it will help you to understand and follow the further discussions in this chapter.

Goals of RESTful API design

From the API examples that we've seen so far, you might have observed that they're straightforward, unambiguous, easy to consume, well-structured, and most importantly accessible with well-known and standardized HTTP methods.

By now, we have a fair understanding of the APIs, and that they are one of the best possible solutions for resolving many digitization challenges out of the box; with our earlier examples, we also know who is consuming those APIs. Now let's ponder how we can create such usable APIs and expose them for consumption. Are there any basic and necessary principles for designing APIs that we must take into account even before we delve into API design? What should the API allow the consumers to do with it? What do the consumers want to do with it? To answer our questions, we will need to understand the following API design goals:

- Affordance
- Loosely coupled
- Leverage existing web architecture

Let's discuss them in a bit more detail.

Affordance

Let's discuss a fundamental design concept called **affordance** as it can yield answers to the various questions that we had. Affordance means how an object and its properties are perceived by its design. Here it provides a clue about its operation:

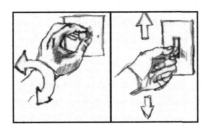

The preceding diagram helps us to understand what affordance is in the design world that we're talking about; among the switches that we see, the first one represents a swivel operation, and another indicates an upward and downward operation. So, by merely seeing those objects, we can perceive what it supports and how. In the case of API design, affordance undoubtedly plays a crucial role, and it is an essential aspect of our API designs.

Loosely coupled

As the whole purpose of an API is to connect heterogeneous clients with the same backend code, it's inevitable that APIs should be as independent as possible and as loosely coupled as possible with the calling clients.

In a loosely coupled design, APIs are independent, and modifications in one won't impact the operation of consumers. Within an API, the components get added, modified, or replaced. However, the loose coupling approach offers clients better flexibility and reusability of APIs while its elements are added, replaced, or changed.

Having a loosely coupled architecture in REST API server designs facilitates the client and server as both follow and respect common semantics. If the API modifies the meaning of its response, then the client needs to be aware of it and act on those new responses accordingly.

Well-designed APIs exhibit loose coupling and well-composed functionalities across service boundaries to maximize scalability factors.

Leverage web architecture

Since its invention by Sir Tim Berners-Lee in 1989, the fundamentals of the web remain as the foundations of all web architecture even today. As you all know, HTTP is the lifeline of the web architecture, and it powers every single client request, server response, and transfer of a document/content over all of the web. So, it is imperative that REST APIs should embrace its bursting power by building interfaces that can be consumed by any device or operating system.

RESTful APIs should use HTTP as a transport layer since the infrastructure, server and client libraries for HTTP are widely available already.

RESTful APIs should take advantage of HTTP methods, or verbs, such as GET, PUT and POST defined by the RFC 2616 protocol.

 RFC 2616 (`https://tools.ietf.org/html/rfc2616`) defines Internet standards for HTTP (the application-level protocol for distributed, collaborative, and hypermedia information systems).

API designer roles and responsibilities

Before we discuss API design goals, principles and practices, let's touch upon the primary roles of a software architect, solution architect, software designer, or anyone who's ready to take responsibility for designing RESTful APIs.

To produce successful APIs, an API designer should have or do the following:

- Be well-versed in REST fundamentals and API design best practices
- Be acquainted with API design patterns to create a modern API design
- Focus on the factors discussed in this chapter such as API design goals and best practices that can improve the application developer's experience
- Translate the business domain into several APIs by having a clear understanding of the business vision and its functions
- Closely work with API developers and help them with their day-to-day constraints and to deal with their existing legacy architecture
- Set up feedback loops that involve developer feedback sessions, prototypes, beta users, release, and versioning
- Use the feedback loops to incorporate acumens in their API design and move faster with API development
- Create best-in-class documentation, reusable code libraries, sample codes, and tutorials

Now that we understand the API designer's roles and responsibilities, let's move on to how one can design successful APIs with some of the industry API best practices in the following section.

API design best practices

Let's think about who the consumers of any web service APIs are. Will it be another system, another software application, or an end-user? Mostly, the consumers of the APIs are another software application or another system itself. So, we can conclude that the customers of any API will be the app developers who give life to the software make it purposeful and usable by their programming codes. So the APIs are heavily dependent on the application developers or app developers.

So application developers should be the primary focus of API design, and for them to consume the APIs, there should be defined and accessible business functions. Please do remember that without any application developer or app developers ready to use the API, the API will cease to exist.

The following is a list of best practices used by API designers to produce APIs that app developers like to use:

- Keep APIs simple and easy to use—simplified, friendly, and intuitive APIs always attract APP developers (clients for our API), get the best out of the APP developer, and make the APP developer's life more comfortable, less painful, and more productive.
- Expose well-defined and instantly recognizable business functions.
- Make APIs accessible with any standard web browsers—exposing APIs with existing web infrastructure (HTTPs `GET`, `POST`, `PUT` , and `DELETE`) and so accessible through a standard browser makes underlying APIs platform independent.
- Abstract service internals and domain models—the best APIs expose only URIs and payloads and not the service internals or domain models. An example is `https://www.googleapis.com/books/v1/volumes`.
- Ensure RESTful API payloads don't have any traces of SOAP payloads as the clients are not the same (machines versus humans).
- Be consistent—API implementations should be free from variation or contradiction; carry consistency across APIs by setting clear standards to help consumers with what to expect from the API, and implement similar behaviours such as searching and filtering (or pagination and limits) in the same way.
- Implement the standard URL pattern—an example of the standard URL pattern is `/collection/item/collection/item` , and the `/collection` can be books, dogs, events (plural), and so on.
- Exercise standard terminology—following standard and meaningful elements in the URI is critical for API success. An example of standard terminology would be `bookId`, `dogId` and `eventId`, and not `bId`, `dId` and `eId`.
- Be flexible—APIs are flexible to accept input from clients. An example would be `/planner/v1/tasks` or `/planner/v1/Tasks` or `/planner/v1/TASKS`; lowercase, uppercase, or camel case in the preceding example should be acceptable and should behave in the same way.
- Be stable—incremental modifications to the APIs are inevitable, but it should be independent of the client applications. In other words, no forced amendments to the clients who consume the APIs that undergo modifications.

Say, `/books/v1/volumes` involves no changes to the clients and provide additional benefits/defect fixes when the volume module goes through some changes.

- There should be a clear handle for errors and error messages—API implementations shouldn't just provide better business functions; it is critical that it handles the errors and error messages well to help clients with useful and human-readable error messages, including diagnostic information that can be understood by the app developer, as error messages give hints and assist the APP developers to resolve issues that may otherwise result in an error.
- Documentation—APIs are discoverable and documented, so publishing the API documentation is a must. API documentation includes a getting-started guide, sample codes, sample requests, sample responses, sample implementations, elaborate explanations about authentication and error handling, information about feedback avenues, and so forth.
- Provide feedback and support mechanism for API users.

Would it be good to have API design practices so you can jump-start the API design? No, not yet. We need to get to know about a few core API design principles, which we will review next.

API design principles

To create flexible, scalable, and secure APIs, an API designer needs a set of guidelines. We'll discuss the following essential principles:

- Ubiquitous web standards
- API flexibility
- API standardization
- API optimization
- API granularity
- API sandbox or playground

By doing so, we will be able to understand how following them will help us to design high-quality RESTful APIs.

Ubiquitous web standards

As we discussed in the *Goals of RESTful API design* section, API designers should embrace the existing web standards and develop their API design and platforms, resulting in ubiquitous communication between the RESTful APIs and clients.

Let's ask ourselves a few questions that will help us to derive better design principles for our APIs:

- Who will be consuming our APIs?
- What are the business functions that the API needs to support?
- How granular should the API be?
- Should APIs always stick to the existing web standards and provide consistency?

The REST architecture style insists on embracing the existing web standards and so leveraging those standards should be the primary focus of any API design. The following diagram depicts a few common web methods, namely, GET, POST, PUT and DELETE , and the interactions with **REST API** by the clients:

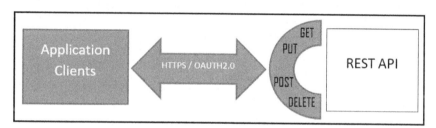

After web methods, there are few essential design aspects that APIs should adhere to, and they address the questions about standardization, consumers of API, and API consistency as well:

- Any application client should be able to use the API ideally without having to refer to much documentation
- Use standard HTTP method call-outs, available on every language and platform, to make requests and retrieve information from APIs
- Don't make any assumptions about the software development technologies used by consumer applications
- Web protocol HTTP and responses such as JSON or ATOM help API clients to find a library that connects to any language or platform

Flexibility

The data from the API should be independent of resources or methods. It implies REST API should handle multiple types of calls and return various data formats, even with some change in the structure representing hypermedia. In other words, the data of the API response isn't tied to the resources or methods.

The GitHub API summary representations and detailed representations may be examples of API flexibility. List of repository API `GET /orgs/myorg/repos` gets the summary representation, and single repository API `GET /repos/myorg/myhelloworld.rb` fetches the detailed description of the indicated repository.

The Salesforce API provides flexibility with its response formats, so API developers can serialize the data in either XML or JSON format.

GraphQL endpoint implementation for API developers is another best example of API flexibility. With GraphQL, developers can request the data that they want based on a predefined schema and so the API can respond according to the predefined schema:

```
{
  book(id: "1000") {
    name
    rating

  }
}
```
→
```
{
  "data": {
    "book": {
      "name": "Architectural Patterns",
      "rating": 3.5
    }
  }
}
```

The preceding screenshot reflects a sample GraphQL request (schema) for specific fields (book name and rating) and response with specified fields.

Granularity

Granularity is an essential principle of REST API design. As we understand business functions divided into many small actions are fine-grained, then business functions divided into large operations are coarse-grained. However, discussions about what level of granularity that needs to be in APIs may vary; we will get distinct suggestions and even end up in debates. Regardless, it is best to decide based on business functions and its use cases, as granularity decisions would undoubtedly vary on a case by case basis.

In some cases, calls across the network may be expensive and so, to minimize them a coarse-grained API may be the best fit, as each request from the client forces lot of work at the server side and, in fine-grained APIs, many calls are required to do the same amount of work at the client side.

Consider the following example. A service returns customer orders (say n orders) in a single call; this is a coarse-grained API in action. In case of fine-grained, it returns only the customer IDs, and for each customer ID, the client needs to make an additional request to get details, so $n+1$ calls need to be made by the clients; these may be expensive round trips regarding its performance and response times over the network.

In a few other cases, APIs should be designed at the lowest practical level of granularity, because combining them is possible and allowed in ways that suit customer needs.

Now, check out this example, an electronic form submission may need to collect an address as well as, say, tax information. In this case, there are two functions one is a collection of the applicant's whereabouts, and another is a collection of tax details. Each task needs to be addressed with distinct API and requires a separate service because an address change is logically a different event and not related to tax time reporting, that is, why one needs to submit the tax information (again) for an address change.

Level of granularity should satisfy the specific needs of the business functions or use cases. While the goal is to minimize the calls across the network and for better performance, understanding the set of operations that API consumers require and how they would give a better idea of the right grained APIs in our designs is important.

Say internal services consumers for those who multiple calls to the API servers are acceptable and those APIs can be designed as fine-grained, and the external consumers and if they need to avoid several round-trips to the API then plan as coarse-grained.

At times it may be appropriate that the API design supports both coarse-grained as well as fine-grained to give the flexibility for the API developers to choose the right APIs for their use cases.

The following points may serve as some basic guidelines for the readers to decide their API granularity levels in their API modelling:

- In general, consider services coarse-grained and APIs fine-grained.
- Maintain a balance between the amount of response data and the number of resources required to provide that data will help to decide the granularity.
- The types of performed operations on the data should also be considered as part of the design when defining the granularity.
- Read requests are normally coarse-grained. Returning all information as required to render the page won't hurt as much as two separate API calls in some cases.
- On the other hand, write requests must be fine-grained. Find out common operations clients need, and provide a specific API for that use case.
- At times, you should use medium-grained, that is, neither fine-grained or coarse-grained. An example could be as seen in the following sample where the nested resources are within two levels deep.

Consider the following snapshot that reflects a medium-grained API response:

```
GET /users/007

{
    "id": "007",
    "name": {
        "first_name": "James",
        "last_name": "Bond"
    },
    "address": {
        "street": "New Bond Street",
        "city": {
            "name": "London",
            "post code": "W1S 1S"
        }
    }
}
```

Let's conclude this section with a broad guideline that helps to determine the right service granularity—identify the vital business entities that the service impacts and model the life cycles accordingly; that is, there should be only one API operation for one business outcome.

The preceding guideline may lead to a number of API deployment units, and this can cause annoyances down the line. There are patterns, especially the API gateway, which brings a better orchestration with those numerous APIs. Orchestrating the APIs with optimized endpoints, request collapsing, and much more helps in addressing granularity challenges.

Optimized APIs

This section discusses adopting better optimization for the API. There's no concept of one-size-fits-all. In the real world, multiple APIs may support the same service as that service might be serving different types of users and use cases. As we quoted earlier in this chapter, the API should be modeled after the design according to the use case it fulfils and not by the backend services or applications it exposes.

So optimization applies to a specific business request in a particular context. Let's take an example, a web service enables its mobile app consumers to clear electricity bills. In the context of the mobile, the constraints of mobile application should be our primary consideration, as a mobile app is sensitive to network latency, numerous network trips, the size of the data compared to a standard web application, and so on. So, our API design should focus on limiting the backend calls and minimize the size of the data returned.

Concerning granularity, let's consider the preceding example will consume few fine-grained independently invokable APIs. On the other hand, to make the payment, the app may need to use a coarse-grained API from another service (which, in turn, may have many fine-grained APIs). So, our mobile app can use a few other fine-grained APIs directly to fetch the due amount, get the user address, and access account details of the bank that the user wants to use to pay the outstanding amount, and may even need more fine-grained APIs to be incorporated in future and so on. So, designers should consider the layered or tiered approach that we discussed in Chapter 1, *Introduction to the Basics of RESTful Architecture*, to orchestrate and manage those fine-grained APIs.

So, API designs can expose fine-grained APIs for consumers who can access them directly, and coarse-grained services on top of them would support broader use cases, so that the service clients may decide to call the fine-grained APIs directly, or they may decide to use the coarse-grained APIs if they need the combined functionality of multiple fine-grained API calls.

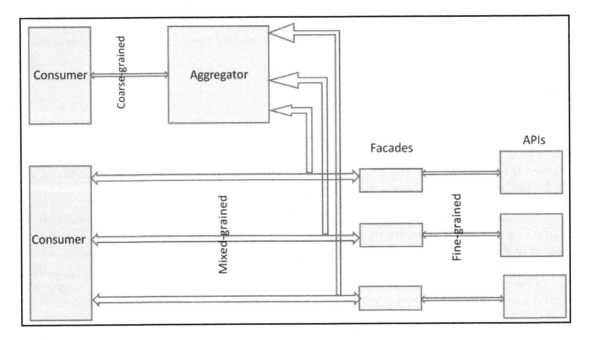

The preceding diagram depicts a logical structure of APIs with their granularities and how those APIs are consumed by the service clients, and it is an example of optimized APIs for the use case that we discussed earlier.

Functionality

This design principle suggests that the API design should support the full process of the life cycle as a single window. For instance, in an e-commerce site, when a consumer purchases an item, they shouldn't have to go to the bank portal to check their balance or to make a payment, and perhaps it should be integrated within that same e-commerce portal. The API used by the e-commerce portal should cover the full process of the life cycle. Partial, unbaked APIs severely affect the user experience.

Another aspect to think about for APIs is to provide full coverage in today's financial world; as the rapid expansion of services in cash management, automatic transfers, stock exchange orders, and so on are inevitable, APIs are the perfect solution for interconnecting these third-party services and banking services.

The same entity life cycle modelling approach that we saw earlier in the section to identify service granularity will also help us to understand which services are necessary to support the full business process life cycle.

Learning about unusual circumstances

In the real world, there are some strange problems that can be solved only with specialized or proprietary technology. Those situations are unusual, and examples of those circumstances may arise in smart home platforms, IoT (fieldbus) implementations with standardized models for B2B, ebMS3/AS4 messaging, and so on.

There are always situations and cases in the pragmatic REST service world where API designers will land in unusual circumstances and need some trade-offs for their API design, for example, enhancing legacy applications to RESTful service scenarios. Practically it isn't feasible to migrate the whole legacy software, especially in the case of propitiatory codes, and we call them special situations. However, there are design principles and patterns such as domain-driven design patterns that come in handy in those particular situations. These unusual or unique situations also come under design principles, and they advise APIs to provide specialized technologies only for such cases where it is absolutely necessary to solve a specific problem and not just because the situation is complicated.

 Applicability Statement 4 (AS4) is an open standard protocol specification for the secure and payload-agnostic **business-to-business (B2B)** documents (OASIS ebMS) using web services.

 You're encouraged to refer the book `Architectural Patterns` published by Packt. It has one dedicated chapter about **domain driven design (DDD)** patterns and discusses many DDD patterns in detail.

Community standardization

Following standards and naming conventions described by open consortiums make our APIs much more usable and interoperable. **Open Travel Alliance (OTA)** and **Open Geospatial Consortium (OGC)** are two examples of these consortiums.

The community standardization principle suggests that API implementations should be designed using industry standard information components when they are available. The iCalendar for calendar invites and events, vCard for the name and address information, and **Keyhole Markup Language (KML)** for geospatial data are a few examples of those well-defined standards our API can make the best use of.

API playgrounds

API providers should develop and expose an associated website/developer portal, for developers to quickly get on board with their APIs. It serves the new clients with documentation, forums, and self-service provisioning with secure API access keys.

APP developers learning about APIs and their offerings, not only with documentation but also with straightforward tools and techniques in an environment in which they can test and manipulate data in a controlled, monitored way, is of paramount importance and brings massive interest among developers to learn and use the APIs.

An interactive and in-browser API playground is one of the best ways for potential users to identify the API endpoints and test their code to experience the API behavior.

Sandboxes, virtualization, and API playgrounds are three different ways that API providers can attract app developers to play with the API functionalities.

An API sandbox is a controlled environment in a limited area with specific rules and provides simple API calls. Virtualization is a mirror image of the real API and offers APP developers production-like environments to do more accurate testing. API playgrounds provide greater capabilities than the sandboxes, yet unlike virtualization, they come as a limited and controlled system emulation. API playgrounds are most suitable for developers to test and get more datasets out of the API; at the same time, the API providers also have better control of those environments.

RESTful API design rules

Now that we understand the roles and responsibilities of an API designer, the API design best practices, and the API design core principles, we can cover one more essential API design aspect called the **rules of APIs**. The best practices and design principles are guidelines that API designers try to incorporate in their API design. However, the rules of API need to be amended in the API design to make our APIs RESTful. So, this section is dedicated to RESTful API rules such as the following:

- Use of Uniform Resource Identifiers
- URI authority
- Resource modelling
- Resource archetypes
- URI path
- URI query
- Metadata design rules (HTTP headers and returning error codes) and representations
- Client concerns (versioning, security, and hypermedia processing)

We're confident that having a clear understanding of these rules will move us closer to design and begin our journey towards delivering the finest RESTful APIs.

Learning about Uniform Resource Identifiers

REST APIs should use **Uniform Resource Identifiers** (URIs) to represent their resources. The resource indications should be clear and straightforward so that they communicate the APIs resources crisp and clearly:

- A sample of a simple to understand URI is `https://xx.yy.zz/sevenwonders/tajmahal/india/agra`, as you may observe that the emphasized texts clearly indicates the intention or representation
- A harder to understand URI is `https://xx.yy.zz/books/36048/9780385490627`; in this sample, the text after *books* is very hard for anyone to understand

So having simple, understandable representation in the URI is critical in RESTful API design.

The following section deals with many such URI aspects for RESTful services.

URI formats

As per RFC 3986, the syntax of the generic URI is `scheme "://" authority "/" path [ "?" query ] [ "#" fragment ]` and following are the rules for API designs:

- **Use forward slash (/) separator**: This is used to indicate the hierarchical relationship between resources, for example, `http://xx.yy.zz/shapes/polygons/quadrilaterals/squares`.

- **Don't use a trailing forward slash**: A trailing forward slash in the URI doesn't have any meaning and may create confusion, for example, `http://xx.yy.zz/shapes/polygons/` and `http://api.examples.org/shapes/polygons` (note the trailing / at the end of the URI). REST API should neither expect trailing slash nor include them in the links that they provide to clients as responses.

- **Use hyphens (–)**: Hyphens improve the readability of URI names, paths, and segments, and help clients to scan and interpret easily, for example, `https://xx.yy.zz/seven-wonders/taj-mahal/india/agra` (note the hyphen segregates the space between seven wonders and Taj Mahal).

- **Avoid underscores (_)**: Designers should avoid _ (underscore) representation in the path, as the character *underscore* may be partially obscured or hidden while rendering on any visual cues due to computer fonts, for example, `https://xx.yy.zz/seven_wonders/taj_mahal/india/agra` (note that we can't make out the underscore as its made as a hyperlink). It should use hyphens instead `https://xx.yy.zz/seven-wonders/taj-mahal/india/agra` (with a hyphen, it's visible even if it is a hyperlink).

- **Prefer all lowercase letters in a URI path**: API designers should give preference to lowercase letters over any other representations, as RFC 3986 defines URIs as case sensitive except for the scheme and host components. Some examples include, `http://xx.yy.zz/shapes/polygons` and `HTTP://XX.YY.ZZ/shapes/polygons` are the same, while `http://xx.yy.zz/shapes/polygons` and `HTTP://XX.YY.ZZ/SHAPES/Polygons` are *not* the same.

- **Do not include file extensions**: As you know, a dot (`.`) prefixed after the filename denotes its file types. However, a URI shouldn't use dots to represent any file extensions; instead, it should rely on media types communicated through a content-type header (refer to the *media types and media type design rules* section).

REST API URI authority

As we've seen different rules for URIs in general, we will discuss the authority (`scheme "://" authority "/" path [ "?" query ] [ "#" fragment ]`) portion of the REST API URI:

- Use consistent sub-domain names:
    - Consistent sub-domain names for an API include the following:
        - The top-level domain and the first sub-domain names indicate the service owner and an example could be `baseball.restfulapi.org`
        - As you see in `http://api.baseball.restfulapi.org`, the API domain should have `api` as part of its sub-domain
    - Consistent sub-domain names for a developer portal include the following:
        - As we saw in the *API playgrounds* section, the API providers should have exposed sites for APP developers to test their APIs called a developer portal. So, by convention, the developer portal's sub-domain should have `developer` in it. An example of a sub-domain with the developer for a developer portal would be `http://developer.baseball.restfulapi.org`.

Resource modelling

Resource modeling is one of the primary aspects for API designers as it helps to establish the API's fundamental concepts.

In an earlier section, we saw details about the URI; let's consider, in general, the URI path always convey REST resources, and each part of the URI is separated by a forward slash (/) to indicate a unique resource within it model's hierarchy.

Let's take the following sample URI designs:

- `https://api-test.lufthansa.com/v1/profiles/customers/memberstatus`
- `https://api-test.lufthansa.com/v1/profiles/customers/accountbalance`

Each resource separated by a forward slash indicates an addressable resource, as follows:

- `https://api-test.lufthansa.com/v1/profiles/customers`
- `https://api-test.lufthansa.com/v1/profiles`
- `https://api-test.lufthansa.com`

Customers, profiles, and APIs are all unique resources in the preceding individual URI models. So, resource modelling is a crucial design aspect, and API designers need to think about the API resource model before they move on to designing URI paths.

Resource archetypes

Each service provided by the API is an archetype, and they indicate the structures and behaviors of REST API designs. Resource modelling should start with a few fundamental resource archetypes, and usually, the REST API is composed of four unique archetypes, as follows:

- **Document**: The document is the base for a resource representation with a field and link-based structure. In the following, each sample URI represents unique document resources, and the first one is also called the doc-root or parent resource (the API endpoint):
    - `https://api-test.lufthansa.com`
    - `https://api-test.lufthansa.com/v1/profiles`
    - `https://api-test.lufthansa.com/v1/profiles/customers`
    - `https://api-test.lufthansa.com/v1/profiles/customers/accountbalance`
    - `https://api-test.lufthansa.com/v1/profiles/customers/memberstatus`

- **Collection**: A collection is also a resource, and it is a directory of resources managed by the API providers or servers. If a collection allows creating a new resource, then the clients can add new resources to the collections. A collection resource decides the URIs of each contained or added resources. In the following, each URI sample found identifies a collection resource:
    - `https://api-test.lufthansa.com/v1/profiles/customers`
    - `https://api-test.lufthansa.com/v1/profiles/customers/accountbalance`
    - `https://api-test.lufthansa.com/v1/profiles/customers/memberstatus`

- **Stores**: A store is a resource repository managed by the client. The store allows the API client to put resources in, choose URIs for the resources that get added, get them out, and delete them when it decides. (URI stores never generate a new URI, and it is the client who chooses when resources initially get added.) Some of the following examples of interaction show a user of a client program of a cart- and song-management API inserting a document resource named carts and playlists respectively against his/her user ID denoted by `{id}`:
  - `http://api.example.com/cart-management/users/{id}/carts`
  - `http://api.example.com/song-management/users/{id}/playlists`
- **Controller**: Controller resources are similar to executable methods, with parameters and return values. REST API relies on controller resources to perform application-specific actions that do not come under any of the CRUD methods. Controller names should always appear as the last segment in a URI path, with no child resources to follow them in the hierarchy:
  - `POST /alerts/245245/resend` is an example of a controller resource that allows a client to resend an alert to a user

URI path

This section discusses rules relating to the design of meaningful URI paths (`scheme "://" authority "/" path [ "?" query ] [ "#" fragment ]`) portion of the REST API URIs.

The following are the rules about URI paths:

- Use singular nouns for document names, for example, `https://api-test.lufthansa.com/v1/profiles/customers/memberstatus`.
- Use plural nouns for collections and stores:
  - **Collections**: `https://api-test.lufthansa.com/v1/profiles/customers`
  - **Stores**: `https://api-test.lufthansa.com/v1/profiles/customers/memberstatus/prefernces`
- As controller names represent an action, use a verb or verb phrase for controller resources. An example would be `https://api-test.lufthansa.com/v1/profiles/customers/memberstatus/reset`.

- Do not use CRUD function names in URIs:
  - **Correct URI example**: `DELETE /users/1234`
  - **Incorrect URIs**: `GET /user-delete?id=1234`, `GET /user-delete /1234`, `DELETE /user-delete /1234`, and `POST /users/1234/delete`

URI query

This section discusses rules relating to the design of the query (`scheme "://" authority "/" path [ "?" query ] [ "#" fragment ]`) portion of the REST API URIs.

The query component of the URI also represents the unique identification of the resource, and following are the rules about URI queries:

- Use the query to filter collections or stores:
  - An example of the limit in the query:
    `https://api.lufthansa.com/v1/operations/flightstatus /arrivals/ZRH/2018-05-21T06:30?limit=40`
- Use the query to paginate collection or store results:
  - An example with the offset in the query:
    `https://api.lufthansa.com/v1/operations/flightstatus /arrivals/ZRH/2018-05-21T06:30?limit=40&offset=10`

HTTP interactions

A REST API doesn't suggest any special transport layer mechanisms, and all it needs is basic Hyper Text Transfer Protocol and its methods to represent its resources over the web. We will touch upon how REST should utilize those basic HTTP methods in the upcoming sections.

Request methods

The client specifies the intended interaction with well-defined semantic HTTP methods, such as `GET`, `POST`, `PUT`, `DELETE`, `PATCH`, `HEAD`, and `OPTIONS`. The following are the rules that an API designer should take into account when planning their design:

- Don't tunnel to other requests with the `GET` and `POST` methods
- Use the `GET` method to retrieve a representation of a resource

- Use the HEAD method to retrieve response headers
- Use the PUT method to update and insert a stored resource
- Use the PUT method to update mutable resources
- Use the POST method to create a new resource in a collection
- Use the POST method for controller's execution
- Use the DELETE method to remove a resource from its parent
- Use the OPTIONS method to retrieve metadata

Response status codes

HTTP specification defines standard status codes, and REST API can use the same status codes to deliver the results of a client request.

The status code categories and a few associated REST API rules are as follows so that the APIs can apply those rules according to the process status:

- **1xx: Informational**: This provides protocol-level information
- **2xx: Success**: Client requests are accepted (successfully), as in the following examples:
    - 200: OK
        - Use for indicating client request success
        - Do not use to communicate the errors in the response body
    - 201: Created
        - Apply for successful resource creation
    - 202: Accepted
        - Use for reporting the successful asynchronous action
    - 204: No content
        - When an API wants to send empty or no content in the response body

- **3xx: Redirection**: Client requests are redirected by the server to the different endpoints to fulfil the client request:
    - 301: Moved Permanently
        - Use for relocated resources
    - 302: Found
        - Please note not to use 302, as it would create confusion among the developers related to the initiation of automatic redirections from the client
    - 303: See other
        - Apply to refer the client to a different URI (in place of 302, it's recommended the API should use 303)
    - 304: Not modified
        - Use so that the client can preserve bandwidth
        - Use in conjunction with conditional HTTP requests
    - 307: Temporarily redirect
        - Use to indicate to the clients to resubmit the request to another URI
- **4xx: Client error**: Errors at client side:
    - 400: Bad request
        - Can be used to indicate generic or nonspecific failures
    - 401: Unauthorized
        - Apply for unauthorized access from the client side or problem with the client credentials
    - 403: Forbidden
        - Use to forbid access regardless of the authorization state
        - Use to enforce application-level permission (allowed to access only a few resources and not all the resources)
    - 404: Not found
        - Must use when client request doesn't map to any of the API resources

- 405: Method not allowed
  - Use when the client accesses unintended HTTP methods
  - Example read-only resource might only support GET and HEAD , and the client tried to use PUT or DELETE
  - Please note that 405 response should be part of the Allow header *(Allow—*GET. POST*)*
- 406: Not acceptable
  - Must use when the server can't serve the requested media type
- 409: Conflict
  - Use for client violation of a resource state
  - An example could be an API returns this error when the client tries to delete a non-empty store resource
- 412: Precondition failed
  - Use to support conditional operations. The client sends one or more preconditions in the request headers to indicate to the API to execute only those conditions that are satisfied; if not, the API should send a 412 error code.
- 415: Unsupported media type
  - Must be used when the API is not able to process the request's payload media type (indicated in the content-type request header)
- **5xx: Server error**: These relate to errors at server side:
  - 500: Internal server error
    - Use to report the API/server-side issues, and when it's certainly not the client's side fault

Metadata design

This section looks at the rules for metadata designs, including HTTP headers and media types.

HTTP headers

As you might already know, HTTP specifications have a set of standard headers, through which a client can get information about a requested resource, and carry the messages that indicate its representations and may serve as directives to control intermediary caches.

The following points suggest a few sets of rules conforming to the HTTP standard headers:

- **Should use content-type**: Client and servers rely on this header to indicate how to process the message's body, as the value of the content-type specifies the form of the data contained in the request or response message body called **media types**.
- **Should use content-length**: The client should know the size of the message body that it is about to read. The other benefit is that the client gets to know how large the response body is that it needs to download, without needing to download the whole response by making a HEAD request.
- **Should use last-modified in responses**: The response should specify the timestamp when the representational state of the required resource was modified or updated so that the client and cache intermediaries can rely on this header to determine the freshness of their local copies of a resource's state representation. The last-modified header should be part of their requests.
- **Should use ETag in responses**: **Entity tag (ETag)** is an HTTP header that helps the client to identify a specific version of the resources they asked for. The server should always respond with the ETag as a header for the client GET requests. The value of the ETag is commonly a digest (hash value, for instance, MD5 hash) of the resource contents so that the server can identify whether the cached contents of the resources are different from the latest version of the resources. ETag differs from the last-modified header by the value (resource content as digest versus timestamp). This header value enables the client to choose whether or not to send the representation again by using If-Non-Match conditionals in the future GET requests. If the ETag value hasn't changed, then the client can decide to save time and bandwidth by not sending the representation again in their subsequent GET requests.
- **Stores must support conditional PUT requests**: REST API can support conditional PUT requests by relying on client requests with If-Unmodified-Since, and/or If-Match request headers. As the store resources use the PUT method for both inserts and updates, the REST API should know the client's intent of the PUT requests. PUT is the same as POST except PUT is *idempotent. Please note that HTTP supports conditional requests with the GET, POST , and DELETE methods; this is an essential pattern for allowing writable REST APIs to help collaboration among API clients.

From a RESTful service standpoint, the idempotent of a service call means the calls that the client makes produce the same results for all calls; that is, multiple requests from the clients produce the same effect as a single request. Please note that the same result or behavior is on the server. However, the response that the client receives may not be the same as the resource state may change between the requests.

- **Should use the location to specify the URI of newly created resources (through** PUT**):** In response to the successful creation of resources through collections or stores, the API should provide the location (URI) of the newly created resource as a response header. The location header can be part of the status code 202 response to direct the clients about the status of their asynchronous call.
- **Should leverage HTTP cache headers:** This is to encourage caching, provide cache-control, Expires, and date-response headers to leverage caching at various levels, such as the API server side, **content delivery networks (CDN)**, or even at the client's network. Some examples are as follows:
    - Cache-Control: max-age=90, must-revalidate (max-age is in seconds)
    - For HTTP 1.0 based caches,Date: Tue, 29 Apr 2018 08:12:31 GMTExpires: Fri, 04 May 2018 16:00:00 GMT

To discourage caching, add cache-control headers with no-cache and no-store, with the following:

- For HTTP 1.0 legacy caches
- Add the Pragma—no-cache and Expires—0 header values

However, unless necessary, REST API should always provoke caching of responses, maybe by shorter duration instead of using a no-cache directive. So the clients get faster responses for frequent access requests by fetching the short-lived response copies.

- **Should use expiration headers with** 200 **("OK") responses:** Setting expiration caching headers in response to the successful GET and HEAD requests encourages caching at the client side. Please note that the POST method is also cacheable, and so don't treat this method as non-cacheable.

- **May use expiration caching headers with 3xx and 4xx responses**: In addition to status code 200 (`"OK": successful responses`), the APIs can include caching headers for 3xx and 4xx responses, also known as negative caching. It helps the REST API server with a reduction in loads due to some redirection and error triggers.
- **Mustn't use custom HTTP headers:** The primary purpose of custom HTTP headers is to provide additional information and troubleshooting tips for app developers; however, for some distinctive cases at the server side, it comes in handy unless those cases do not change the behavior of the HTTP methods. An example could be an API that makes use of the X-cache header to let app developers know whether the resource is delivered by the origin server or by the edge server. If the information that should go through a custom HTTP header is critical in that it needs an accurate interpretation of the request or response, then it is better for it to be included in the body of the request or response or in the URI used for that request.

Media types and media type design rules

As you saw in the *Manipulation of Resources* section of `Chapter 1`, *Introduction to the Basics of RESTful Architecture*, media types help to identify the form of the data in a request or response message body, and the content-type header value represents a media type also known as the **Multipurpose Internet Mail Extensions (MIME)** type.

Media type design influences many aspects of a REST API design, including hypermedia, opaque URIs, and different and descriptive media types so that app developers or clients can rely on the self-descriptive features of the REST API.

The following points discuss the rules of media type design in brief:

- **Uses application-specific media types**: REST APIs treat the body of an HTTP request or response as part of an application-specific interaction. While the request or response body is built with languages such as JSON or XML, it typically has semantics that requires special processing beyond merely parsing the language's syntax. An example representation of such a REST API URI is `https://swapi.co/api/planets/1` that responds to the `GET` requests with a representation of the *Star Wars* planet resource that's formatted using JSON.

- **Supports media type negotiations in case of multiple representations**: The client may require different formats and schema by submitting the desired media type as part of the `Accept` header, so the API should allow the clients to get the response in the desired format.Following is an example representation of the media type negotiations from `developer.atlassian.com` for the following `Accept` header:

```
Content-Type: application/json
 Accept: application/json
```

Observe the following curl execution:

```
curl -i -u application_name:application_password --data '{"value":
"my_password"}' http://testapi.com
/crowd/rest/usermanagement/1/authentication?username=my_username --header
'Content-Type: application/json' --header 'Accept: application/json'
```

We can conclude the following:

- Support media type selection using a query parameter:
  - To support clients with simple links and debugging, REST APIs should support media type selection through a query parameter named accept, with a value format that mirrors that of the accept HTTP request header
  - An example is REST APIs should prefer a more precise and generic approach as following media type, using the `GET` `https://swapi.co/api/planets/1/?format=json` query parameter identification over the other alternatives

 Windows OS users can use MobaXterm (`https://mobaxterm.mobatek.net/`) or any SSH clients that supports Unix commands.

Representations

As we know, machine-readable description of a resource's current state with a request or response is a representation, and it can be in different formats. The following section discusses the rules for most common resource formats, such as JSON and hypermedia, and error types in brief.

Message body format

REST API communications in the distributed environment are most often as a text-based format, and we will discuss the JSON text-format representation rules as follows:

- Use JSON for resource representation and it should be well-formed
- You may use XML and other formats as well
- Don't create additional envelopes or any custom transport wrappers and leverage only HTTP envelopes

Hypermedia representation

As we have understood from `Chapter 1`, *Introduction to the Basics of RESTful Architecture*, REST API clients can programmatically navigate using a uniform link structure as a HATEOAS response, and following are a few rules related to hypermedia representations.

The following screenshot helps us to recollect from `Chapter 1`, *Introduction to the Basics of RESTful Architecture*, the HATEOAS representation:

```
Without HATEOAS:                       With HATEOAS:
 1   Request:                       1   Request:
 2   [Headers]                      2   [Headers]
 3   user: jim                      3   user: jim
 4   roles: USER                    4   roles: USER
 5   GET: /items/1234               5   GET: /items/1234
 6   Response:                      6   Response:
 7   HTTP 1.1 200                   7   HTTP 1.1 200
 8   {                             8   {
 9       "id" : 1234,               9       "id" : 1234,
10       "description" : "FooBar TV",    10       "description" : "FooBar TV",
11       "image" : "fooBarTv.jpg",  11       "image" : "fooBarTv.jpg",
12       "price" : 50.00,           12       "price" : 50.00,
13       "owner" : "jim"            13       "links": [
14   }                             14           {
                                   15               "rel" : "modify",
                                   16               "href" : "/items/1234"
                                   17           },
                                   18           {
                                   19               "rel" : "delete",
                                   20               "href" : "/items/1234"
                                   21           }
                                   22       ]
                                   23   }
                                   24   }
```

Also, it can help us to relate to the following rules:

- Use a consistent form to represent links, link relations, and link announcements
- Provide a self-linking representation in a response message body
- Minimize the number of the advertised *entry point* or API URIs
- Use links to advertise any resource actions in a state-sensitive manner

Media type representation

A GET request won't have a request body, and the response body is always a resource representation. So, for every client request, except for GET requests, the API should define the media type in the request body and response body. The API media type relates to features such as sorting, filtering, paginating, and linking. So, media type formats and schemas should be consistent.

Errors representation

Error status codes of HTTP methods (4xx and 5xx) can carry client-readable information in the response body. The following rules present consistent forms of errors and error responses:

- Errors and error responses should be consistent
- Error types for generic and for common error conditions should also be consistent

The following diagram depicts a sample JSON response and addresses how errors and error codes predominate in API responses:

```
       401 UNAUTHORIZED                    404 NOT FOUND

{                                    {
  "error": {                           "error": {
    "errors": [                          "errors": [
      {                                    {
        "domain": "global",                  "domain": "global",
        "reason": "required",                "reason": "notFound",
        "message": "Login Required",         "message": "Not Found"
        "locationType": "header",          }
        "location": "Authorization"      ],
      }                                  "code": 404,
    ],                                   "message": "Not Found"
    "code": 401,                       }
    "message": "Login Required"      }
  }
}
```

Client concerns

As we know from the *API design best practices* section, the REST API clients in the REST API world are APP developers and REST APIs are designed to suit the needs of their client programs (APP developer code). This section deals with a set of REST API design principles to address common client concerns.

Versioning

A REST API is a collection of interlinked resources or resource models. The representational resources communicate their state through the versions. So versioning is one of the essential design principles, and we will look at the versioning of APIs before we state the rules for versioning.

APIs should be versioned (increase the major version) when it undergoes a breaking change; breaking changes include the following:

- Response data changes
- Response type changes
- Removing any part of the API

APIs should undergo version changes even when it involves minor or non-breaking modifications, such as adding new endpoints or new response parameters. Minor versions help to track the APIs' small changes and assist in customer support, who may be receiving cached versions of data or may be experiencing other API issues. Following are a few of the rules about REST API versioning:

- Use new URIs to introduce new models or conceptions
- Use schemas for managing representational form versions
- Make use of ETags to manage representational state versions

 The general versioning practices follow schematic versioning (`https://semver.org/`); however, the versioning practices in RESTful API attract lots of discussions, and please be aware that, as API designers, we may need to make decisions aligned with business needs and impacts.

Security

REST APIs may expose resources that contain secure information intended to be revealed only to restricted clients, and the following rules help to secure resources:

- Use OAuth, an HTTP-based authorization protocol, to protect resources
- Use API management solutions, such as reverse proxy, to protect resources

We've provided a sample implementation as an example in the next chapter.

Response representation composition

When REST APIs evolve with new features, the client may require new resources from its supporting REST API. However, for many practical reasons, the client may need new resources from the REST API. So a REST API can provide a measure to control the composition of its response representations. It's crucial that REST APIs maintain a consistent resource model design, so clients can benefit from the composite responses. The following two rules enable the client to tune the responses:

- It should support partial response by using the query component of a URI
- It should embed linked resources by using the query component of a URI

For examples, you may refer back the *URI query* section of this chapter.

Processing hypermedia

We discussed earlier two hypermedia structures, link and link relation. They help clients to process the response structure using a consistent algorithm.

The client should interact with a specific REST API response representation link. The following points discuss a simple flow:

- The client processing program starts by looking up the link using its relation's name, and interacts with the link lookup using the appropriate HTTP request method
- The client code inspects the method field of the link's relation document resource and decides whether the content should be submitted in the request message body or not

JavaScript clients

It's most common that JavaScript clients wish to interact with REST APIs. However, there are restrictions imposed (sandboxed) by the web browsers same-origin, also known as **same domain policy**. It restricts the JavaScript client from accessing resources if the resources aren't from the same domain/own source. The URI scheme, host, and port components indicate whether the resource origin is from the same domain. The browsers impose the same-origin policy to prevent leaking of confidential user data.

However, in most cases, the REST API needs to provide multi-origin read/write access from JavaScript for its JavaScript clients, and we will see how the following rules enable such flexibility:

- Support multi-origin read access with **JSON with padding (JSONP)** from JavaScript
- Support **cross-origin resource sharing (CORS)** to provide multi-origin read/write access from JavaScript

Summary

As part of design strategies, we looked at what an API is and its importance for connecting devices with various other devices and technologies in the digitization era. We examined a few essential API design characteristics, such as affordance, leveraging, and maximizing existing web infrastructure, along with API design goals, such as consistency, simplification, flexible yet stable APIs, and how it is essential for an API designer to focus on the APP developers—the consumers of the APIs.

We also briefly discussed the role of an API designer and how they need to follow design principles and rules, so that they can create better RESTful APIs. We concluded this chapter by giving the necessary rules for RESTful APIs, along with some dos and don'ts.

So, we've set a strong foundation and the path for you to get your hands on API programming in our next two chapters as they deal with hands-on REST API programs implementations, with various RESTful API design patterns and applications.

Further reading

We encourage readers to refer to `https://www.packtpub.com/all` for various reference materials and a vast collection of books on RESTful services and APIs.

Essential RESTful API Patterns 3

This chapter provides both the concepts and code examples of common and fundamental design patterns of the RESTful API so that you can pick up these examples and replicate and power their RESTful API services.

As design patterns provide generic, time-tested, proven, and reusable solutions to familiar yet recurring design problems, API design patterns are essential for software designers to learn and adapt in their RESTful API applications. API design patterns provide a description or templates to solve specific, recurring API design problems that any software architects and API designers would like to adopt in their API designs. Adopting patterns provides much flexibility to developers and helps them focus on business logic implementation and deliver the service with high quality.

As part of this chapter, we will learn the following common yet essential API design patterns, along with a few sample pieces of code as well. However, please note that there is no specific order to the following patterns and each pattern addresses the RESTful constraints. We also need to ensure that these essential patterns are accounted and ingrained as needed for our API designs and implementation patterns:

- Statelessness
- Content negotiation
- URI templates
- Design for intent
- Pagination
- Discoverability
- Error and exception logging
- Unicode

Technical requirements

As we will take a plunge into the code and samples, and a few pattern implementations in this chapter, the readers are expected to have a Java programming language and understand the basic concepts of Java 1.8. Our examples are implemented with Spring Boot and we have provided instructions to download and run the sample codes anywhere. However, for those who want to execute and test the code samples provided in this chapter, they may need to have the basic and necessary understanding of data formats such as JSON and XML, and also have a basic understanding of a Maven build process and client-server or web services development.

The following is the GitHub link for this chapter: `https://github.com/PacktPublishing/Hands-On-RESTful-API-Design-Patterns-and-Best-Practices.git`.

For the code to run in your computer, you need Java 8, Spring 4 (1.4.4), and Maven 3.x. Please follow the following instructions to get started. The following are the prerequisites for this chapter:

- Java 1.8
- Maven 3.2
- Your favorite IDE (optional)
- Command-line
- Postman

To start with, please download or clone the samples from GitHub. There are various online help resources available in case anyone needs help in downloading the samples to their local machines.

Beginning with the installations

If you don't have JDK or Maven installed in your environment yet, you may want to install it now by following their respective installation instructions. We need Maven installed on our machines, and we can run the program with IDEs as well. The following instructions cover how to run these samples with Windows command-line, along with the maven command line.

If you need Maven installation instructions, please follow the link and steps defined in the installation document. The Maven installation guide is available at `https://maven.apache.org/install.html`.

The following section provides instructions on how to run the examples of this chapter, along with screenshots that the author was able to set up and run in his Windows-based laptop:

- Download the build script from `Hands-On-RESTful-API-Design-Patterns-and-Best-Practices/scripts/buildMyExamples.bat`.
- Run the downloaded `buildMyExample.bat` script in your Windows Command Prompt and observe your output, which should be similar to what you can see in the following screenshot:

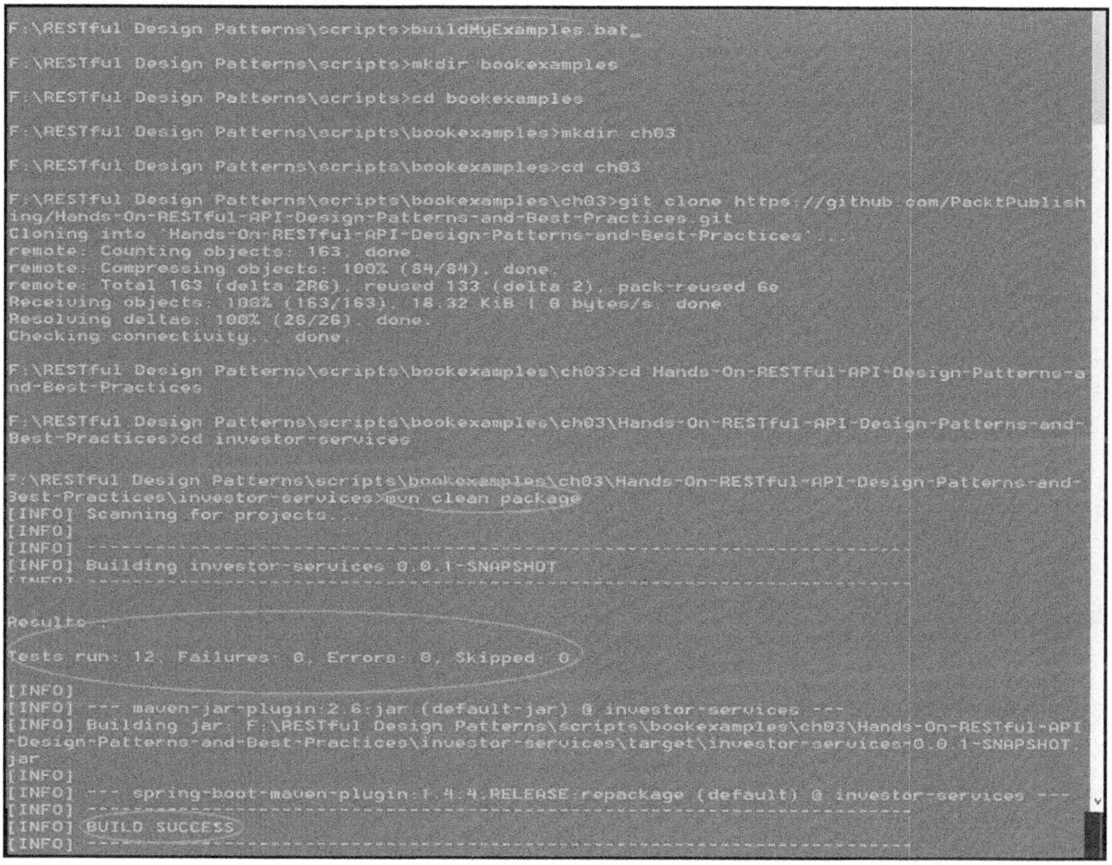

- Download the run script from `Hands-On-RESTful-API-Design-Patterns-and-Best-Practices/scripts/runMyExamples.bat`. Observe the following screenshot and match it with your Windows command-line output:

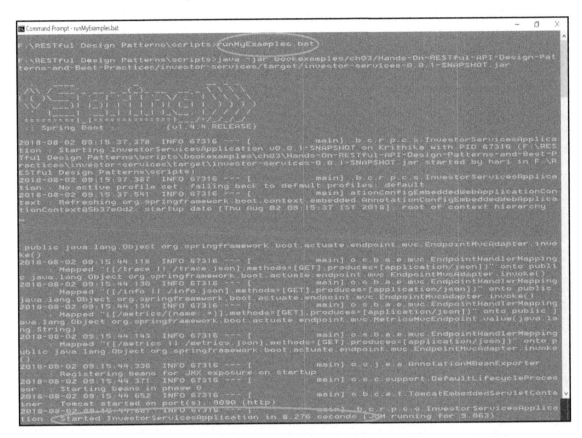

- Once your local server has started, you can download the sample Postman collections for this book from the following GitHub link: `https://github.com/PacktPublishing/Hands-On-RESTful-API-Design-Patterns-and-Best-Practices/blob/master/scripts/book-examples.postman_collection.json`. Import the collection to your local Postman tool, then run the mentioned examples in this chapter and witness the results in your Postman as you see in the following screenshot:

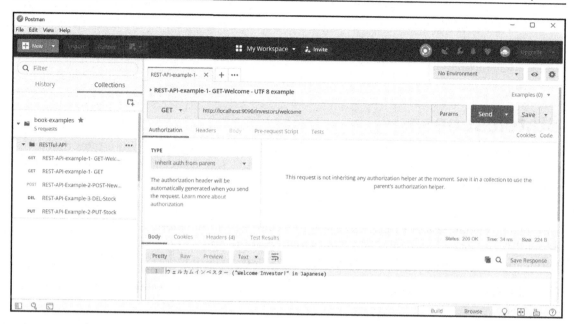

If you need help on installing Postman, you may find this link useful: `https://learning.getpostman.com/docs/postman/launching_postman/installation_and_updates/`. If you need help importing the Postman collections to your local Postman installation, you may find this link useful: `https://learning.getpostman.com/docs/postman/collections/data_formats/#exporting-and-importing-postman-data`.

Beginning with RESTful API patterns – part I

This chapter covers the most common and necessary REST services design patterns to aid API designers and developers in API development in various domains. The design patterns included in this section are as follow:

- Statelessness
- Content negotiation
- URI templates
- Design for intent
- Pagination

- Discoverability
- Error and exception logging
- Unicode

Statelessness

Statelessness refers to servers being free from application states, that is, the states that are stored at the server side and help to identify the client's requests, client's last interaction details, and their current context information.

The REST architecture enforces the server *not* to maintain any client states at the server side and insists on statelessness between the server and the calling client. Any API developer certainly does not want to store state information at the application server side. So, the application server should always be designed as state-free (in most cases).

Let's observe a few responsibilities for both the client and server so that we can achieve statelessness:

Client	Server
A client should provide all necessary information to the server as part of its request to the server.	The server understands the client's request and should include all the necessary information as a response that a client needs to create a session on its side.
Session states should entirely be managed and kept at the client side.	The server does not store the client state and doesn't rely on its stored context.
The client is responsible for storing and handling all its states and sends state information to the server whenever it is needed.	No session affinity or session stickiness on the server is to be maintained.

To comply with RESTful constraints, and for the service to be genuinely stateless, the servers don't even store the authentication/authorization information of the client and make clients provide credentials with their request. So, each request is understood separately by the server and there is no impact on the current request due to previous requests from the same clients.

In our chapter code example, we can observe that none of our requests and responses are associated with/carry any state information and they are entirely independent. Even in later sections when we will develop authentication examples, our code will still evolve and maintain statelessness across its life cycle.

For stateless constraints, how do we code? Spring Boot's REST API framework provides out-of-the-box implementation; our responsibility as a developer is to ensure we follow URI constraints and provide the necessary implementation for the URI. In the following code snippet from our example, `InvestorController.java`, we have a URI (`/investors/{investorId}/stocks`) defined for fetching the stock of an investor by the investor ID; that's all—we do not have any specific implementation, session validation, and so on:

```
@GetMapping(path = "/investors/{investorId}/stocks")
public List<Stock> fetchStocksByInvestorId(@PathVariable String investorId,
  @RequestParam(value = "offset", defaultValue = "0") int offset,
  @RequestParam(value = "limit", defaultValue = "5") int limit) {
    return investorService.fetchStocksByInvestorId(investorId, offset,
limit);
}
```

As the path element doesn't have any indications of state, and the code expects an `investorId` along with a few other parameters, our implementation is fulfilling the stateless constraints. This will be more interesting when we deal with authentication (also with statelessness) in the next chapter.

Let's also observe the necessities and a few advantages of enforcing statelessness in RESTful services through the following table:

Advantages	Details
Scalability	Achieve scalability by having server code that's been deployed to multiple servers so that any server can handle any requests as there is no session stickiness/affinity to be maintained by the server. This occurs since the client's requests will have all the necessary information in each request for to the server manage.
Reduced complexity	There is reduced complexity as the server can get rid of server-side state synchronization logic and implementations (leads to simplified application design).
Easy cache-ability, so improved performance	The intermediate software can cache the results of specific HTTP requests by looking at the client's requests. Also, there are no uncertainties and concerns about the state information of the previous requests.
Traceability	The server never loses track of where each client is in the application as the client requests themselves have all the necessary information.
Best use of HTTP/HTTPS	As HTTP itself is a stateless protocol. REST implementation becomes seamless with HTTP protocols (it adheres well to REST constraints).

Content negotiation

The resources in the RESTful APIs need to deal with different type of representations—not just XML or **JavaScript Object Notation (JSON)**, as different clients may need different representations. In fact, as we build our complex APIS, we may find that XML/JSON is too limiting, and we may need to move to another type of content in an entirely different format (Instagram and Flickr use JPEG and PNG images, while media houses use MP3/MP4), and that's how we get to content negotiation.

Content-negotiation is a mechanism or process that services and clients can select as their resources representation format for their communication and handshakes during their usual course of communication.

As we saw in Chapter 2, *Design Strategy, Guidelines, and Best Practices*, in the *HTTP headers* section, the HTTP specification comes up with a set of standard headers, through which the client can get information about a requested resource and carry the messages that indicate its representations.

So, for content negotiation, REST services need to use HTTP headers; that is, when the client makes requests, it includes the accepts header, the list of file types that the client and server can handle with no additional steps to the client requests, the server processes, and replies.

If the response representation selection is determined at the server-side, then it is server-driven negotiation or proactive negotiation using request-headers. If the same selection is at the client side, then it is agent-driven content negotiation or reactive negotiation using distinct a URI. For most practical purposes, server-side negotiations are more complex and lead to make many assumptions about client requirements. So, most of the REST API implementations follow agent-driven content negotiations that rely on the HTTP request headers or resource URI patterns.

Let us look at a quick and live example of content negotiation by going to the following link: http://www.w3.org/StyleSheets/TR/logo-REC. Observe that logo-REC is an image file; however, it does not have any file extension (that is, w3.org serving images without a file suffix), and the log-REC is not just one file, but two—loge-REC.gif and logo-REC.png. So, with content-negotiation the w3.org server serves two different files. The following screenshot explains a bit more about the request and response headers for the same:

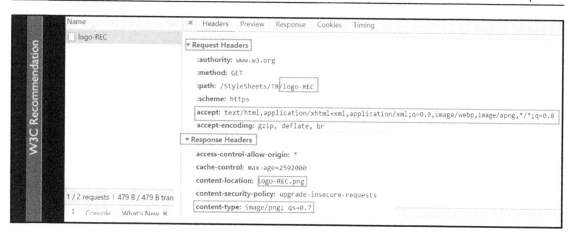

Please observe the highlighted pieces from the preceding screenshot. The URL path, `http:/ /www.w3.org/StyleSheets/TR/logo-REC`, does not say any file extension; however, in the response headers, observe the **content-location** and the **content-type** as `image/png`. The highlighted rectangles are quick examples of some of the content negotiation. Also please observe reactive negotiation through the request header accept.

Let's get into the details about content negotiation and the way the services/clients use them in the following paragraphs.

Content negotiation with HTTP headers

With our earlier example, we have seen that the server understands the content-types of incoming requests and entities with HTTP request header content-types.

In our code example, we have implemented the following content type and, by default `application/JSON`, and to represent what content type that the client desired to get, we use `application/JSON` as the **Accept** header.

Please note that if no **Accept** header is present in the request, the server will send a pre-configured default representation type. In our example, it is always `application/JSON`, as shown in the following screenshot:

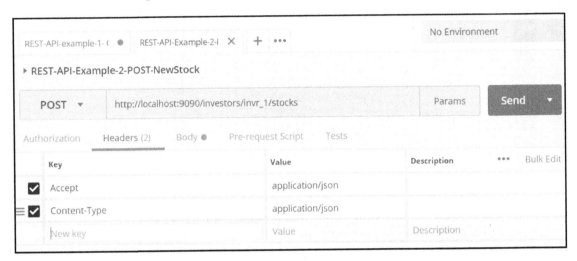

The preceding screenshot depicts the **Content-Type** and **Accept** headers from our examples.

If we want to implement our earlier example of a w3c image within our investor service application in a similar fashion, all we need to do is add the following dependency to `pom.xml`:

```
<dependency>
    <groupId>com.fasterxml.jackson.dataformat</groupId>
    <artifactId>jackson-dataformat-xml</artifactId>
</dependency>
```

Modify the `@GetMapping` annotation in the controller class as follows:

```
@GetMapping(path="/investors/{investorId}/stocks/{symbol}",
produces={MediaType.APPLICATION_JSON_VALUE,
MediaType.APPLICATION_XML_VALUE})
```

So, by using the accept request header, the client either gets the response as XML or as JSON. Cool, isn't it?

With Postman, we will get either a XML or JSON response according to the `application/XML` or `application/JSON` **Accept** header value:

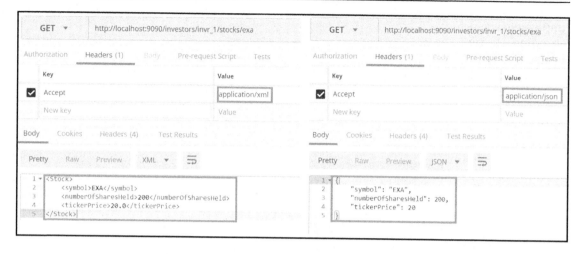

Two other ways that we can pass the content type information to the server are as follows:

- Using specific extensions in resource URIs:
  - `https://xxx.api.com/v1/students/course.xml`
  - `https://xxx.api.com/v1/students/courses.json`
- Using parameters for representing an extension:
  - `https://xxx.api.com/v1/students/course?forrmat=xml`
  - `https://xxx.api.com/v1/students/courses?forrmat=json`

The following table provides a quick reference guide of a few other content-negotiation examples as server and client may need to deal with many other aspects of content-negotiation:

Content-Negotiation	Implementation
Indicate client preference—allows clients to indicate their capabilities (such as media types and languages)	`Accept:application/json,application/xml;q=0.9,*/*;q=0.8` `(support json or xml, q -> preference order)`
Implement media type—how to decide which media type to use for representation in a response	According to the **Accept** header from the client (Accept: `application/atom+xml`), the server can respond with a content-type, that is, `Content-Type: application/atom+xml;charset=UTF-8`

Implement character encoding—know what character encoding to use for textual representations in responses	`Content-Type: charset=UTF-8` (use content-type charset)
Support compression—know when to enable the compression of representations	# Request `Accept-Encoding: gzip` # Response `Content-Encoding: gzip Vary: Accept-Encoding`
Send **Vary** header—know how to use the **Vary** header to indicate to clients how the server chooses a particular representation	# Response `Content-Language: en Vary: Accept-Language`
Handling negotiation failures—know whether to serve a default representation or return an error	# Request `Accept: application/json,*/*;q=0.0` (client cannot process anything other than JSON) # Response `406 Not Acceptable` (the server returns an error code as it does not support JSON. `@GetMapping` our chapter examples throws this error when the client expects only an XML responses as our example serves the JSON and not XML, except for one—a `GET` mapping) Link: `<http://www.example.org/errors/mediatypes.html>;rel="help"` `{"message": "This server does not support JSON. See help for alternatives."}` (additional help)

URI templates

As we saw in Chapter 1, *Introduction to the Basics of RESTful Architecture*, a **Uniform Resource Identifier (URI)** is often used to identify a specific resource within a common space of similar resources. For instance, if we pick up the Star Wars API example from Chapter 1, *Introduction to the Basics of RESTful Architecture*, the films resource is represented by the URIs https://swapi.co/api/films/2, https://swapi.co/api/films/3, and so on. It is always the case that the client may need to include some additional information in their request, and how the server lets the client include that information about resources in the URIs. Server-side developers require the ability to describe the layout of the URIs that their services will respond to.

The answer to this is URI templates. URI templates provide a way to describe a set of resources as variables. So, let's observe the following table with our more general examples before we move on go to this chapter's code examples:

Resources	URI templates
People: https://swapi.co/api/people/ **Planets:** https://swapi.co/api/planets/ **Films:** https://swapi.co/api/films/ **Species:** https://swapi.co/api/species/	https://swapi.co/api/{resource_id}/
https://swapi.co/api/films/2/ https://swapi.co/api/films/6/	https://swapi.co/api/{resource_id1}/{resource_id2}

So, it is clear that if we need to define the URI template for the preceding list with variables or resource identifiers, we need to provide those variables within curly braces.

Now, we will see examples from the code implementation of this chapter which have been picked up from the investor-service controller class:

`@GetMapping("/investors/{investorId}/stocks")` `@GetMapping("/investors/{investorId}/stocks/{symbol}")`	The client would need to send an investor ID and a stock symbol for `GET`
`@DeleteMapping("/investors/{investorId}/stocks/{symbol}")`	The client would need to send an investor ID and a stock symbol for `Delete`

The `@PathVariable` annotation of spring boot does the magic of applying the URI template for the resources that the client needs. Please take note of the following code snippet from our code (`InvestorController.java`) as an example:

```
. . . . . . . .
. . . . . . . . .
public ResponseEntity<Void> updateAStockOfTheInvestorPortfolio(
    @PathVariable String investorId,
    @PathVariable String symbol,
    @RequestBody Stock stockTobeUpdated)
{
        Stock updatedStock =
investorService.updateAStockByInvestorIdAndStock(investorId, symbol,
stockTobeUpdated);
. . . . . . . . . .
. . . . . . . .
```

The `@PathVariable` annotation provided by Spring Boot help us implement the URI template pattern in our code seamlessly. As we can see, `investorId` and the symbol variables are picked up as parameters by our methods.

Please note that there are other REST frameworks that do a good job and provide out-of-the-box URI templating.

Design for intent

Imagine our car getting repaired without even taking it to an automobile service centre. A few years back, Tesla, the car manufacturing company, famously did that when it issued an over-the-air repair to their cars. Tesla's software got updated to detect charging problems and help decrease the charging rates (cascading effect) to avoid overheating and hence avoid engine fires.

Design for intent is a term that's used in structural and automobile fields for parameterized changes, and we will learn how it benefits REST API services as well.

Design for intent is a method that expresses the different relationships between objects so that changes to one object automatically propagates changes to others. In Tesla's case, the decreased number of charging cycles (cascading effect) helped to avoid overheating of the engine.

In a RESTful API world, the API should be developed to ensure they meet the requirements of the use cases, provided and faced by the users, but without exposing the internal business objects. Design for intent is a strategic design pattern that's intended to influence or result in specific and additional user behaviors.

To relate the design for intent implementation within our investor service example, we should provide the mechanism to update the investor's portfolio automatically whenever the new (type) stocks get added to the investor object:

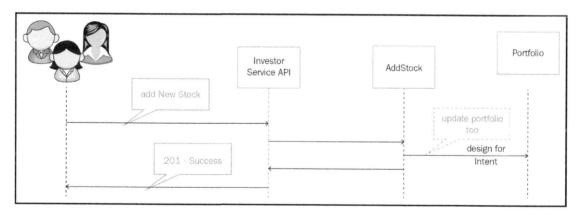

As you can see in the preceding diagram, the intention of the API is to add a new stock; however, it should have a cascading effect on the investor's portfolio as well—maybe a new stock type should get added, the total number of stocks needs to be updated, and so on. This is abstract to the app developer. The same applies when stocks are deleted as well.

Please recollect the granularity of APIs discussion from Chapter 2, *Design Strategy, Guidelines, and Best Practices,* as choosing the right granularity of APIs plays a vital role in the design for intent strategy. In this chapter's example, we have provided a simple update method for adding the stock types to the investor's portfolio, and readers are encouraged to develop more functionalities as part of this pattern ensures having the right granularity (coarse-grained versus fine-grained) of APIs for the update and delete stock types within an investor's portfolio. Consider the following code:

```
........
public Stock addNewStockToTheInvestorPortfolio(....) {
   if (......)) {
       designForIntentCascadePortfolioAdd(investorId);
       return ......;
   }
......
}
.........
.........
public boolean deleteStockFromTheInvestorPortfolio(....) {
   ......
   if (....) {
      ....
      designForIntentCascadePortfolioDelete(investorId, deletedStatus);
      return .......;
      }
.........

private void designForIntentCascadePortfolioAdd(...) {
         .....
      }
private void designForIntentCascadePortfolioDelete(...) {
         ........;
      }
   }
```

The output of the preceding code is as follows:

The preceding screenshot and code is the sample implementation (code snippets) that we can see in InvestorService.java. This also shows a console message when the Delete and Add APIs are called with the Postman tool.

Pagination

When a client tries to fetch a list of objects that run into pages, we have to think about how the server can manage to serve the clients with such a massive response without hampering its performance.

Pagination is a concept that helps in serving only part of the data as a response, however, with information about how to access all the data from the server, page by page, without much load and high computation for the server to serve the whole data.

Should we consider a page (of results) as a resource or just a representation of resources? Considering the page as a representation and not as a resource is what we are going to discuss in this section.

As we decided pagination is a resource representation, we will include the pagination information as part of the URI query, that is, `xxx.api.com/stocks?page=2`.

Please note that pagination as part of the URI path is not an option (as we consider that it is not a resource but resource representation), that is, `xxx.api.com/stocks/page/2`, as we may not be able to uniquely find the resource between calls.

One problem that we need to solve in the case of pagination for URI queries is encoding, and we can use the standard way of encoding the paging information to do this.

Before we jump into the code, let's have a look at some better API pagination examples in the industry and a few pagination types as well.

Facebook's API uses offset and limit (`fields=id, message& amp;limit=5`), linkedIn uses start and count (`.../{service}?start=10&count=10`), and Twitter uses records per page or count (`api.twitter.com/2/accounts/abc1/campaigns?cursor=c-3yvu1pzhd3i7&count=50`).

There are three variants of resource representation ways of pagination, and they are as follows:

- **Offset-based**: When a client needs responses based on page count and page number. For example, `GET /investor/{id}/stocks?offset=2&limit=5` (`returns stocks 2 through 7`).

- **Time-based**: When a client needs responses between a specified timeframe and can have a limit as well as part of the parameter to represent the max number of results per page. For example, `GET` `/investor/{id}/stocks?since=xxxxxx&until=yyyyy (returns stocks between a given dates)`.

- **Cursor-based**: A technique where a pointer (a built-in bookmark with breadcrumbs) reference of the remaining data is served a specific subset of data as a response and is let off. However, the rest of the data is still needed for later requests until the cursor reaches the end of the records. For example, `GET` `slack.com/api/users.list?limit=2&token=xoxp-1234-5678-90123`. The following code explains this:

```
@GetMapping(path = "/investors/{investorId}/stocks")
  public List<Stock> fetchStocksByInvestorId(
      @PathVariable String investorId,
      @RequestParam
      (value = "offset", defaultValue = "0") int offset,
      @RequestParam
      (value = "limit", defaultValue = "5") int limit) {
    return investorService.fetchStocksByInvestorId(investorId, offset,
limit);
      }
```

The output of the preceding code is as follows:

The preceding blocks shows offset-based pagination implementation within our investor service code. We will implement and touch upon other pagination methods, along with sorting and filtering in the next chapter when we discuss versioning and other patterns involving a database.

Discoverability

As we have discussed in the earlier chapter, API developers are the raison d'être of APIs. Helping them find the right APIs and helping them figure out programmatically whether the site that's being accessed has an API enabled or not will be the most critical responsibility of the API.

The primary step to connect with a site is to find out if the site is API enabled by simple URLs that are be using as user input to help us verify the API's availability. They also help us find out how to access them.

Discoverability of the API is all about the descriptive capability of the server to instruct the client on the usage of the API.

Let's look at the two types of discoverability in the following section and their implementation in our code examples (as screenshots):

1. **By valid HTTP methods**: When clients call REST services with invalid HTTP methods, the response of that request should end up in the 405 HTTP error code; that is, 405 Method Not Allowed. In addition to the error code, the response header should provide flexibility to the client to find the supported methods that allow headers in its response. The code for this is as follows:

```
@DeleteMapping("/investors/{investorId}/stocks/{symbol}")
public ResponseEntity<Void> deleteAStockFromTheInvestorPortfolio(
  @PathVariable String investor,
  @PathVariable String symbol) {
    if
(investorService.deleteStockFromTheInvestorPortfolio(investorId,
symbol)) {
      return ResponseEntity.noContent().build();
    }
    return ResponseEntity.ok(null);
}
```

The output of the preceding code is as follows:

2. **By providing the URI of the newly created resource**: Including the URI as part of the location header as the response to the newly created resource is another method of discoverability. The returned URI as a location will be available through GET. The code for it is as follows:

```
@PostMapping("/investors/{investorId}/stocks")
public ResponseEntity<Void......) {
  Stock insertedStock = investorService.addNewSto...;
  if (insertedStock == null) {
    return ResponseEntity.noContent().build();
  }
  URI location = ServletUriComponentsBuilder.....
  return ResponseEntity.created(location).build();
}
```

The output for the preceding code is as follows:

Please note that, as our examples are using spring boot, we are leveraging the capabilities of spring boot's seamless and out-of-the-box implementations for discoverability (with @GetMapping, the servlets URI components builder, and so on).

One more type of discoverability (yet to be standardized, though) can be implemented through valid link headers. While responding to the client's particular resources through GET, you must provide the client with clues about what they can do next as well; that is, providing a list of all available resources as a list through the link header:

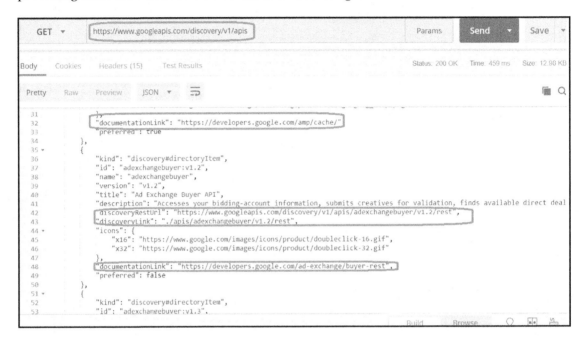

As a live example of discoverability, the preceding screenshot depicts one of Google's APIs.

Error and exception logging

As we keep on emphasizing when we discuss the importance of API developers when it comes to the consumption of our services, error handling and exception handling should be taken care of without any compromises. Services are the black boxes to the API developers, and therefore service providing errors and exceptions provide clients with a clear context and visibility to use our APIs.

Let's take some real-world and very popular APIs and how they are handling these errors in a sample error scenario. This is shown in the following table. We will also look at the way we handle these errors and exceptions within our investor service code:

APIs	HTTP code	Sample message	Remarks
Facebook	200	{"type":"OAUTH exception","message":"...."}	Note that 200 indicates success. However, the API decides to send an error message as a response and still provide a success (200) code for an API call.
Twilio	401	{"status":401,"message":"Authenticate","code":"....".. }	Leverages the existing HTTP code as it is.
InvestorService	405	{"Status":405,"error":"Method Not Allowed"....	Leverages the existing HTTP code as it is.

We also have a sample implementation of a custom exception class called InvestorNotFoundException in our sample repository. The code snippet and output sample (from Postman) is as follows:

```
public class InvestorNotFoundException extends RuntimeException{

........
    public InvestorNotFoundException(String exception)
    {
            super(exception);
    }
}
```

The output of the preceding code is as follows:

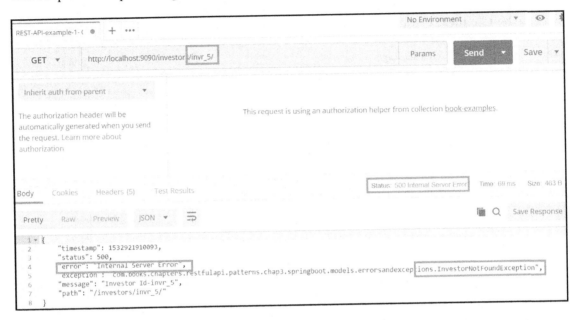

From our earlier examples, we can observe we have done a fair job regarding managing errors and exceptions with existing HTTP standard error codes. However, we can go further by providing more customized errors and messages to the caller; for instance, it would be more proper for the caller to receive a 404 error instead of a 500 error. Maybe we will implement a few customized error messages in the next chapter while we build some more patterns.

Unicode

A simple yet powerful way to make our API support multiple languages is to enable the API to support Unicode.

Unicode is an encoding standard that support an international character set. It has a unique number for every character across multiple languages including Chinese, Korean, and Arabic and their scripts. The unique number makes almost all characters identifiable and accessible across platforms, programs, and devices.

So, in short, we can simplify our REST API that supports multiple languages by supporting Unicode as part of their headers. The following code depicts this:

```
@GetMapping(value="/investors/welcome",
produces="text/plain;charset=UTF-8")
  public String responseProducesConditionCharset() {     return "
ウェルカムインベスター (\"Welcome Investor!\" in Japanese)";
}
```

The output for it is as follows:

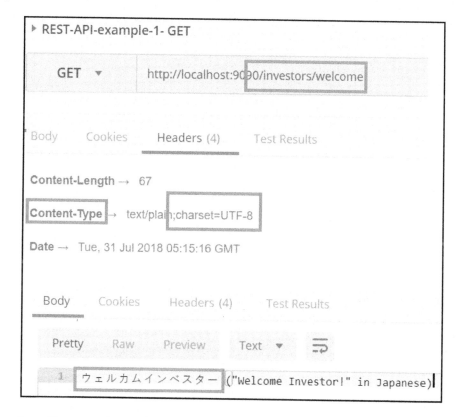

The preceding diagram shows the code snippet of the (`InvestorController.java`) accept-encoding charset in the header and the Postman results for the same.

Summary

With a sense of our hands dealing with real code examples of statelessness, content-negotiation practices, URI templates definitions, service design for intent, discoverability, and a type of pagination. Then, we discussed error and exception handling in detail before finally concluded with a Unicode implementation for internationalization (supporting multiple languages with our services).

This chapter should be an excellent start for anyone who wants to get their hands on the RESTful services; not just the basics, but the essential patterns as well. In the next chapter, we will see more advanced pattern implementation and examples to enable our readers to increasingly utilize best practices and implementations.

4
Advanced RESTful API Patterns

Every software designer agrees that design patterns, and solving familiar yet recurring design problems by implementing design patterns, are inevitable in the modern software design-and-development life cycle. In general, there are various API design patterns, and in our earlier chapter, we covered a few fundamental RESTful API patterns. We'll delve into few advanced API design patterns in this chapter, as those patterns are necessary for real-time RESTful services and what the software industry needed at this moment.

This chapter is part two of API design patterns; the intention is to cover a number of advanced design patterns, such as versioning, and backend for frontend. Once readers have gone through this chapter, they should know how to implement the following patterns:

- Versioning
- Authorization
- Uniform contract
- Entity endpoint
- Endpoint redirection
- Idempotent
- Bulk operations
- Circuit breaker
- API facade
- Backend for frontend

 Please don't forget to go through the Investor Service code examples and learn the advance pattern implementations as well.

Technical requirements

As this chapter deals with advanced patterns, we expect that readers have knowledge of a few basic software design patterns and practices, Java's programming ability, Spring framework, and RESTful services.

To run this chapter's sample code, please refer to `Chapter 3`, *Essential RESTful API Patterns*, for the additional technical requirement and information on how to run the sample codes provided here.

RESTful API advanced patterns

We covered few critical RESTful patterns in the earlier chapter; now it's time to get into more advanced patterns and get our hands dirty to provide our customers and app developers with the best-possible RESTful services implementation. Let's start learning how to implement versioning for our services.

Versioning

Many books and articles recommend avoiding versioning APIs if possible. However, it's not practical to believe that we'll develop one API that caters to almost every requirement within the first release and never changes, so we avoid versioning altogether. A few others recommend providing different URIs for different (major) version changes. Ideally, we'd manage APIs just like website URLs (most of the time the URL address never changes, regardless of any changes/implementations).

The general rules of thumb we'd like to follow when versioning APIs are as follows:

- Upgrade the API to a new major version when the new implementation breaks the existing customer implementations
- Upgrade the API to a new minor version of the API when the new implementation provides enhancements and bug fixes; however, ensure that the implementation takes care of backward-compatibility and has no impact on the existing customer implementations

Let's consider that we need to manage the versions in our API; there are four different ways that we can implement the versioning, and we will see each type in the following sections.

Versioning through the URI path

The major and minor version changes can be a part of the URI, for example, to represent v1 or v2 of the API the URI can

be http://localhost:9090/v1/investors or http://localhost:9090/v2/investors, respectively.

The code implementation of the URI path versioning within our investor service examples is shown in the following code snippet:

```
@GetMapping({"/v1/investors","/v1.1/investors","/v2/investors"})
    public List<Investor> fetchAllInvestors()
    {
        return investorService.fetchAllInvestors();
    }
```

The output of this code is as follows:

The preceding screenshot shows the Postman execution of the URI path-versioning example.

URI path changes according to the version violates the RESTful principles of URI and its resource representation (two different URIs represent the same resources—the only difference is v1, v2, and so on, in our example). However, URI path versioning is a popular way of managing API versions due to its simple implementation.

Versioning through query parameters

The other simple method for implementing the version reference is to make it part of the request parameters, as we see in the following examples—`http://localhost:9090/investors?version=1`, `http://localhost:9090/investors?version=2.1.0`:

```
@GetMapping("/investors")
public List<Investor> fetchAllInvestorsForGivenVersionAsParameter(
@RequestParam("version") String version)
throws VersionNotSupportedException {
if (!(version.equals("1.1") || version.equals("1.0"))) {
throw new VersionNotSupportedException("version " + version);
}
return investorService.fetchAllInvestors();
}
```

The output of this is as follows:

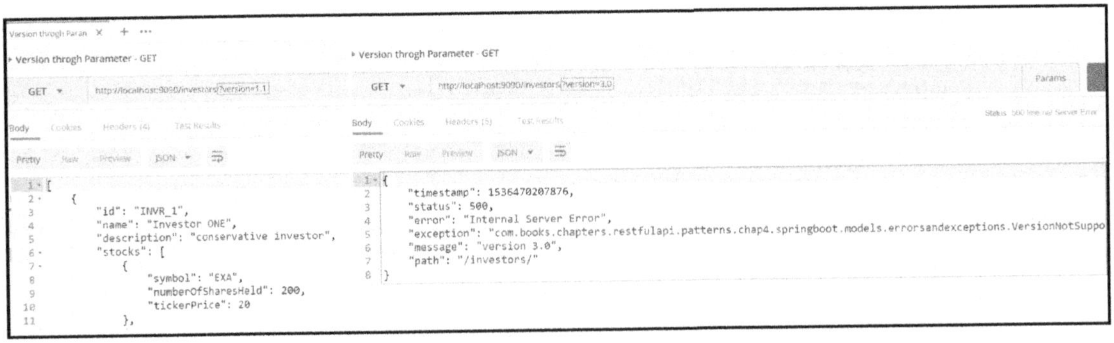

The preceding screenshot shows the implementation of versioning through parameters within our sample.

Versioning through custom headers

Define a new header that contains the version number in the request as part of request header itself. A custom header allows the client to maintain the same URIs, regardless of any version upgrades. This implementation is the kind of content-negotiation that we saw in Chapter 2, *Design Strategy, Guidelines, and Best Practices* and we'll see it in the next section as well. The following code snippet will help us understand the version implementation through a custom header named x-resource-version. Please note that the custom header name can be any name; in our example, we name it x-resource-version:

```
@GetMapping("/investorsbycustomheaderversion")
public List<Investor> fetchAllInvestors...(
@RequestHeader("x-resource-version") String version)
throws VersionNotSupportedException {
return getResultsAccordingToVersion(version);
}
```

The output of the preceding code is as follows:

The preceding screenshot is an example of versioning through the `x-resource-version` custom header and executing the same code example with postman.

Versioning through content-negotiation

Providing the version information through the **Accept** (request) header along with the content-type (media) in response is the preferred way as this helps to version APIs without any impact on the URI. As we've already learned about content-negotiation, in Chapter 2, *Design Strategy, Guidelines, and Best Practices*, let's jump to a code implementation of versioning through **Accept** and **Content-Type**:

```
@GetMapping(value = "/investorsbyacceptheader",
headers = "Accept=application/investors-v1+json,
application/investors-v1.1+json")
public List<Investor> fetchAllInvestorsForGiven..()
throws VersionNotSupportedException {
return getResultsAccordingToVersion("1.1");
}
```

The following screenshot is the output of the preceding code:

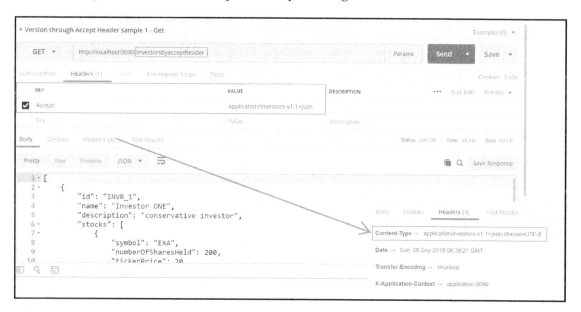

The preceding screenshot of the postman tool depicts the execution of our investor service app versioning through the **Accept** header. Please observe the response header content-type as well.

As we have seen, each type of versioning methodology has advantages and disadvantages, so we need to determine the right approach on a case-by-case basis. However, the content-negotiation and custom headers are a proponent of RESTful-compliant services. We will move on to one of the essential pattern authentication and authorization.

Authorization

So far, we've built a sample application investor service with various incorporated patterns. Now, how do we ensure our REST API implementation is accessible only to genuine users and not to everyone? In our example, the investor's list should not be visible to all users, and the stocks URI should not be exposed to anyone other than the legitimate investor. Here comes the Authorization header to help us out. We'll use a scheme called **basic authentication** as it solves our current requirement. Please note that there are different schemes, such as basic authentication, **hash-based message authentication** (HMAC), **JSON Web Token** (JWT), and OAuth 2.0 bearer authentication token scheme, that are available to secure the REST APIs. However, for this section, we are implementing simple basic authentication through the authorization header, and we'll cover OAuth 2.0 in detail in Chapter 6, *RESTful Services API Testing and Security*.

Let's start with a simple overview of basic authentication. It's a standard HTTP header (RESTful API constraint compliant) with the user's credentials encoded in Base64. The credentials (username and password) are encoded in the format of username—password. Please note that the credentials are encoded not encrypted, and it's vulnerable to specific security attacks, so it's inevitable that the rest API implementing basic authentication will communicate over SSL (https).

We will also need to understand authentication versus authorization. The authentication verifies who (user) is accessing the APIs, and authorization is whether the accessing user has privileges or is authorized to access the API resources. Admin users of our investor service example are authorized to see all the investors, and individual users aren't authorized to see other investors' information.

The Spring security framework provides an out-of-the-box security implementation, and we'll use Spring-provided functionalities to secure our API. As we are going to discuss more security implementations in Chapter 9, *A More In-depth View of the RESTful Services Paradigm*, we'll stick to a basic authentication implementation in this chapter.

Authorization with the default key

Securing the REST API with basic authentication is exceptionally simplified by the Spring security framework. Merely adding the following entries in `pom.xml` provides basic authentication to our investor service app:

```
<dependency>
<groupId>org.springframework.boot</groupId>
<artifactId>spring-boot-starter-security</artifactId>
</dependency>
```

Now rebuild (`mvn clean package`) the application and restart it. It's time to test our APIs with the postman tool. When we hit the URL, unlike our earlier examples, we'll see an error complaining `Full authorization required to access this resource`:

The preceding error is due to the addition of spring-security into our `pom.xml` file. How are we going to access our REST API now? Don't worry, on the console where we started our app, we can observe a text using the default security password or search for it in our log file. That's the key for anyone to access our API. The following screenshot shows this:

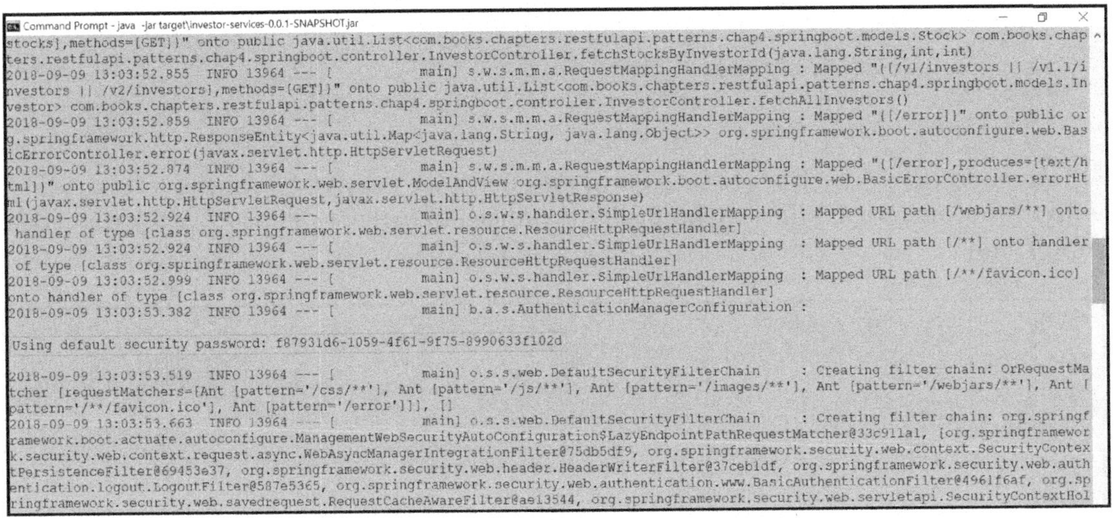

As we see in the preceding screenshot, our console displays the password that we can use to access our API, and so let's use it for the same URL that we have got error earlier:

As we observe in the previous screenshot, we need to provide **BasicAuth** as the **Authorization** header for the API that we are accessing; we will see the results now without any authentication errors. Please note that the **Authorization** header that carries the XYZKL... token prefixed with Basic, as we use the HTTP **Authentication** header to enforce REST API authentication.

Authorization with credentials

In many real-time situations, we need to use specific credentials to access the API and not the default one; in such cases, we can enhance our investor service application and secure it with our custom credentials by using few additional out-of-the-box spring modules.

In our investor service, we will have a new class, called `PatronAuthConfig.java`, which helps the app to enforce the credentials to the URLs that we would like to secure:

```
@Configuration
@EnableWebSecurity
public class PatronsAuthConfig extends WebSecurityConfigurerAdapter {
.....
```

As we see in the preceding code block, with a few annotations, we can implement the security. The following code snippet shows an override method implementation as well as a few lines of code:

```
@Override
protected void configure(AuthenticationManagerBuilder authMgrBldr) throws
Exception {
   authMgrBldr.inMemoryAuthentication()
.passwordEncoder(org.springframework.security.crypto.password.NoOpPasswordE
ncoder.getInstance())
.withUser(DEFAULT_USER_ID).password(DEFAULT_USER_SECRET).authorities....
      }

@Override
protected void configure(HttpSecurity httpSec) throws Exception {
httpSec.csrf().....
.....
```

The following code does the magic of forcing authorization headers to validate for credentials in each request:

```
httpSec.csrf().disable().authorizeRequests().and()
.authorizeRequests().antMatchers(NO_RESTRICT_WELCOME_URI)
.permitAll().antMatchers("/investors/admin")
.hasAuthority(DEFAULT_ADMIN_ROLE).antMatchers("/investors/invr*/**")
.access("hasAuthority('"+DEFAULT_USER_ROLE+"')").anyRequest()
.authenticated().and().httpBasic().and().logout();
```

Please note that our example uses the following username and password along with two roles. We've provided the sample execution script and postman scripts to execute various scenarios by just clicking the labels:

User Id	Password	Role
admin	admSecret	ADMIN
user	usrSecret	USER

Now, please observe the following screenshot:

The preceding screenshot depicts a sample run of one rest API call that needs admin credentials as the authentication header and shows result for valid credentials. On the left-hand side, we can see various test cases; each one has the necessary prerequisites. Now we need to run them one by one and observe the results of each case. Ensure to see the authentication headers as well for each execution.

> The only difference between the investor services example in `Chapter 3`, *Essential RESTful API Patterns,* and this authentication example is that we have added a new class, `PatronsAuthConfig.java`, that extends the configuration for authentication with the **Authorization** header implementation.

Uniform contract

As we mentioned earlier in the *API versioning* section, services will always evolve with additional capabilities, enhancements, and defects fixes, however, now a service consumer can consume the latest version of our services without the need to keep changing their implementation or REST API endpoints. Also, the service consumer needs to be aware of the latest and evolving details of those service contracts.

The uniform contract pattern comes to the rescue to overcome these problems. The pattern suggests the following measures:

- Standardize the service contract and make it uniform across any service endpoints
- Abstract the service endpoints from individual services capabilities
- Follow the REST principles where the endpoints use only HTTP verbs, and express the underlying resources executable actions only with HTTP verbs

Please refer to the API versioning examples in the *API versioning* section as the implementation is already available and it has the flavor (please refer our investor service examples with GET, POST, DELETE, and so on) of the uniform contract.

Entity endpoints

If service clients want to interact with entities, such as investors, and their stocks without needing them to manage a compound identifier for both investor and stock, we need a pattern called **entity endpoint**. Entity endpoints suggest exposing each entity as individual lightweight endpoints of the service they reside in, so the service consumers get the global addressability of service entities:

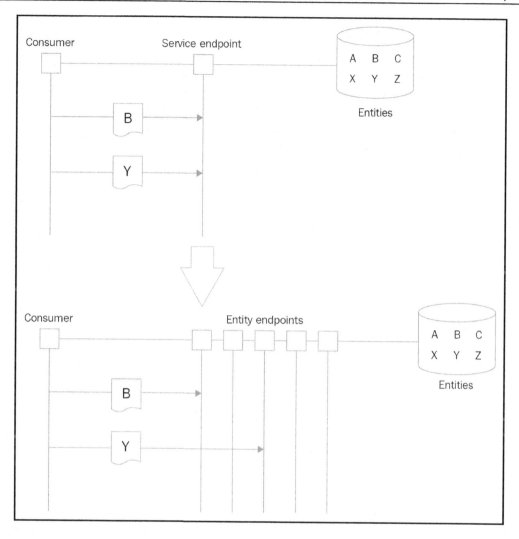

The preceding screenshot illustrates how a service consumer can access individual entity endpoints instead of service endpoints. The entity endpoints expose reusable enterprise resources, so service consumers can reuse and share the entity resources.

Our rest service, the investor service, exposes a couple of entity endpoints, such as `/investors/investorId`, and `investor/stockId`, and they are few examples of entity endpoints that our service consumer can reuse and standardize.

Endpoint redirection

Changing service endpoints isn't always ideal, However, if it needs to, will the service client know about it and use the new endpoint? Yes, with standard HTTP return codes, `3xx`, and with the **Location** header, then by receiving `301 Moved permanently` or `307 Temporary Redirect`, the service client can act accordingly. The endpoint redirection pattern suggests returning standard HTTP headers and provides an automatic reference of stale endpoints to the current endpoints:

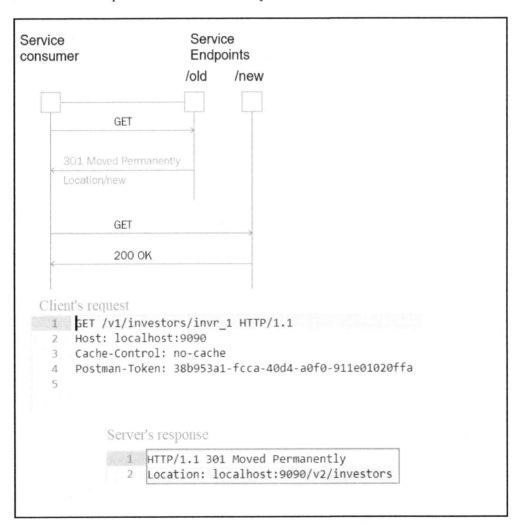

As we can see, the service consumers may call the new endpoints that are found in the **Location** header.

Please refer to our investor service example for header implementations if you want to play around with 3xx codes and **Location** headers.

Please note that with the HATEOAS implementation at the services, the client could potentially avoid these endpoint redirections.

Idempotent

Imagine a bank's debit API failed immediately after deducting some amount from the client account. However, the client doesn't know about it (as it didn't get any response from the server) and reissues the call to debit! Alas, the client loses money. So how can a service implementation handle messages/data and produce the same results, even after multiple calls?

 The dictionary meaning of idempotent is *representing an element of a set that is untouched when it involves some operations or is otherwise operated on by itself.*

Idempotent is one of the fundamental resilience and scalable patterns, as it decouples the service implementation nodes across distributed systems. Whether dealing with data or messages, the services should always have designed for sticking to Idempotent in nature.

There is a simple solution: use the idempotent capabilities of the HTTP web APIs, whereby services can provide a guarantee that any number of repeated calls due to intermittent failures of communication to the service is safe, and process those multiple calls from the server without any side effects.

Please refer to Chapter 3, *Essential RESTful API Patterns*, for examples of DELETE, PUT, and PATCH, as those are all typical implementation of idempotent services; that is, even after we call DELETE multiple times for the same stock, it's safe; and the same applies to PUT as well.

When it comes to dealing with concurrency, the services can be enhanced with E-Tag and send back a 409 conflict response to inform the client that the resource called is in an inconsistent state.

Bulk operation

We have seen many REST API patterns and their implementations. However, we have yet to discuss an essential pattern, called **bulk operations**, within the REST API. It's inevitable that our design should thrive, which will reduce performance bottlenecks, such as response time, and the number of round trips between the server and clients.

Marking a list of emails as read in our email client could be an example of a bulk operation; the customer chooses more than one email to tag as Read, and one REST API call does the job instead of multiple calls to an underlying API.

Let's take our investor service API: if a client wants to create a set of stocks for their portfolio rather than one by one, the client needs to call our REST endpoint as many times as the number of stocks that they wanted to create. If they need to update 100 stocks, they need to call the endpoint 100 times, and indeed, it isn't an elegant solution. The bulk operations pattern comes to the rescue in such scenarios, without compromising the REST principles. Let's see how our investor services can be modified to provide bulk operations.

The investor service accepts PATCH for a single element, and we need to think about enhancing the same resource to also accept multiple insertions, or we can have another separate URI to support a bulk operation. Having another URI for the same resource isn't a clean approach as it may deviate from the RESTful principle, and so let's move ahead with the same PATCH request to support the update of more than one stock through the request. The following two approaches are suggested for implementing bulk operations:

- Content-based bulk operation
- Custom-header action-identifier-based bulk operation

Our code example follows both approaches; please note that we don't use any specifics of the framework-provided annotations for the bulk operation. However, we continue to use the custom header and the enhanced request body to support a list of stocks in the client request. The following screenshot depicts the difference in the requests for a non-bulk operation and bulk-operation patch request along with headers:

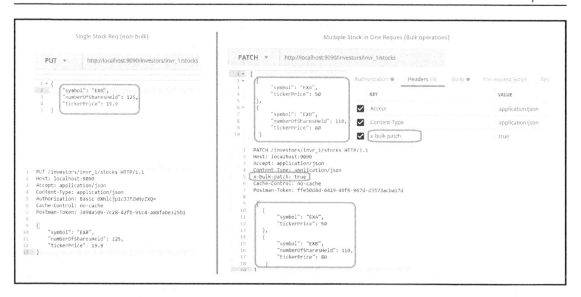

The following code snippet from the InvestorController class enforces the custom header, and the list of the Stock object, unlike the PUT example in Chapter 3, *Essential RESTful API Patterns*, (accepts only one Stock object):

```
@PatchMapping("/investors/{investorId}/stocks")
  public ResponseEntity<Void>
updateStockOfTheInvestorPortfolio(@PathVariable String investorId,
@RequestHeader(value = "x-bulk-patch") Optional<Boolean> isBulkPatch,
@RequestBody List<Stock> stocksTobeUpdated) throws
CustomHeaderNotFoundException {
        // without custom header we are not going to process this bulk
operation
        if (!isBulkPatch.isPresent()) {
            throw new CustomHeaderNotFoundException("x-bulk-patch not
found in your headers");
        }
    investorService.bulkUpdateOfStocksByInvestorId(investorId,
stocksTobeUpdated);
        return ResponseEntity.noContent().build();
    }
```

By running our PATCH example, we can understand the bulk operations of the RESTful API by grouping multiple items in one request. Please note that the bulk operations may involve many other aspects, such as E-tag, asynchronous executions, or parallel-stream implementation to make it effective. However, we aren't covering these special topics here, and we encourage readers to refer to the *Sources, references, and further reading* section for resources.

Bulk operations versus batch operations

Bulk operations deal with a single target operation on a varied list of business objects within a single REQ, and batch operations (not covered in this chapter) deal with a heterogeneous and homogeneous list of business objects, but with multiple REQs.

Circuit breaker

We regularly encounter circuit breakers; the circuit breaker is an automatic switch designed to protect entire electrical circuits from damage due to excess current load as a result of a short circuit or overload.

The same concept applies when services interact with many other services. Failure due to any (network) issue can potentially create catastrophic effects across the application, and preventing cascading impacts is the sole aim of a circuit-breaker pattern. Hence, this pattern helps subsystems to fail gracefully and also prevents complete system failure as a result of a subsystem failures:

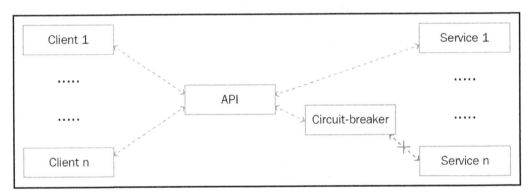

The preceding screenshot illustrates the circuit-breaker concept in which one of the downstream services is non-communicable. However, the circuit breaker implementation handles it in such a way that the **API** continues to serve its multiple clients.

Before we delve into the implementation, let's understand the three different states that constitute the circuit breaker:

- **Closed**: This is when all the service interconnections are intact (closed), and all the calls go through intended services. This state needs to keep track of failures to determine threshold limits. If the number of failures exceeds threshold limits, the services will move to the open state to avoid cascading impacts.

- **Open**: The open state of the services is responsible for returning errors without really executing their intended functions.
- **Half-open**: Once the services land in the open state, it should periodically (timeout) check for failures that made the services be in the open state. Moreover, if those failures are still occuring, it continues to keep the services in the open state until the next check. If the failures are no longer detected, the responsibility of this state is to trigger back to the closed state for the continuous function.

It's time to get our hands dirty with the circuit-breaker implementation. We'll use spring annotations, along with an incredibly dominant open source library called **hysterix**, and we can implement the entire concept with very little effort.

We need to have a minimum of two services to explain the circuit-breaker implementation, so we are creating circuit-breaker-service and circuit-breaker-consumer services, which will have the circuit-breaker pattern implemented. The following sections elucidate the investor services implementation of circuit-breaker.

Bring up any service that we've already developed, or, to simplify we have a lightweight service called **circuit-breaker-service**, and please note that this service doesn't have any specific implementation for circuit-breaker.

Now for the critical part of our implementation; that is, a new service called **circuit-breaker-service-consumer**, which will have all the necessary circuit-breaker implementations, along with a call to our first service (circuit-breaker-service). Let's perform the following steps:

Add the hysterix dependency to our `pom.xml` (`circuit-breaker-service-consumer/pom.xml`):

```
<dependency>
<groupId>org.springframework.cloud</groupId>
<artifactId>spring-cloud-starter-netflix-hystrix</artifactId>
<version>2.0.1.RELEASE</version>
</dependency>
```

Annotate `InvestorController` to enable circuit-breaker and introduce a new method for us to test (`circuit-breaker-service-consumer/com/**/InvestorController.java`):

```
@EnableCircuitBreaker
@RestController
public class InvestorController {
@Autowired
private InvestorService investorService;
```

```
// call the downstream service circuit-breaker-service
@GetMapping(value="/welcome", produces="text/plain;charset=UTF-8")
public String welcomePageWhichProducesCharset() {
return investorService.circuitBreakerImplWelcome();
}
```

Use the *Hystrix* command and create a method for the circuit-breaker implementation as well as a fallback method, as can be seen in the following code block. We will have two methods: one for the actual call (InvestorService.java/circuitBreakerImplWelcome) and another for fallback (InvestoreService.java/welcomeUrlFailureFallback), so that in case there are failures with the actual call, the app will call the fallback method:

```
@HystrixCommand(fallbackMethod="welcomeUrlFailureFallback")
public String circuitBreakerImplWelcome() {
logger.info("reached circuit breaker consumer circuit breaker impl");
RestTemplate restTemplate = new RestTemplate();
URI circuitBreakerServiceURI = URI.create(CIRCUIT_BREAKER_SERVICE_URL);
return restTemplate.getForObject(circuitBreakerServiceURI, String.class);
}
// fall back method for welcome page failures
public
 String
 welcomeUrlFailureFallback
 () {
logger.info("lucky we have a fallback method");
return WELCOME_URI_FALLBACK_MESG;
}
```

Cool, isn't it! Implementing the circuit-breaker with *Hysterix* is that simple. Now, let's build and run our services by following these steps:

1. Open a terminal and build circuit-breaker-service (mvn clean package of circuit-breaker-service)
2. Bring up circuit-breaker-service
3. Open a new terminal and build circuit-breaker-service-consumer
4. Bring up circuit-breaker-service-consumer
5. Open Postman and run http://localhost:9090/welcome
6. Observe the Japanese welcome text
7. Now, execute the circuit-breaker experimentation
8. Stop the circuit-breaker-service that we started in step 2
9. Run step 5 again, and now observe the English message

Yes, the circuit-breaker fallback is activated, and so we see the English message, not the Japanese message, as the circuit-breaker-service is down. However, the /welcome URI didn't break.

The following screenshot captured various phases for verifying the circuit-breaker implementation:

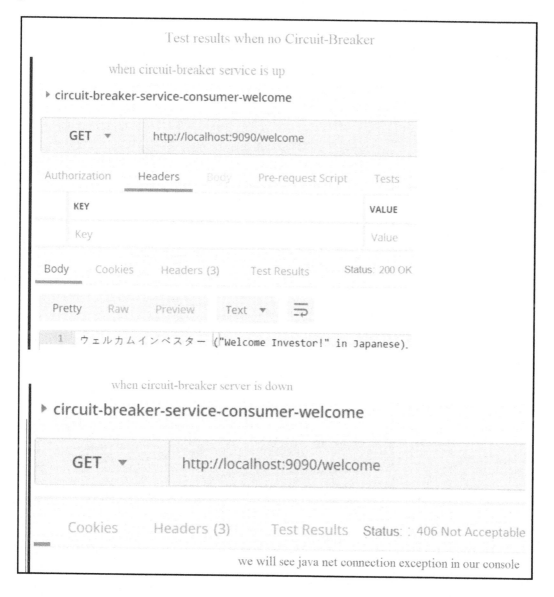

The following screenshot is another phase of this:

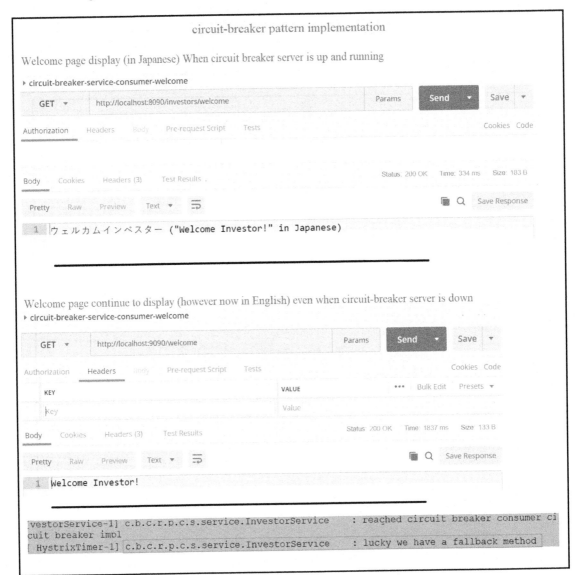

As we can observe in the preceding screenshots, in the pre-implementation of circuit-breaker, the `/welcome` call is failing and shows console message connection errors as well. However, after we implement circuit-breaker, the same call shows the content from the fallback method, even though the connections with the circuit-breaker-service are still failing.

Readers and designers are encouraged to test and enhance circuit-breaker-consumer with more fallback methods for other method calls as well.

> The downside of the circuit-breaker pattern is that the applications/services involved may experience slight performance hits. However, it's a good trade-off for many real-world applications.

Combining the circuit pattern and the retry pattern

As software designers, we understand the importance of gracefully handling application failures and failure operations. We may achieve better results by combining the retry pattern and the circuit breaker pattern as it provides the application with greater flexibility in handling failures.

The retry patterns enable the application to retry failed operations, expecting those operations to become operational and eventually succeed. However, it may result in a **denial of service (DoS)** attack within our application. The circuit-breaker pattern prevents an application from performing an operation that's likely to fail. How about an intelligent retry mechanism that's sensitive to any failures returned by the circuit breaker that indicates no transient failures, and so the application abandons any further retry attempts?

API facade

We knew the pattern called **facade** from GoF, which abstracts the complex subsystem from the callers and exposes only necessary details as interfaces to the end user. API facade' is also aligned with the same definitions and implementations.

Let's have a look at the following diagram, which depicts a simple implementation of multiple service calls from a client with and without the API facade pattern implementation:

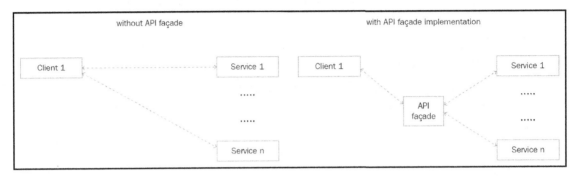

As we can see in the preceding diagram, the client is calling one API facade to make it simpler and more meaningful in cases where the clients need multiple service calls. However, that can be implemented with a single API endpoint instead of the client calling multiple endpoints. The API facades provide high scalability and high performance as well.

Our investor services have implemented a simple API facade implementation for its delete operations. As we saw earlier, the delete methods call the design for intent methods. However, we have made the *design for the intent* method abstract to the caller by introducing a simple interface to our investor services. That brings the facade to our API.

The interface for the delete service is shown as follows:

```
public interface DeleteServiceFacade {
    boolean deleteAStock(String investorId, String stockTobeDeletedSymbol);
    boolean deleteStocksInBulk(String investorId, List<String>
stocksSymbolsList);
}
```

The implementation for the delete service interface is shown in the following code snippet:

```
@Component
public class DeleteServiceFacadeImpl implements DeleteServiceFacade {
    private static final Logger logger =
LoggerFactory.getLogger(InvestorService.class);
    private InvestorServicesFetchOperations investorServicesFetchOperations
= new InvestorServicesFetchOperations();
        @Override
        public boolean deleteAStock(String investorId, String
stockTobeDeletedSymbol) {
                boolean deletedStatus = false;
```

```
            ,          Stock stockTobeDeleted =
investorServicesFetchOperations.fetchSingleStockByInvestorIdAndStockSymbol(
investorId,
                        stockTobeDeletedSymbol);
            if (stockTobeDeleted != null) {
                Investor investor =
investorServicesFetchOperations.fetchInvestorById(investorId);
                deletedStatus =
investor.getStocks().remove(stockTobeDeleted);
            }
            designForIntentCascadePortfolioDelete(investorId,
deletedStatus);
            return deletedStatus;
        }
. . . . .
. . . . .
```

As a simple exercise, we encourage the reader to implement our circuit breaker service call as an API facade and to also complete the bulk delete method within the delete service.

Backend for frontend

So far, we have developed various restful service APIs and endpoints so that any app developer can start to use it. However, we need to ensure those services will cater to various types of devices, since its real purpose is to serve any customer using any device, and not only for desktop users or as web-based applications.

Providing a better user experience across any device is vital, regardless of its backend services, and having figured out all possible best practices of developing RESTful services become meaningless if we aren't providing a better mechanism to use those services by heterogeneous end users and to their devices.

Backend for frontend (BFF) is a pattern first described by Sam Newman; it helps to bridge any API design gaps. BFF suggests introducing a layer between the user experience and the resources it calls. It also helps API designers to avoid customizing a single backend (services) for multiple interfaces:

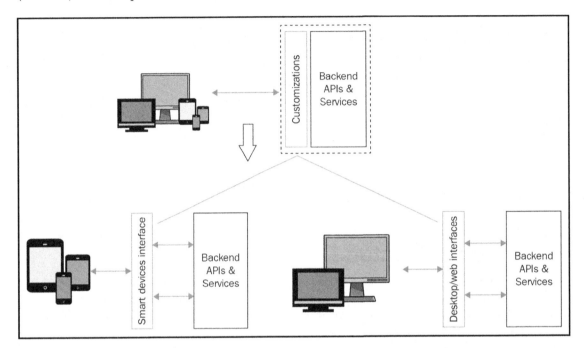

The preceding diagram depicts a simple implementation of the BFF pattern in the form of exclusive interfaces for both desktop and mobile devices. Each interface can define its necessary and unique requirements that cater to frontend requirements without worrying about impacting other frontend implementations.

Let's examine a number of specific requirements of each interface so that we understand why we need to have multiple interfaces for the same backend services:

- Response payload formatting and size may differ for each client
- Performance bottlenecks and optimization requirements due to the number of calls to be made to services
- When in need of shared or general purpose backend services, but with less development and maintenance overhead

BFF may not fit in cases such as multiple interfaces making the same requests to the backend, or using only one interface to interact with the backend services.

Please note that there are drawbacks with BFF, and exercise caution when deciding on separate, exclusive APIs/interfaces, as it warrants additional and lifelong maintenance, security improvement within layers, additional customized designs that lead to lapses in security, and defect leaks.

Summary

Learning the patterns with a few code examples always provides us with great insights. In this chapter, we discussed versioning our APIs, securing APIs with authorization, and enabling the service clients with uniform contract, entity endpoint, and endpoint redirection implementations. We also learned about Idempotent and its importance, which powers APIs with bulk operations. The most important part of this chapter is the circuit-breaker implementation with *Hysterix*, where we envisioned and implemented the resiliency patterns of API designs.

Having covered various advanced patterns, we concluded the chapter with the BFF pattern, and we learned how it reduces churns within the cross-implementation team by helping them to develop an exclusive interface for target environments.

In the next chapter, we'll cover RESTful API gateways, which should be an equally exciting read for API designers.

Further reading

- RESTful Java Patterns and Best Practices: `https://www.packtpub.com/application-development/restful-java-patterns-and-best-practices`

Microservice API Gateways
5

As microservices are typically fine-grained, any large-scale application has to consist of many microservices. With hundreds of microservices in an IT environment, the IT complexity is bound to escalate. The operational, monitoring, measurement, and management complexities of microservices are definitely greater, and hence the idea of leveraging API gateways originated and has flourished for not only mitigating rising complexity, but also for abstracting away all kinds of common capabilities from microservice source code. In this best practices chapter, we explain the role and responsibility of API gateways in the microservice era. Further on, you can also see how the reliability of microservice applications is ensured through the smart leveraging of an API gateway infrastructure.

Technical requirements

This chapter mainly talks about the crucial contributions of API gateway solutions to empower microservices to be the right and rewarding ingredient for producing enterprise-scale, mission-critical, cloud-hosted, service-oriented, event-driven, innovation-filled, process-aware, production-grade, and business-centric applications. We discuss popular API gateway solutions in this chapter. We also implement an aggregation service through the API gateway. The source code for the microservices (order service, customer service, and aggregation service) are deposited in the book's GitHub. The GitHub link for the book is `https://github.com/PacktPublishing/Hands-On-RESTful-API-Design-Patterns-and-Best-Practices`.

About microservice architecture

Legacy applications are inflexible, closed, monolithic, massive, and much more. Bringing forth business and technology modifications is beset with a number of issues and risks. Third-party service integration is a tough affair. Incorporating additional interfaces such as web, mobile, and cloud is another difficult thing for legacy systems. There are several access channels emerging these days, and our applications need to have the innate capability to work with multiple channels. In future, businesses will demand more with less from their IT teams and partners. In short, the development and operational complexities of legacy applications are prohibitively large. **Microservice architecture (MSA)** is all about achieving speed and safety at scale, and the MSA ecosystem is continuously growing to provide scores of competent technologies, tools, and frameworks for efficiently implementing a range of business applications and IT services. This approach etches and elevates IT as a viable and value-adding business partner. That is, business-centric IT is the new normal owing to a raft of noteworthy advancements in the IT space. The previously held thought (IT is cost-centric) is changing fast, and IT is being proudly announced as the profit-centric paradigm.

Any software application based on a microservice architecture simply consists of a suite of small, modular, and easily manageable services. Each service runs in a unique process and communicates through well-defined APIs. RESTful interfacing is the most popular and lightweight entrance for services to find, bind, and use one another. API-enabled microservices smoothly align with the business to deal with changes in an agile fashion, match business changes with an agile response, and deliver solutions in a decentralized manner. Microservices are independently deployable, horizontally scalable, composable, interoperable, publicly discoverable, network accessible, technology-agnostic, modular (loosely coupled and highly cohesive), fine-grained, and so now. The convergence of containerization and microservices results in big savings and benefits for businesses and technology professionals. All kinds of microservices are being methodically containerized and hosted in **bare metal (BM)** servers and **virtual machines (VMs)**. The lightweight nature of containers along with business-centric and purpose-specific microservices brings a number of crucial advantages for the business world. There are other technological advancements in the form of container orchestration and management solutions in order to form container/service clusters to realize multi-container, business-aware, mission-critical, adaptive, and composite applications.

With microservices emerging and becoming established as the simple and optimal building block for designing, developing, deploying, and managing production-grade business applications and IT platforms, existing monolithic applications are being meticulously partitioned into a number of interactive and insightful microservices. The proven technique of divide and conquer is doing extremely well, even now through MSA conundrum. The individual yet interconnected microservices can be separately advanced and deployed without bringing down other microservices. There are a number of business, technical, and user advantages and hence there is a zeal among business executives, technology professionals, and IT operators to embrace MSA. New applications are being built using the salient features of the MSA from the ground up. In the following sections, we will see how an API gateway infrastructure is paramount for achieving the intended success of microservices architecture.

We have written about the widespread success of the RESTful service paradigm in the other chapters of this book with a bevy of practical examples. The gist is that RESTful APIs allow consumers/user applications to progress through an application (web, cloud, mobile, business, IoT, and so on) by appropriately selecting links (resources), such as `/product/book/`, and through specific HTTP operations (methods), such as `GET`, `DELETE`, `POST` or `PATCH`. This results in the next resource, which actually represents the next state of the application. REST stands for representational state transfer. And this new state gets transferred to the consumer for its subsequent use.

The prominent infrastructure modules in microservice-centric applications

Horizontal scaling and independent deployment are being touted as the key hallmarks of microservices. Microservices and their instances can be easily replicated, replaced, refactored, and restored to adapt to incoming traffic. Fresh applications are being designed, developed, and deployed as microservices, while legacy applications are being systematically partitioned into a pool of microservices working together. It is therefore clear that MSA is the prime architectural pattern and style for next-generation software applications. In this section, we will discuss the key infrastructure components of MSA-compliant systems.

Service registry

Microservices are increasingly dynamic and widely dispersed. Thus, for leveraging microservices and for enabling service discovery (static as well as automated), we need a centralized service registry/repository mechanism in place. The service registry is designed to keep track of the registered microservice instances in order to give correct information about the services and their latest locations. This registry is a sort of a database for accurately containing and maintaining the network locations of the service instances. If there is a movement, then the microservices have to consciously approach and update the service registry. The API gateway, on getting requests from client microservices, connects and tries to procure the location details of the serving microservices. If there is any deviation or deficiency, then there is the possibility of an unwanted failure. Every microservice instance has to register itself with the centralized service registry on startup and does the reverse by de-registering on shutdown. The registration of service instances is typically refreshed periodically using a heartbeat mechanism. The service registry module has to be highly available and for that high-availability requirement, the overwhelmingly recommended approach is to have a cluster of the service registry module. It is not recommended to cache the network location details obtained from the registry at the API gateway or the registry-aware client. If location details are cached at the API gateway, then it may turn out to be degrading the performance of the API gateway. It is the sole responsibility of microservice instances to update the registry about their changing status (availability). The role of the service registry is illustrated in the following figure:

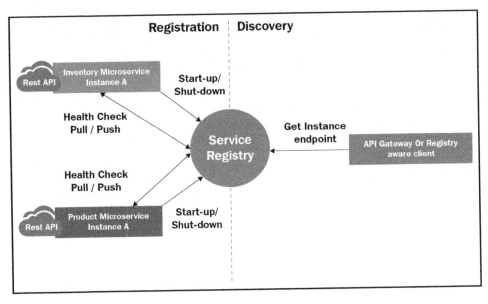

The microservices, service registry, and API gateway interactions

Service discovery

We explained how the service registry solution comes in handy when pinpointing the location details of microservices and their instances. In a monolithic application, finding and calling application components happen through one of the language-level methods. If application components are being run in different process spaces, then there are **remote method invocations (RMIs)**, **remote procedure calls (RPCs)**, **distributed component object model (DCOM)**, and so on. In a traditional legacy IT environment, applications run at fixed and well-known locations. That is, the hosts and ports are fixed in order to be found and used. Applications, therefore, can easily call one another using any one of the standard communication and data transmission protocols. However, in the agile and adept microservices era, the number of microservices and their instances are changing frequently. Further on, in order to bring about much-desired optimization, microservices and their instances are being redeployed in other locations. Therefore, client microservices need to use an advanced service discovery mechanism to get to know the latest status of microservice instances. For simplification, there are two main service discovery patterns—client-side discovery and server-side discovery.

For client-side discovery, the client will get the location of a service instance from service registry, as the registries has the information of latest locations of all the services. The client knows the address of the **Service Registry**. The client then uses a load balancing algorithm to select the optimal service instances and makes a request.

For server-side discovery, the **Client** makes a request to the **API Gateway**. The **API Gateway** then queries the **Service Registry** to get the network location of the desired microservices. Based on that location information, the API gateway makes an attempt to connect and leverage the ability to serve microservices.

The following diagram illustrates the differences between client- and server-side service discovery:

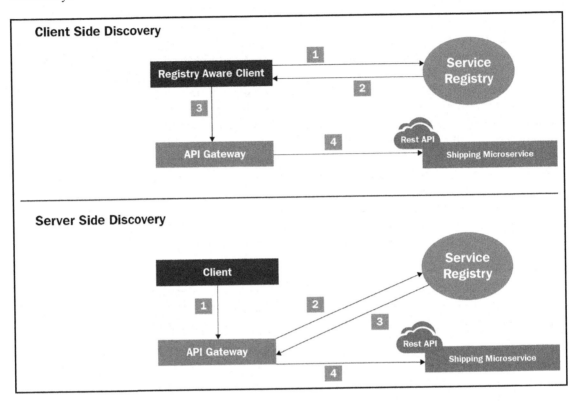

Composition/orchestration

Microservices primarily implement business functionality. For creating composite, business-centric, and process-aware applications, microservices must be linked together. For ensuring composition, there are two methods—orchestration and choreography. Also, there are static and dynamic compositions. The API gateway can act as the orchestration module. The other option is to code the orchestration logic and keep it as a separate utility service. The following diagram clearly depicts how service orchestration builds composite services, which are process-aware and business-centric:

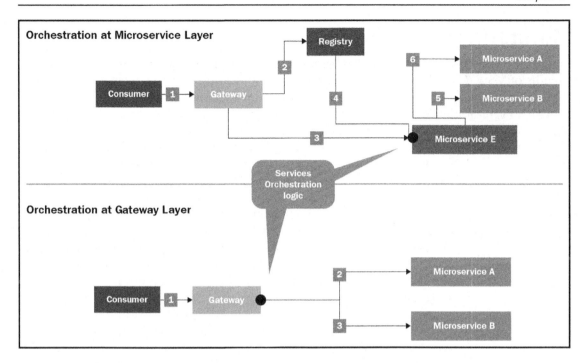

Transformation

There are several different types of, such as client applications on IoT devices, browsers for resource-constrained devices, web and mobile applications, and so on. With the input/output device ecosystem is consistently on the rise, the client side of any application and service has to be worked out separately. Client applications on heterogeneous devices follow different data representation, exchange, and persistence formats. Also, they follow different data transmission protocols. Then there are synchronous and asynchronous communication protocols. The data format and protocol translation requirements are bound to increase in a heterogeneous environment. The API gateway facilitates translation and other transformation needs quite comfortably. Transformation adapters can be freshly baked in, based on emerging needs, and deposited in a centralized place to be readily found and used. With purpose-agnostic and specific devices, optimal data formats and protocols are being continuously developed; there is a need for fresh data and protocol translators to enable them to join in mainstream computing.

Monitoring

Monitoring system resources and microservices is becoming vital for realizing the original benefits of MSA. There are service and application monitoring tools. As most microservices are being containerized, container monitoring tools have gained prominence recently. There are even monitoring tools for Kubernetes, which has gained the top slot and spot as the container life cycle management platform. As this chapter has been specially prepared to explain everything about API gateways, it is logical to write about API gateway monitoring. API gateways are paramount and pertinent for the intended success of microservices in delivering a variety of functionalities. Every service request/response gets routed through them. The monitoring and measurement of the API's operation, performance, health condition, scalability, security, and log data are critical for meeting the agreed SLA and OLA parameters. The much-insisted health monitoring is done to make sure the gateway is up and running all the time. Monitoring is indispensable for ensuring service reliability and stability. The aspect of observability is vital for service availability, adaptability, and analytics. For minutely monitoring the health of systems, resource parameters such as processing power, memory capacity, and I/O rates (network and storage) are the main focus. The other important things to be precisely monitored and measured are the connectivity (network), security alerts, secure backups, recovery (data and disaster), and so on. Finally, logging data plays a very important role in supplying a lot of useful and usable information to the concerned in solidifying and shaping up the distinct goal of business continuity.

The other important factor is nothing but the traffic monitoring. Gathering and deeply analyzing traffic data will enable the operations team to consider, contemplate, and carry out correct measures in time, with all the clarity and confidence. The essential metrics to be faithfully considered include the total number of requests being sent out for an API for a period of time, the performance/throughput value, the number of successful and exception messages received, the number of blocked messages by API gateway, and so on. Also, request categorization is taken into consideration. This deeper and deft analysis helps to easily predict traffic situations with greater accuracy so that any kind of spike and surge can be taken care of without any kind of breakdown or slowdown.

Load balancing and scaling

This is an important ingredient for ensuring the extended availability of software systems. The goal of achieving application scalability (horizontal) through infrastructure elasticity is accomplished by leveraging a **load balancer** (**LB**) (software or hardware). We need traffic information to predict and prescribe the correct countermeasures in time. Deeper real-time analysis of traffic data helps us to understand and estimate the load on the applications. The insights from load data helps cloud administrators and operation teams to collectively and concisely formulate viable policies and rules for application scalability. Additional infrastructure modules can be readied in time in order to take up extra load. The API gateways can also scale horizontally as well as vertically so that the high availability of an API gateway solution is guaranteed. Otherwise, an API gateway can become a single point of failure. To have a clustered API gateway setup, we can have a LB in front of the API gateway. What this means is that multiple instances of an API gateway solution can be leveraged to ensure continuity, and all those instances can run the same configuration; this uniformity helps in virtualizing the same APIs and to execute the same policies. If there are multiple API gateway groups, then the capability (load balancing) can be elegantly extended and accurately accomplished across groups.

The API gateway does not mandate any additional requirements on LBs. That is, the user and data loads are balanced based on widely recommended characteristics including the response time, the system load at that point of time, and so on. API gateways are maintained in a stateless fashion in order to ensure they are not weighed down by state information. This also enables service messages to take any route to reach the appropriate and assigned services. Some prominent components such as caches and counters, which are typically held on a distributed cache, are meticulously updated for every unique message. This setup ultimately helps the API gateway to complete its obligations without any problem across modes (sticky and non-sticky).

The distributed nature of API gateways poses a certain restriction during active/active and active/passive clustering. For example, to lose any counter and cache state, the system has to be designed in such a way that at least one API gateway is active at all times. Precisely speaking, to ensure high availability and reliability, as previously indicated, multiple API gateway instances have to run in a connected and clustered manner. The API gateway is able to maintain zero downtime by having the configuration deployment in a steady and continuous fashion. Generally, an API gateway instance in the cluster takes a few seconds to update its configuration. And when it is getting updated, that particular instance does not entertain any new request. Still, all the existing in-flight requests are fully honored. However, the other API gateway instances in the cluster can ceaselessly receive and process new requests and deliver the results. The key role of the **Load Balancer** here is to ensure all the incoming requests are pushed to the correct API gateway instances that are receiving and processing fresh requests. Thus, API gateway clustering is important for continuously receiving and responding to service messages and the **Load Balancer** plays a vital role in fulfilling this, as illustrated in the following diagram:

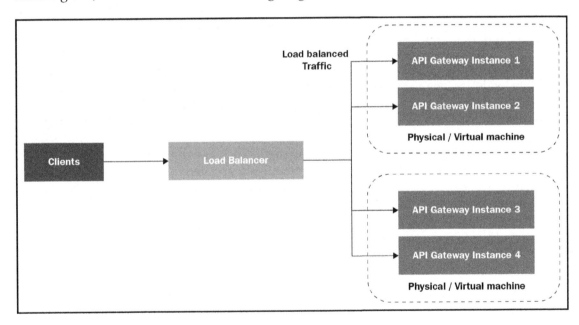

High availability and failover

In the era of microservices, guaranteeing high available through fault tolerance, fault detection, and isolation is an important thing for architects. In the recent past, API gateway solutions emerged as a critical component for the microeconomic era. Microservice architecture is being touted as as the soul and savior for facilitating the mandated business adaptivity, process optimization, and automation. API gateways are the only entry point for microservices to find and talk with one another to fulfill business tasks. This broker/middleware solution is blessed with a number of common features so that microservices can just focus on business functionalities. The **non-functional requirements (NFRs)** and the **quality of service (QoS)** attributes are achieved through gateway solutions. To achieve high availability and stability, the recommended action and approach is to deploy the API gateway in **high availability (HA)** mode. As previously described, API gateway instances are usually deployed behind a standard LB. The LB continuously probes the API gateway instances to understand whether they are alive or not. The health condition and performance level of each of the instances are captured and used by the LB to embark on the appropriate remedy in time, so that the continuity of the system does not get affected in any way. If the LB comes to know that an API gateway is not functioning, then the LB redirects and routes inbound traffic to the gateway instance that is functioning and delivering on its obligations.

Timely alerts are configured in order to get relevant notifications in the case of untoward incidents. If an alert is triggered, then the issue along with its metadata can be understood, as the data analytics capability is an important feature of any API gateway product. Generally, API gateways are kept as a stateless entity as they are designed and destined to be bombarded with millions of service request messages every second. However, API gateways can maintain cached data, which can be replicated across a cluster of API gateways. Such an arrangement helps to maintain the peer-to-peer relationship among API gateway instances.

HA and failover guidelines

Experts have produced a series of guidelines and best practices to ensure the high availability of systems:

- In order to guarantee maximum availability, an API gateway has to be used in proven active/active mode.
- There is a need for deeper and decisive analysis on traffic data. The insights from this analysis help operators and others manning production environments to plan and protect against message flooding.

- Tool-supported automated network infrastructure monitoring and management are essential for ensuring the highest availability. Not only collecting operational and log data, but also subjecting them to a variety of investigations unravels a lot of useful and usable information. All the knowledge thus discovered and disseminated goes a long way in empowering the network infrastructure to work in prime and pristine condition. The analytics feature intrinsically embedded in an API gateway solution comes in handy in analyzing and articulating what to do to prevent any kind of failure and faltering. There are specific as well as agnostic monitoring tools, which can be integrated with knowledge visualization/report generation tools.

Governance

As the number of APIs keeps on increasing, it is essential to establish policies and to put other mechanisms in place for effective monitoring and management. The policies can broadly be categorized as design-time and runtime governance. The policies are highly influenced by business objectives and goals. Increasingly, IT is being upgraded to meet changes in business sentiments. Thus, IT policies have to be synced with business expectations to produce solid and smart governance.

About API gateway solutions

In a nutshell, an API gateway is a multifaceted proxy that accomplishes a variety of integration, intermediation, and enrichment tasks. It has all the information about the main microservice endpoints in order to correctly and cognitively mediate, route, and invoke a respective endpoint. This is performed after the initial request verification, content filtering, authentication, and authorization.

A typical API gateway has to have the following ingrained and serviceable competencies. The common features of any API gateway solution include authentication and authorization, message enrichment, remediation, process-based composition, traffic routing and management, and service monitoring.

An API gateway is bound to provide a single and unified API entry point across one or more internal APIs. There can be different distributed sources, such as client applications, services, and devices, trying to access the API gateway. Clients send a variety of requests and expect appropriate responses. The gateway is supposed to do a variety of initiation, intermediation, and implementation tasks. One of them is to *unify* these requests and work with the backend services. All kinds of proxy and aggregation activities are accomplished through API gateways, which also ensure rate limiting and security needs are met as well. In the microservice era, there can be hundreds of services, and hence the need for API gateways and management platforms is bound to grow further. In short, an API gateway can help provide a unified entry point for external consumers. The orchestration/choreography, brokerage, discovery, routing, enrichment, policy enforcement, governance, concierge jobs, and so on are performed by standardized API gateway solutions. On the other hand, API management adds additional capabilities such as analytics and life cycle management. In future, there will be attempts to meet QoS and NFRs such as availability, scalability, high performance/throughput, security, and reliability through replication and fault tolerance, through a combination of API gateways, cluster and orchestration platforms, service mesh solutions, and so on.

API gateways for microservice-centric applications

The unique contributions of API gateways for operationalizing microservices in a beneficial fashion are growing as days pass. The main features of an API gateway are the following:

1. **Adds flexibility**: API gateways are supposed to hide internal concerns from external clients. An API gateway decouples external APIs from internal microservice APIs. This abstraction facilitates the addition, replacement, displacement, and substitution of advanced microservice implementations in place of legacy ones. The APIs of internal microservices can be changed without affecting the requesting microservices. Services can be freshly registered and referenced in a service registry or repository. The service discovery of newer services can be smooth and error free. Services can be versioned.

2. **Adds an additional layer**: As microservices are not contacted directly, the security of services is greatly strengthened. Through using an API gateway, it is possible to stop all kinds of malicious attacks on internal microservices. Every microservice has its own data store. Thus, not only service security but also data security is enabled. Through rate limiting/throttling offered by API gateways, distributed DoS attacks can be thwarted easily.

3. **Enables support for data and protocol translation**: There are disparate data transmission and communication protocols. There are synchronous and asynchronous communications and their corresponding protocols. Besides HTTP, there are other protocols such as ProtoBuf (`https://developers.google.com/protocol-buffers/docs/reference/overview`), AMQP (`https://www.amqp.org`), COAP, and more, for integrating with third-party applications and services in order to produce and sustain integrated applications. This is the essence of API gateway solutions. Precisely speaking, all the common capabilities of microservices are safely abstracted and incorporated into API gateways. The idea is to have the business logic in any microservice implementation. This best practice keeps microservices simple and easy to manipulate. All the security, networking, third-party integration, adding volumes, fulfilling QoS attributes, and other cross-cutting concerns are accumulated together and accomplished through API gateways, which act as a centralized and clustered middleware solution.

The following diagram illustrates how an API gateway solution links microservices with service clients:

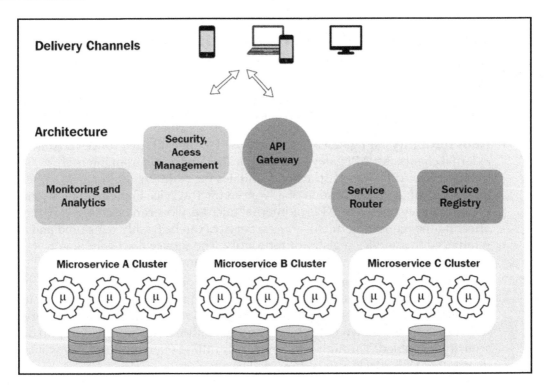

Essentially, the **API Gateway** is a reverse proxy to microservices and serves as the single point of contact for the growing list of clients to enter into the system. This implements the age-old facade pattern for the microservice era. Further on, API gateway solutions simplify and standardize API design, implementation, and management. The consistency of microservices, their instances, and the software infrastructure is ensured. Because of this consistency, it is quite easy to establish and enforce the service level and security requirements of microservices. Formulating and firming up policies at different layers and levels of the system stack become vital for the intended success of microservice architecture. The gateway ultimately helps to address the key challenges and concerns such as security, caching, monitoring, and much more. It can handle heterogeneous clients, multiple backend microservices, and their instances. Service discovery is automated through the API gateway. The following diagram shows various features and functionalities of an API gateway solution:

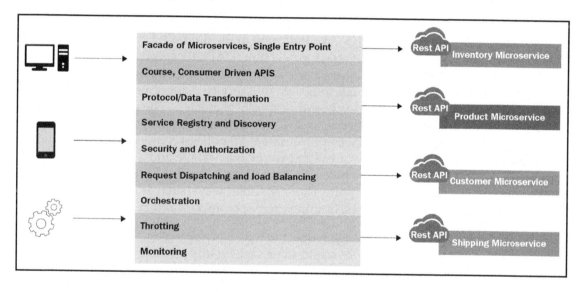

The issues with microservice API gateways

We have listed several key benefits and contributions of API gateways toward microservice-centric business applications. However, there are a few drawbacks too. As we all know, this gateway infrastructure is an additional abstraction layer, so all the control and the data flows happen via this middleware solution; therefore, there is the possibility of system performance degradation. This introduces an additional hub through which service requests and responses pass. Not only is it a single point of contact but also a single point of failure. When the number of microservices goes up significantly, complications will increase steadily. Service-to-service communication resiliency is not provided by API gateways. There are service mesh solutions, which guarantee the much-needed service resiliency that, in turn, results in reliable applications. With the widespread use of technologically advanced cloud infrastructures, we can safely expect lots of reliable systems and environments.

Policy configuration in API gateways—we indicated in the preceding section that the API gateway is capable of doing **content attack protection (CAP)**. By specifying and modifying security policies, API gateways can thwart any security attacks. Content attacks are primarily performed by inserting malicious data into service request messages. The most widely known content attacks include inserting special characters. The other prominent content attack methods are text patterns, and SQL and XPATH injections. The way to surmount this type of attack is to have appropriate CAP policies configured for inbound as well as outbound traffic. These measures can protect against SQL and XPATH injection attacks. The other considerations include security attacks being forbidden by limiting the HTTP versions, methods, and URL path. There are other ways, such as defining a whitelist of domain names, client IP addresses, limiting query parameters and HTTP headers.

The IoT device (client) sends a message request to microservice via an API gateway. An inbound CAP policy scans the service request message for any possible content-based attacks. If there is any violation, then the API gateway sends an error message back to the IoT device client. If everything is perfect, then the API gateway passes verified and validated messages to the service mediation layer for identity verification and authentication, authorization. Then, the right microservice endpoint is invoked and messages are processed. The microservice in turn calls one or more microservices. Then, the outbound CAP policy scans the reply message for any content-based attacks. If there is no violation, then the response is delivered to the requested client.

Security features of API gateways

Security plays a critical part in any distributed IT environment. Data integrity, confidentiality, and availability are the most important parameters for ensuring impenetrable data security. There are several mechanisms such as encryption and decryption, digital signature, hashing for securing data while in transit, persistence, and usage. For microservice-centric applications running on cloud infrastructures, the security aspect starts with identification, authentication, and authorization. Security policies are another solution widely used in public cloud environments. **Hardware security modules (HSMs)** are prevalent these days as it is not easy to break in while guaranteeing higher throughput. Then there are several security appliances such as firewalls, intrusion detection, and prevention systems. Unified threat modeling and management solutions are also getting a lot of attention these days, considering the severity of security threats and vulnerabilities in the microservice era. As mentioned previously, API gateways form an important phenomenon for the intended success of microservice architecture. Considering the strategically sound significance, API gateway solutions are being stuffed with security-enablement properties. A bevy of unique security characteristics are being incorporated into API gateways to ensure utmost and unbreakable security. Let's take a look at these security features.

Federated identity is the widely preferred way for service authentication and authorization. As we all know, microservices exclusively focus on business functionality. The supporting functionalities and facilities are attached when needed. The proven technique of divide and conquer is still working wonders in the IT world, which is becoming hugely complicated yet sophisticated owing to the consistently evolving and erudite trends and transitions in the IT space. Especially, identity management, being the prime security requirement, is being delegated to third-party solutions and services. That is, each microservice does not need to obtain and store user credentials in order to authenticate them during subsequent requests.

Instead, the identity management system takes care of the authentication well. The following diagram shows the role authorization servers play in the authentication and authorization processes. The attached database stores all the user credentials in clustered mode. Also third-party authentication and authorization management systems are closely coupled with API gateways in order to seamlessly and smoothly do the initial security-enablement tasks:

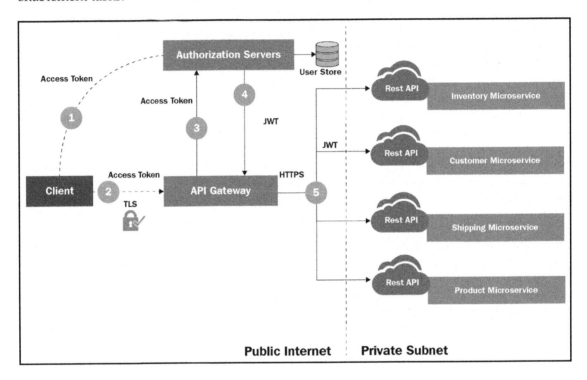

There are three key protocols enabling the federated identity:

- OpenID
- SAML
- OAuth

The flow is as follows. The application client first sends a request and grabs a **JWT** access token from the third-party authentication and authorization server by supplying the mandated credentials. Once the mandated credentials are obtained, the client then embeds the access token in the Authorization HTTP header of the API request. The **API Gateway** then validates the access token supplied by the client with the authorization server. Once validated by the third-party authentication server, the API gateway passes the **JWT** access token to the appropriate backend microservices to initiating the business tasks. If there is a need for other downstream microservices to fulfill the service request, then the same **JWT** token is shared across to all the participating and contributing microservices. Microservices that are in collaborating mode have to attach the **JWT** access token to their request messages:

- **Confidentiality**: Data security and privacy are very much demanded owing to the remote storage. Also the pervasive, public, and open internet, which turns out to be the world's largest communication infrastructure and information powerhouse, is the data carrier. Keeping data safe and secure is the foremost requirement for business entities and their IT divisions. That is, the confidentiality of data cannot be compromised at any cost. Primary data protection is done by the API gateway. The other option is that the database server is totally insulated from other servers. As a way of ensuring data privacy while data is being persisted, data is encrypted and the encryption key is managed separately. Data servers are not allowed to be accessed by clients directly. Every data access request is routed through a frontend service.

- **Integrity**: The service messages comprising confidential, customer, and corporate information cannot be hacked and manipulated. A compromised message can be used for the wrong purposes, such as bringing down servers or stealing private information. To ensure better integrity for messages and data, a number of purpose-specific and agnostic checks are done on messages while the messages are passed through a host of intermediary servers from the source to the sink. Typically hashing algorithms are used in order to identify whether there has been any kind of data modification.

- **Availability**: Service availability is very important for attaining success with microservice architecture. There are hackers attempting to bring down services. The API gateway provides the first defense against this. Then, there are LBs to ensure the service continuity. Clustered and cloud servers come in handy in guaranteeing the high availability of services. **Distributed denial of service (DDoS)** attacks on services can be thwarted through the application of the throttling/rate limiting pattern.

- **Secure communication**: Communication has to be secured through the SSL/TLS mechanism. Microservices and API gateways are, therefore, mandated to be SSL/TLS-compliant. Such a setup easily safeguards against man-in-the-middle attacks. Also, the widely used message and data encryption method secures against peeking at and tampering with service messages and data.

Apart from other functionalities, API gateways are predominantly leveraged to secure microservice-based applications. Security acquires special significance as microservices are deployed in geographically distributed server environments. Also, with web-scale applications, microservices and their distinct instances are being frontended by LBs. API gateways represent a growing collection of advanced services that enable microservices to contribute to business automation and augmentation.

Prominent API gateway solutions

There are a few competent API gateway solutions (open source as well as commercial grade).

Kong (https://konghq.com/) is an open source **API** gateway solution. The Kong server can run in front of any RESTful API. Kong fully supports popular REST APIs. Due to their lightweight and versatile nature, RESTful is the widely used API standard for all kinds of web, mobile, embedded, and cloud applications. The current capability of the Kong API gateway can be substantially extended through plug-ins, which bring in extra functionality to meet evolving needs. That is, the core features and facilities offered by Kong can be supplemented through additional functionalities provided by versatile plug-ins. That is, Kong natively supports plug and play architecture. Small, medium, and large-scale business enterprises across the globe are using this innovation-field product suite in production-grade IT environments. Kong can be deployed in on-demand, online, and off-premises clouds. Also, it can run on on-premises private clouds. As illustrated in the following diagram, OpenResty and Nginx are the core engines of Kong. OpenResty is a high-performance web platform that integrates the standard `Nginx` core, `LuaJIT`, and a host of libraries. Kong uses either Cassandra or PostgreSQL as the data store. The popular features accentuated by Kong include authentication, monitoring and analytics, and request/response translation and logging.

To better understand how Kong works, here is a typical request workflow of an API that uses Kong:

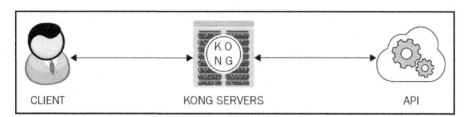

Once Kong has started to run, every request made to the **API** will hit the Kong server first. And the Kong server acts as the proxy to send the request to the **API** of the requested service. In short, everything in the microservice world gets initiated and implemented through an API gateway. When everything uses an **API**, the role of API gateway, management, and analytics solutions is bound to escalate in the days to unfold:

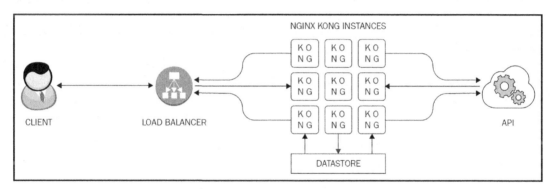

Red Hat 3scale APIcast gateway (https://www.3scale.net/tag/open-source/)—the APIcast gateway is also Nginx-based and made available as an open source software solution. This API gateway is configured within 3scale's Admin Portal. The gateway is a crucial part of 3scale API management, which is a **software as a service (SaaS)** offering. The Admin Portal has a number of customization and configuration functionalities, such as allowing customers to define desired authentication methods, setting rate limits, getting analytics done on API usage data, and creating a developer portal for their API consumers. The 3scale APIcast gateway lets you deploy the API gateway service on a cloud environment with a few clicks. This deployment is much faster than others because there is no need for any kind of code modification at the backend. APIcast is emerging as the perfect solution for low or medium volume APIs. Enterprises widely use APIcast in staging environments and this speeds up the process of testing.

Tyk (`https://tyk.io/`) is also an open source API gateway. This solution intrinsically takes care of API management activities. The Tyk package consists of an API gateway and an API management dashboard. It also has the API analytics feature. A developer portal is another interesting module of this package. Tyk can be installed in on-premises clouds. It is available in leading public clouds and can be purchased and used as a cloud service. Not only that, it integrates private and public clouds to contribute as the API gateway solution for hybrid clouds. Under load, this API gateway can do the full key validation, security verification, quota management, and data analytics, without any hitch or hurdle. The developer portal is made available to empower the development community.

Moesif (`https://www.moesif.com/`) is primarily an API analytics solution. This has the capability to understand how developers use APIs and to know why certain errors occur and repeat sometimes. Also, it helps to notify API providers of any hidden issues before the customers see them. Thus, this solution is a helping hand for service providers. As we tend toward the API economy, the API analytics solution plays an important role.
Today, thousands of developers process billions of API calls through Moesif for debugging, monitoring, and understanding API usage. The first and foremost requirement to build a great API (whether it is REST, GraphQL, or JSON-RPC API) is to precisely and concisely measure how developers use the APIs. Product teams use the API analytics capability offered by this solution to understand how their APIs are being used. By leveraging the proven and potential **machine learning** (**ML**) techniques, Moesif API insights enable data-driven teams to continuously improve their API and **developer experience** (**DX**).

Ambassador (`https://www.getambassador.io/`) is a popular open source and Kubernetes-native API gateway for the microservice world. This gateway solution can do several things for the container world. Ambassador can authenticate all kinds of incoming requests before intelligently routing them to backend services. It natively supports TLS termination. In addition to that, Ambassador supports rate limiting/throttling via an external third-party service. This rate limiting is facilitated through the Envoy proxy's rate limiting capabilities. A key feature of Envoy is the observability feature, which is enabled by exposing a multitude of statistics about its own operations. Ambassador makes it easy to disseminate that knowledge to statistics and monitoring tools such as Prometheus, Datadog, and so on. Ambassador generally relies on the fast-evolving Kubernetes platform for ensuring service reliability, availability, and scalability.

Envoy (`https://www.envoyproxy.io/`) was originally built by Lyft. Envoy is a high performance C++ distributed proxy designed for single services and applications. Envoy turns out to be a competent solution as a communication bus. For microservice-centric applications, this contributes as the universal data plane. Finally, it is a core engine for service mesh solutions. Envoy runs alongside every application and abstracts the networking complexity by providing all the common network features in a platform-agnostic manner. By leveraging the Envoy mesh solution, it is possible to visualize and pinpoint problem areas because features such as consistent observability, tuning overall performance, and adding a substrate are made available in a single place.

Tree gateway (`http://treegateway.org/`) is a free and open source solution. This can create a complete and customizable pipeline to handle service requests. Tree gateway makes it easy to create and sustain big clusters. In addition to this, it supports the ready formation of Redis clusters to share configurations, circuit-breaker states, and cached content. Any API configuration can be changed at any point in time, and all configurations get propagated to other tree gateway cluster nodes, without any problems. This comes with an advanced circuit breaker module that can *fast fail* responses when any API fails, falls, and falters. Furthermore, it innately supports real-time monitoring and analytics. A pluggable engine allows any kinds of transformations or verifications to any API requests.

Gravitee.io (`https://gravitee.io/`) is a flexible, lightweight, blazingly fast, and open source API management solution. This tool helps any business enterprise to control who, when, and how users access the APIs in a finely grained manner.

API Umbrella (`https://apiumbrella.io/`) is a proxy solution that sits in front of any API. It can seamlessly add API gateway and analytics functionalities, such as API keys, rate limiting, and so on.

Express gateway (`https://www.express-gateway.io/`) is a microservice API gateway, which is built on Express.js. It is typically fast, flexible, and community driven.

API gateway solutions are very important for API-enabled microservices. RESTful APIs are the most prevalent and powerful. RESTful APIs are overwhelmingly used by web, mobile, cloud, and IoT applications and services. Not only software applications but also resource-constrained and intensive embedded devices are being linked with one another via RESTful APIs. With microservices quickly proliferating and as everything is stuffed with APIs, there is a mandate for advanced API gateway solutions to form integrated and orchestrated applications, which businesses increasingly prefer these days. API management and analytics capabilities are also attached with gateway solutions to make them comprehensive. A variety of plugins and utility services are being built and incorporated on demand. Furthermore, API gateway solutions are being integrated with third-party tools for monitoring, measurement, management, and visualization. The well-intended approach is to have a dynamic pool of modular (loosely and lightly coupled and highly cohesive) API gateway services instead of a monolithic API gateway solution, which is difficult to manage, inflexible, and closed.

Service mesh versus API gateway

We have discussed API gateway solutions extensively in relation to the success of the MSA paradigm. We all know that in order to increase the resiliency of microservices, the service mesh solutions are being pampered. And in this section, we are to discuss the key differences between API gateways and service meshes.

Firstly, the API gateway, as explained in the preceding section, the key objective of using an API gateway is to express and expose microservices to the outside world. With the attachment of API management modules, APIs are managed well. API data is captured and subjected to a variety of investigations to produce insights to steer API gateways in the right direction:

- API services call the downstream microservices that can be atomic and composite. The noteworthy capability of API gateways is to fuse multiple downstream services into something that is useful for the requesting services. That is, services are blended as per the stated requirements to produce process-aware, mission-critical, and composite services.
- API gateways also come with inbuilt support for service discovery, analytics, and security. The observability capability for capturing various metrics along with monitoring, distributed logging, and distributed tracing is the key differentiator for gateway solutions.
- API gateways closely work with several other software solutions, such as API management, marketplace/store, and portals in order to be comprehensive for the microservice era.

Secondly, service mesh—this is relatively a new solution type and approach for providing the resiliency characteristic, which is becoming an important one for microservice-based applications. As we all know, services ought to interact with one another in order to realize bigger and better business-scale services. When services talk to one another, several things can go wrong. In order to guarantee service communication resiliency, the IT industry is leaning towards embracing the new concept of a service mesh, which is a kind of network and communication infrastructure to ensure service resiliency. Service mesh implementations have embedded resiliency-enablement patterns such as circuit breaker, retry, timeout, and throttling/rate limiting. There are service mesh solutions such as Istio, Linkered, and Conduit. Advanced functionalities such as service discovery and observability are being incorporated into these solutions. The functionalities of API gateways and service mesh solutions are clearly demarcated. It is also possible to use both of them in a production environment.

The service mesh is used alongside most other service implementations as a sidecar. A service mesh provides a stream of utility and horizontal functionalities for enabling service resiliency.

In conclusion, API gateways facilitate API communications between a client application and a server application. Also, microservices within an application can be integrated through the API gateway solution. An API gateway operating at layer 7 (HTTP) enables internal as well as external communication. Other noteworthy services include user authentication, throttling/rate limiting, transformations, logging, and so on.

Service mesh solutions such as Istio, Linkered, and Conduit are for enabling service communication resiliency. That is, they mainly focus on routing internal communications. A service mesh operates primarily at layer 4 (TCP). All the resiliency and reliability design patterns such as circuit breakers, timeouts, retries, and health checks are intrinsically implemented and incorporated into service mesh solutions.

Summary

Microservices are being proclaimed as a groundbreaking architectural style for producing and sustaining business and IT applications and platforms. Cloud environments are filled up with bare metal servers, virtual machines, and containers. Microservices can be hosted on these and run to extract and supply their unique functionalities. As the number of microservices is growing rapidly, we need technology-sponsored and complexity mitigation solutions and services. API gateway solutions are being presented as the viable and venerable infrastructure (software or hardware) solutions for that bring a kind of abstraction to reduce dependency-induced problems. This chapter detailed the various features of API gateway solutions and how they come in handy for resolving various microservice-specific issues. The key gateway solutions (open source and commercial grade) and their unique properties were documented for your benefit. The next chapter is about how microservices have to be tested in a systematic manner and speed up the testing needs through scores of automated testing tools.

6
RESTful Services API Testing and Security

Any software that claims to be enterprise-ready must have gone through rigorous testing cycles, be quality assurance certified, and have met several quality measures so that it gets used on production servers. The security of a software application is another critical aspect that determines whether or not it will be used on production servers.

To equip readers with an understanding of different aspects of production and enterprise-ready RESTful APIs, this chapter will discuss various aspects of those quality and security measures.

This chapter's intention is to take readers on an API testing journey. These are the milestones or topics we will cover as we go along:

- Types of API tests
- Challenges in API testing
- Security in API testing
- In addition, we will give you a glimpse of various API testing tools, API security tools, and frameworks

Midway through the API testing journey, readers will be taken on a detour to be introduced to some security issues and API vulnerabilities and learn how to expose them as part of API testing.

An overview of software testing

Any product, be it simple safety pins or majestic airplanes, needs to go through a process to ensure that it solves the purpose of its creation, and so does software, too. Software testing is a process to confirm the accuracy and quality of software through the verification and validation of its purpose, end-to-end.

So, the primary focus of any software product or application is verification (checks for consistency and alignment according to the documented requirements) and validation (checks the accuracy of the system and validates the end user's needs versus the actual outcome).

Let's list a few essential outcomes of software testing and move on to focus more on API testing in the upcoming sections:

- Assert and ensure that there are no differences between the realities and the expectations of the requirements
- Assert and ensure software product continuity and availability, regardless of the amount of end users
- Foresee and uncover concealed problems
- Assert and ensure that offerings function seamlessly with anticipated end user platforms, browsers, and so on

RESTful APIs and testing

As this book deals with RESTful APIs, this chapter is intended to take readers through a few essential best practices and API testing principles, along with a couple of testing frameworks. With integration tests (both manual and automated), we can accomplish most critical API testing strategies for distributed applications and help those applications to be production-ready, deployable, and part of CI/CD, as well as to assert their scalability and stability for every release.

The following section introduces the basics of API testing, API testing approaches, their types, and so on.

Basics of API testing

A software application product, that we discussed in an earlier section, has various software layers such, as the **user interface** (**UI**), the business logic layer, middleware, and a database. **API testing** and certification primarily focuses on data integration tests on the **Business layer**. **API testing** is software testing that involves direct **API testing**, unlike other generic tests, which primarily involve the UI:

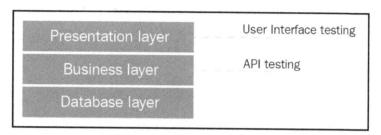

The preceding diagram depicts the typical layers of software, with **API testing** on the **Business layer** and the functional or UI testing on the **Presentation layer**.

Understanding API testing approaches

Agreeing on an approach for API testing when beginning API development is an essential API strategy. Let's look at a few principles of API testing:

- Clear definition of the scope and a good understanding of the functionality of the API
- Common testing methodologies such as boundary analysis and equivalence classes are part of API test cases
- Plan, define, and be ready with input parameters, zero, and sample data for the API
- Determine and compare expected and actual results, and ensure that there are no differences

API testing types

In this section, we will review the various categories of API testing and move on to best practices as well.

Unit tests

Tests that involves the validation of individual operations are unit tests. In our investor services API examples in `Chapter 4`, *Advanced RESTful API Patterns*, we covered numerous unit test cases, and the following is one of the sample code snippets of a specific unit test case that validates getting all the investors from the API:

```
@Test
public void fetchAllInvestors() throws Exception{
    RequestBuilder requestBuilder =
        MockMvcRequestBuilders.get(
            "/investors").accept(
            MediaType.APPLICATION_JSON);
    MvcResult result =
        mockMvc.perform(requestBuilder).andReturn();
    MockHttpServletResponse response =
        result.getResponse();
}
```

API validation tests

All software needs quick evaluation and to assert its purpose of creation. The validation tests need to be run for every function that is developed, at the end of the development process. Unlike unit tests, which focus on particular pieces or functions of the API, validation tests are a higher-level consideration, answering a set of questions so that the development can move on to the next phase.

A set of questions for validation tests could be the following:

1. A product-specific question, such as, is it the necessary function that is asked for?
2. A behavioral question, such as, is the developed function doing what is intended?
3. An efficiency-related question, such as, is the intended function using the necessary code, in an independent and optimized manner?

All of these questions, in essence, serve to validate the API in line with the agreed acceptance criteria and also to ensure its adherence to standards regarding the delivery of expected end goals and meeting user needs and requirements flawlessly.

Functional tests

Tests that involve specific functions of the APIs and their code base are functional tests. Validating the count of active users through the API, regression tests and test case execution come under functional tests. We saw many examples of functional tests executed with the Postman tool earlier, in `Chapter 3`, *Essential RESTful API Patterns*, and `Chapter 4`, *Advanced RESTful API Patterns*. The following screenshot may refresh your memory of one such functional testing example of investor service validation for user authentication:

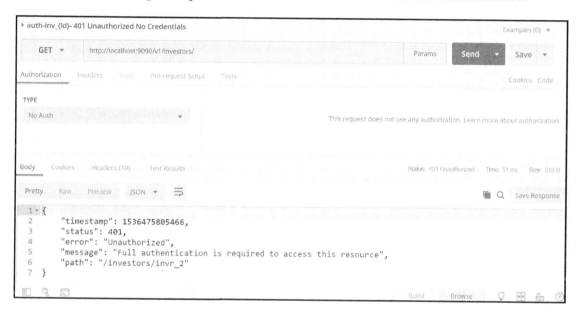

UI or end-to-end tests

Tests that involve and assert end-to-end scenarios, including GUI functions and API functions, which in most of the cases, validate every transaction of an application, are grouped under end-to-end tests.

Load testing

As we know, an increase in the number of end users should not affect the performance of the functions of an application. Load testing will uncover such issues and also validate the performance of an API in normal conditions too.

Runtime error detection tests

Tests that help to monitor the application and detect problems such as race conditions, exceptions, and resource leaks belong in the runtime error tests category. The following points capture a brief about those factors.

Monitoring APIs

Tests for various implementation errors, handler failures, and other inherent concerns inside the API code base and ensures it does not have any holes that would lead to application insecurity.

Execution errors

Valid requests to the API return responses and asserting them for expected valid responses is common, however, asserting invalid requests for expected failures is also essential as part of an API testing strategy, and those tests come under execution errors:

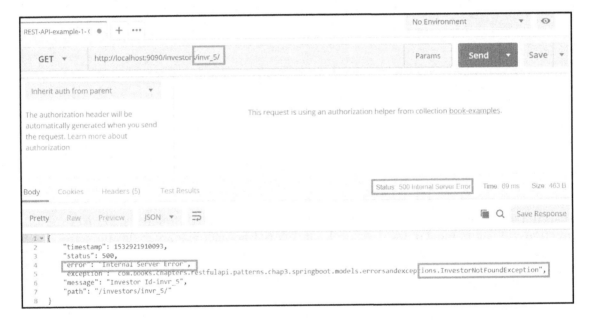

The preceding screenshot depicts the `Chapter 3`, *Essential RESTful API Patterns*, example of expecting an error when the user gives an ID that is not present on the system.

Resource leaks

Negative tests to validate the underlying API resource malfunctions by submitting invalid requests to the API. The resources, in this case, are memory, data, insecurities, timeout operations, and so on.

Error detection

Detect network communication failures. Authentication failures from giving the wrong credentials is an example error detection scenario. These are tests ensure the errors are captured and then resolved as well:

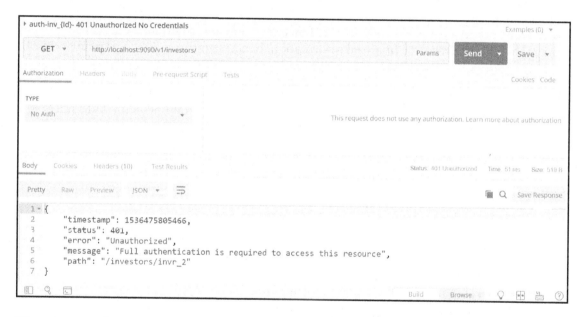

We saw an authentication error in our `Chapter 4`, *Advanced RESTful API Patterns*, investor-service example, and the previous screenshot depicts this, as the code returns `401` (as it should); this is an example of an error detection test.

REST API security vulnerabilities

APIs are popular and widely used because they are simple, schematic, fast to develop, and quick to deploy. This naturally brings challenges in terms of ensuring that implementations are secured from various threats, such as **man-in-the-middle-attacks** (**MITM**), a lack of XML encryptions, insecure endpoints, and API URL parameters.

REST APIs have similar vulnerabilities as web applications; we will present the most common API attacks and vulnerabilities in the following sections, then move on to security tests.

Exposing sensitive data

The first and foremost essential security aspect of testing a REST API (or any application) is to evaluate and determine the categories of data and the need for data protection when they are in transit or in a persisted state. For instance, personal information, credit card information, health records, financial information, business information, and many other such categories of information need protection.

Moreover, data is fundamentally protected through encryption, as exposing sensitive data with no encryption could lead to an attacker stealing sensitive data, which would not just be limited to personal data, credit card numbers, identity theft, and so on.

There are many preventative measures and means of protection sensitive data you can apply according to the classification (of data) and data protection needs. Some of these protection measures are listed here:

- Classify data and apply controls according to data classification.
- Do not store sensitive information unless necessary and discard it as soon as possible. Use tokenization and truncation methods to prevent the exposure of sensitive data.
- Encryption is a necessary and crucial protection measure.
- Do not implement a cache for sensitive data (or disable caches for sensitive data transactions).
- Use salts and adaptive (with a configurable number of iterations) hashing methodologies for passwords.

Understanding authentication and authentication attacks

Authentication is a process to determine the identity of an entity (a process, a machine, or a human user) to either disallow or allow that entity to access underlying application functionalities.

Logon authentication, network authentication, IP authentication, remote authentication, basic authentication, and client certificates are a few authentication types.

Authentication attacks are processes with which hackers attempt to exploit an authentication process and gain unauthorized access. Successfully penetrating an authentication system and gaining unauthorized access will allow a hacker to steal sensitive information and alter, corrupt, or delete valuable data. Imagine a hacker assumes someone's identity; this is identity theft and can lead to personal damage and monetary theft. Worse, if the hacked identity is of a network or server administrator, then the damage may be beyond our imagination.

Authentication-type attacks include bypass attacks, brute-force attacks (for passwords), verify impersonation, and reflection attacks.

While we are discussing authentication attacks, it may be good to recollect an example implementation of basic authentication `Chapter 4`, *Advanced RESTful API Patterns*. The investor service has some necessary security measure such as basic authentication, authorization with a default key, and also authorization with credentials to restrict API access only to genuine users. We also touched upon how to test and validate those security measures with Postman.

The following screenshot depicts one such scenario (**Authorization** with a default key) and how we validate access using a default security key:

Understanding authorization and OAuth2 schemes

As we now understand, proving a correct identity is authentication, and allowing a specific action by authenticated users is authorization. In this section, we will present a brief about OAuth—an industry-standard protocol for authorization – along with a few authorization schemes. When we mention the OAuth IETF OAuth Working Group (`https://tools.ietf.org/wg/oauth/`) in this section, it's OAuth 2.0, which focuses on client-developer simplicity (a RESTful principle) while providing specific authorization flows for various application use cases such as desktop applications, web applications, mobile phones, and even IoT-enabled living room devices.

Before we move on to OAuth 2.0 schemes, let's understand why you would choose OAuth-based authorization over traditional cookie-based authorization with the following list:

- Cookie-based authorization is mostly stateful, that is, the server has to keep a record of active user sessions. To manage active sessions, the server would need multiple database calls to maintain the state. Also, a few other server-side overheads make it difficult to decouple the authorization process from the application server (to be stateless).

- Cookie-based authentication and authorization involve domains, as applications may interact with multiple domains, and so the underlying server needs a few additional configurations, resulting in maintenance and security overheads.

- Integration of third-party clients such as Google+ and Facebook. Authorization for the application with cookie-based authorization is not a feasible solution in many cases.

- Cookie-based authorization is considered a maintenance nightmare (in some cases, such as native mobile apps) and so is not a preferred choice for many applications, especially when relying on mobile-based authentication.

OAuth addresses these concerns by allowing arbitrary clients (for example, a first-party iOS application or a third-party web application) to access user's (resource owner's) resources on resource servers via authorization servers with secure, reliable, and effective methods:

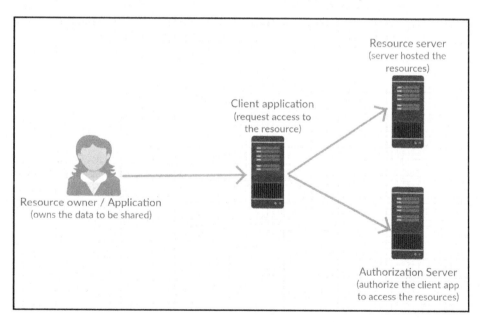

The preceding diagram depicts OAuth authorization stakeholders and their roles.

Now, let's look at a few OAuth 2.0-based authorization schemes and the situations or business cases you would choose those specific schemes for, with the following table:

Schemes / Flow	Client type	Brief description
Implicit	**Single-page application (SPA)** such as Google Fonts.	Application requests access tokens from the gateway and the user grants permission
Client-credentials	Machine-to-machine non-interactive programs such as services, daemons, and so on	The application passes the client credentials and gets the access token from the gateway server
Authorization code	Less trusted apps (third-party apps requesting access to your application)	The application sends a temporary authorization code it receives from the gateway and gets it validated (by the same gateway)

Resource owner password credentials	Highly trusted apps (first-party apps)	The client will ask the user for their authorization credentials (usually a username and password), then the client sends a few parameters (`grant_type`, `client_id`, `client_secret`) to the authorization server

As part of this chapter, we have provided OAuth 2.0 example code that implements the **Resource Owner** password credentials flow and is available on GitHub for anyone to download and execute.

The following diagram depicts the typical sequence of a resource owner password credential OAuth scheme, before we move to the section that explains how to run that example code:

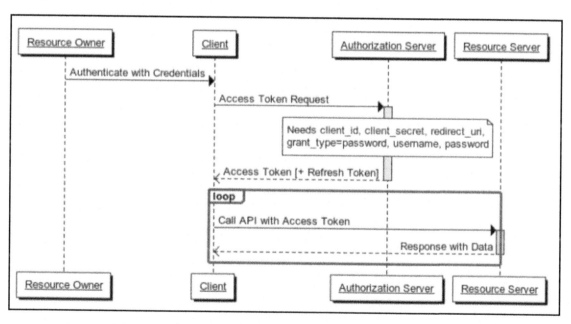

The following steps and a few screenshots of the Postman tool will be useful if you want to run and test that example code on your system:

1. Download the code from GitHub (you may want to refer to the *Technical requirement* section `Chapter 3`, *Essential RESTful API Patterns*).

2. Open the Terminal and `cd` to `downloaded_loc/Hands-On-RESTful-API-Design-Patterns-and-Best-Practices\Chapter06\oauth2-sample`.

3. Run `mvn clean install` and wait for the `BUILD SUCCESS` message.

4. Run the application by running the `java -jar target\ oauth2-sample-0.0.1-SNAPSHOT.jar` command.

5. Open the local Postman tool and test the URLs (in the `Chapter06` folder of Postman collections).

6. you will see the following screenshots when you run the different scenarios.

7. Try error conditions and other scenarios as well (by providing incorrect credentials, user credentials instead of admin credential, and so on).

8. Run the sample with the `java -jar` command:

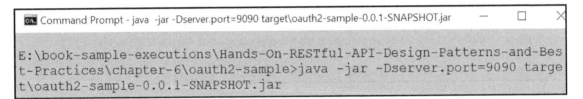

9. Wait for the local server to start and be ready to accept requests:

10. Open the Postman tool, run the collections in the `Chapter06` folder, and observe the client credentials (required for the **Authorization** server):

11. Now enter user credentials for the **Authorization** server to provide the necessary token:

12. Get the access-token from the **Authorization** server so that we can use it to access the necessary resources in the next step:

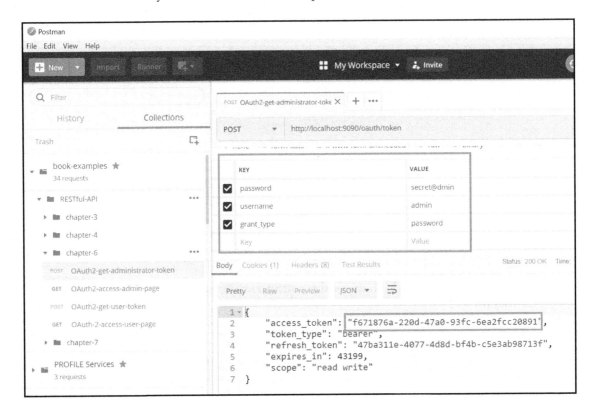

13. Use the access token that we got in the last step and access the admin (resource) API. Notice the response body:

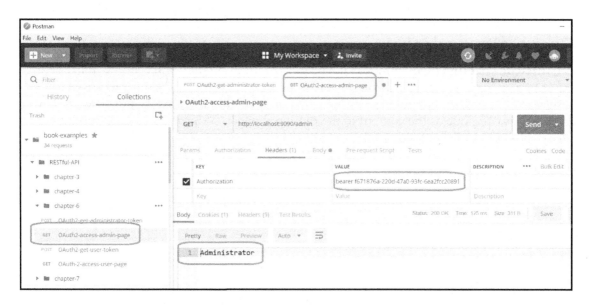

14. Repeat the same steps for user resources with the necessary user credentials (notice the user name in the input):

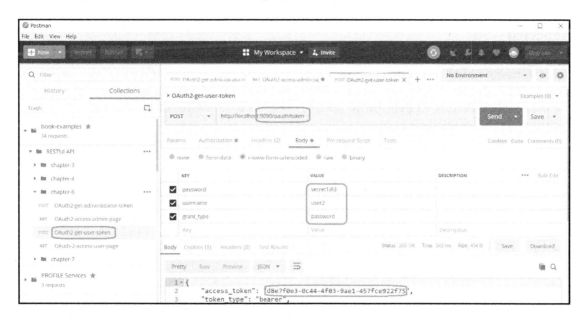

So, you can execute different scenarios (not provided as part of this chapter) such as error messages and different HTTP error codes (`403`, `302`, and so on) with the sample code.

Cross-site scripting

A **Cross-site scripting** (**XSS**) attack is the process of injecting malicious code as part of the input to web services, usually through a browser. Once injected, the malicious script can access any cookies, session tokens, and sensitive information retained by the browser, and can even masquerade as the content of the rendered pages. XSS can be categorized into server-side XSS and client-side XSS.

Traditionally, XSS is one of three types:

- Reflected XSS
- Stored XSS
- DOM XSS

 An exciting read about stored XSS on the word-press REST API defect can be found here: `https://threatpost.com/wordpress-rest-api-bug-could-be-used-in-stored-xss-attacks/124294/` and here: `https://threatpost.com/wordpress-silently-fixed-privilege-escalation-vulnerability-in-4-72-update/123533/`.

Reflected XSS

Successful reflected cross-site scripting happens when an application allows an attacker to inject browser-executable code (such as JavaScript, Applets, Action Scripts, Flash) within a single HTTP response. You may be aware the injected code is non-persistent and impacts the users only when they open the maliciously crafted link or URL or third-party web page that renders the affected response.

Stored XSS

Stored XSS, also known as persistent XSS, often considered harmful and high risk, occurs when a malicious script is injected into a vulnerable application as input and is viewed by another user or an administrator at a later time.

DOM XSS

The third type (developed by Amit Klein and available since 2005), DOM XSS, occurs when client-side code uses insecure references to DOM objects that are not entirely controlled by server-provided pages. Generally, but not limited to, APIs that dynamically inject attacker-controllable data to a page and JavaScript frameworks. Single-page applications are vulnerable to DOM XSS.

> XSS protection needs to filter malicious content from user input and also needs encoding (escape).

Cross-site request forgery

Cross-site request forgery (CSRF), Sea Surf, or XSRF, as it's known, is a one-click attack vulnerability that web applications exposes the possibility of the end user being forced (by forged links, emails, and HTML pages) to execute unwanted actions on a currently authenticated session.

> The synchronize token pattern, cookie-to-header token, double submit cookie, and client-side safeguards are common CSRF prevention methodologies.

Denial-of-service attack

A **denial-of-service** (DoS) attack is intended to make the targeted machine reach its maximum load (capacity to serve requests) quickly by sending numerous false requests so the target system denies further genuine requests.

Flood attacks and buffer overflow attacks are two categories of DoS. With flood attacks, the attacker saturates the target server by generating enormous traffic to the server, causing the target server to end up in DoS.

On the other hand, a buffer overflow attack is intended to target a machine and make that machine consume all available memory or hard disk space, or cause high usage of the CPU. This result in various consequences, such as the system becoming slow to respond or sluggish in its behavior, and there may even be a situation in which the targeted system will crash, creating potentially catastrophic results.

Please note that, generally, DoS attacks happen on networks where the malicious user (attacker) has more available bandwidth than the target server. Smurf attacks, ping floods, and ping of death attacks are some actual DoS attacks.

Distributed denial of service

DoS attacks on distribution systems are known as **distributed denial of service (DDoS)** attacks. DDoS attacks achieve success by employing multiple compromised computer systems, including network resources such as IoT devices, as sources of attack traffic.

Injection attacks

One of the most harmful and dangerous attacks is an injection attack. The attacker supplies untrusted input to the application, which gets executed/processed as a part of a command or query, thus resulting in the partial or complete discourse of the application behavior and leading to consequences such as data theft, data loss, loss of data integrity, and DoS. It can even lead to full-system compromise.

The following table captures a few common injection attack types, brief descriptions for each, and their potential impact:

Type of Injection	A brief description	Potential impacts
Code injection/OS command injection	Execute operating system commands with application code	Gains higher privileges with higher privilege escalation vulnerabilities and lead to full-system compromise
CRLF injection	Injects an EOL/carriage return character in an input sequence	Results in splitting the HTTP header to facilitate arbitrary content injection in the response body, including XSS
Email (Mail command/SMTP) injection	Injects IMAP/SMTP statements to a mail server	Personal information disclosure and relay of SPAM emails
Host header injection	Abuses the trust of the HTTP Host Header by dynamically generating headers based on user input	Cache poisoning—manipulates the caching system and serves malicious pages Password reset poisoning—exploits with password reset email and delivers malicious content directly to the target
LDAP injection	Injects **Lightweight Directory Access Protocol (LDAP)** statements and executes them	Modifies contents of LDAP tree and grants illegitimate permissions, privilege escalations, and bypass authentication
SQL injection	Injects fabricated SQL commands to exercise database read or modify data	Leads to data loss, data theft, data integrity loss, DoS, and can even result in full system compromise due to advanced variations of SQL injections

XPath injection	Executes fabricated XPath queries by injecting false data into an application	Results in information disclosure and bypass authentication

Insecure direct object references

Insecure direct object references (IDOR) are equally as harmful as the other top API vulnerabilities; they occur when an application exposes direct access to internal objects based on user inputs such as ID and filename.

Let's look at a quick example of IDOR with the following diagram. In it, Bob is getting his file having ID 1001 from the app does make sense, but what about he is getting Alice's document with ID **1003**?

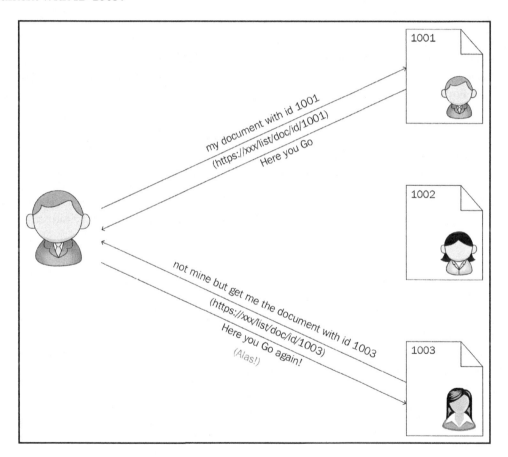

A direct object reference is happening, as the developer exposed a reference to an internal implementation object – here, in the preceding example, it is a file (an object reference may be a directory, an image file, a database key, and so on) – with the application.

So, not having a validation mechanism, allowing Bob (the attacker) to manipulate these references to access unauthorized data is called an IDOR vulnerability.

One can test for IDOR vulnerabilities by mapping out all of the endpoints where the user input is a direct reference (as depicted in the example diagram) and used as a reference object. Its always recommended two ore more users to cover direct objects and functions.

Missing function-level access control

Another aspect of IDOR is missing functional level access rights. The application might have missed implementing function-level access rights, and so anyone with network access will be able to send a request and get a response rather than just the specific user who has privileges. For instance, an admin URL should not be available to a user who does not have admin-level access rights.

APIs with insufficient protection for sensitive request handlers within an application fall into the category of missing functional-level access rights vulnerability, and so allow hackers to penetrate the application without the necessary authorization.

Testing aspects of this vulnerability should focus on two essential scenarios—whether the user can directly browse a resource, and whether the UI accessing the API resources expose an unauthorized resource to that UI.

Man-in-the-middle attacks

An MITM attack is an attack by a perpetrator who has placed themselves in the middle of a network or communication between a genuine user and an application server. They intend to steal, eavesdrop on, impersonate and secretly relay, intercept, or alter communications, including API messages, between two communicating parties, all while it appears as though a normal exchange of information is underway:

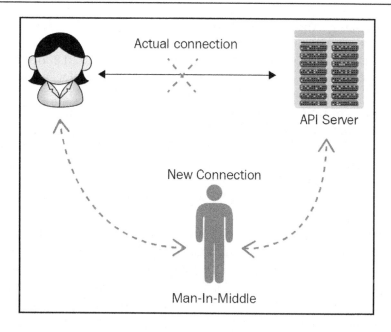

The preceding diagram depicts a typical MITM attack, where the eavesdropper impersonates and relays communications/responses to the caller as they come from the server, and they will appear genuine.

An example of an MITM attack could be communication between an API that issues a session token as part of an HTTP header and a perpetrator acting as a man in the middle between the user's browser and the HTTP header (session token). So, it's easy to intercept that session token as it opens up access to the user's account, then the damage can be done depending on that account's privileges.

Common types of MITM attacks and protection measures

There are a few common MITM attacks, as found in the following list, that you need to be aware of, and also a few protection measures against those attacks:

- **Sniffing**: Sniffing, also known as packet sniffing, in which attackers use widely/freely available packet capture tools by using specific wireless devices to inspect and monitor packets communicated over a network.
- **Packet injection**: Injecting malicious packets into data communication streams in such a way that they blend in with valid data streams and appear as part of the original/intended communication.

- **SSL stripping**: Altering HTTPS network communication to HTTP on the fly and making the communication insecure is another form of MITM attack (the user may not even realize that they are redirected to unsecured endpoints) and, leaking sensitive information as plain text, which attackers get onto it quickly.
- **Email hijacking**: A very common type of MITM attack, in which attackers mimic a trusted site (for example, a bank's website) send an email with instructions to the targeted account and convinces the account holder to follow the instructions in the email, resulting in the catastrophic effect of losing their money/personal information and so on.
- **Wi-Fi eavesdropping**: This involves setting up exclusive Wi-Fi access points to lure users to get connected and make them use the network. Once the user is connected to those Wi-Fi access points, attackers will intercept and gain their credentials, credit card information, and much more sensitive information.
- **Session hijacking**: Once the user logs in to an application with their credentials, the application will generate a temporary token so that user does not need to provide credentials again to access subsequent pages. However, an attacker can sniff and pick up that session token and use it to gain access to the user's account.
- **Protection measures**: Protection against MITM attacks are as follow:
    - **Secure/Multipurpose Internet Mail Extensions (S/MIME)**
    - **Public key infrastructure (PKI)** based authentication certificates
    - SSL/TLS certificates
    - System and server configurations
    - **HTTP Strict Transport Security (HSTS)**

Replay attacks and spoofing

Replay attacks, also known as playback attacks, are network attacks in which valid data transmissions (supposed to be once only) are repeated many times (maliciously) by the attacker who spoofed the valid transaction. While a server is expecting a valid transaction, it will not have any doubts as to whether requests are valid transactions. However, these are a masqueraded request and lead to catastrophic effects for clients:

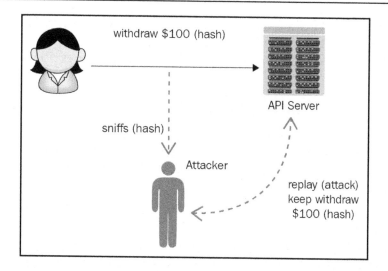

The previous diagram depicts a replay attack example where the legitimate user sends a valid request, but the attacker spoofs it and resends/replays it to the APIs.

As RESTful APIs are stateless, the chances of getting those APIs into replay attacks are high (they're an easy target). So, it is evident that API designers/developers need to have countermeasures in their APIs for all replay attacks. Protection measures include a one-time password with session identifiers, **time-to-live (TTL)** measures, MAC implementation on the client side, and including timestamps in requests, along with secure protocol such as Kerberos protocol prevention, secure routing, and the **challenge-handshake authentication protocol (CHAP)**.

Causes of vulnerabilities

As we have looked at a few of the vulnerabilities in the previous section, let's also familiarize ourselves with a few common concerns and issues that cause APIs to be vulnerable to various attacks in the following paragraphs.

API design and development flaws

Missing or not adhering to API security principles and best practices may lead to defects that expose business-critical data. Another aspect of design and development is to keep APIs as simple as possible, as complexity may lead to less coverage and vulnerability. Poor user input validation, SQL injection loopholes, and buffer overflows are a few other causes.

Chapter 2, *Design Strategy, Guidelines, and Best Practices*, discussed various aspects of design strategies and RESTful API design practices. Understanding and implementing those design principles and practices in APIs helps reduce design and development flaws.

Poor system configuration

Even the best design and development is not necessarily enough to safeguard a system if the system configurations (where the APIs are) do not adhere to security compliance. This will also lead to loopholes and attackers stealing information.

Human error

Non-adherence to organization security compliance and inadequate knowledge of security measures such as document-shredding policies, secure coding practices, strong passwords, maintaining the confidentiality of passwords, periodical resetting passwords, and preventing access to unknown/unsecured sites creates loopholes in the API that can lead to security breaches.

Internal and external connectivity

As APIs are part of unsecured internal and external networks, the connectivity of APIs in an unsecured network is another major cause of vulnerability. Also, APIs' exposure to large and unique channels, such as mobile networks, poor risk management, and lenient authorization practices within a network are a few examples from this category of vulnerability.

Security tests

Security tests ensure APIs are secure from external threats and protected from the vulnerabilities that we have discussed in earlier sections. The primary focus of API security tests and security testers is to find the vulnerabilities of the API they intend to test by running penetration tests, fuzz tests, validations, sensitive data exposure determination, and so on.

Security functional testing and security vulnerability testing are two categories of security tests. A functional test executes manual tests and manually checks for the presence of security mechanisms within API's implementation. Security vulnerability tests execute automated test cases that may expose vulnerabilities.

The ultimate goal of the tester should be to understand the system behavior by studying error messages and expose any security vulnerability such as gaining unauthorized access, IDOR, MITM, and replay attacks.

You can fulfil security test goals by running penetration tests and fuzz tests along with various manual tests.

This section discusses penetration tests and fuzz tests in detail and also discusses the tools/frameworks that provide out-of-the-box support for security tests so that API testers can make use of tools to get security assurance for underlying APIs.

Penetration tests or pen tests

One of the imperatives in API testing is penetration tests, also known as pen tests. Pen tests are the process of simulating cyber attack against a the system or API to expose/determine exploitable vulnerabilities such as intra-network loopholes, XSS attacks, SQL injections, and code-injection attacks.

Pen tests asses the threat vector from an external standpoint, such as supported functions, available resources, and the API's internal components as well.

Let's discuss more details about pen testing—its stages, testing methods, frameworks that support pen testing, and a few criteria for selecting the best penetration tool in the following sections.

Importance of penetration tests

Before we delve into the details, the following rationalizations will help us understand why pen tests are so crucial in API testing:

- No compromise to data privacy
- Guaranteed and secured financial transactions and financial data over the network
- Discover security vulnerabilities and loopholes in APIs and in underlying systems
- Simulate, forecast, understand, and assess the impacts of attacks
- Make APIs fully information security compliant

Pen testing lifecycle

Now that we have a good understanding of vulnerability causes from the earlier section, let's look at the five stages of pen tests in this section:

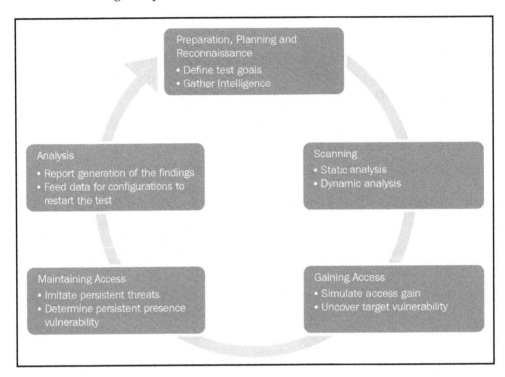

The preceding diagram depicts the life cycle of pen tests, involving five phases of activities such as Preparation, **Scanning**, **Gaining Access** and **Maintaining Access**, and reporting.

Let's look at each phase in more detail in the following sections.

Preparation, planning, and reconnaissance

The first phase of the life cycle involves the following two parts:

- Scope, scope definitions, defining the goals of the tests to be carried out, and defining the testing methods and systems to be addressed
- Gathering intelligence such as the domain and endpoints, and understanding how the target API works, along with its exposure to vulnerabilities

Scanning

Understanding the target application's response to various intrusion attempts with static and dynamic analysis is the focus of the **Scanning** phase.

Gaining access

This involves attempting to uncover API vulnerabilities with application attacks such as XSS, SQL injections, code injections, and backdoors. Once those vulnerabilities are uncovered, exploiting them with privilege escalations, data stealing methods, and traffic interceptions are part of the **Gaining Access** scope, as well as assessing the damage that API vulnerability could cause.

Maintaining access

An illicit, long-term intruder presence in a network may cause irreversible damage to the system, as they may be present in the system for a long time, which facilitates highly sensitive data mining (especially on government, military, and financial networks) in steady, well-researched, and meticulously planned attacks.

Assessing the long-term presence abilities, and the chances of them gaining in-depth access to systems/APIs is the primary intention of this **Maintaining Access** phase.

Analysis

The final phase of the life cycle focuses on compiling and presenting the results of penetration tests as a report. These reports generally contain a specific vulnerability that was exploited as part of pen tests, details of compromised/accessed sensitive data as part of the pen test exercise, and, most importantly, the duration of the time that you were able to remain in the system undetected. These results and reports will act as a feed/input security configurations across the organization to prevent any future attacks.

Pen testing types for API testing

We discussed the importance of penetration tests in security testing, and APIs are no exception; they all need to go through these penetration tests and ensure that underlying APIs are not exposing any vulnerabilities. Please note that there are three categories of pen tests in practice and they are—black-box pen tests, grey-box pen tests, and white-box pen tests.

Black-box and grey-box testing assumes testers have only limited knowledge about the underlying API. We shall briefly cover white-box testing in this section, as it's essential for API security testing, and why it is preferred for API penetration tests in the following section.

White-box penetration testing

White-box testing is also known as **structure-testing**, open-box, clear-box, and glass-box testing. The white-box pen test is a comprehensive testing methodology, as you get a whole range of information about the schema, source code, models, and so on, before starting the testing. White-box tests are intended to scrutinize the code and catch any design and development errors. They are simulations of internal security attacks.

API pen tests rely on white-box testing for the following reasons:

- The tests run on all of the independent paths of a module
- The tests confirm and verify all logical decisions (`true`/`false`) inside the code
- The tests execute syntax checking, and so find typographical errors that are critical to finding code injections and SQL injection attacks
- The tests find design errors caused by a mismatch of the logical flow of the program and the actual execution (design for intent)

There are plenty of open source tools available and commercial versions that can scan code, check for malicious code, find security loopholes using data encryption techniques, and even find hardcoded username and passwords. A few of the tools are listed in the following table (both commercial and open source versions):

Tool	Type	Providers
Nmap	OpenSSL	Pure Hacking
Nessus	Cain and Abel	Torrid Networks
Metasploit	THC Hydra	SecPoint
Wireshark	w3af	Veracode

Let's summarize this section by stating that pen tests for APIs should expose API vulnerabilities before real attackers find them, and move on to fuzz tests.

Fuzz tests

Fuzz testing, also known as fuzzing, is one of the most widely used testing practices in the quality assurance phase. It involves massive amounts of random data (noise or fuzz) as input to the target system with the intention of targeting APIs to exhibit buffer overflow or any other unwanted behaviors, or even to provoke the system to crash.

Barton Miller at the University of Wisconsin introduced fuzz testing (in 1988, as part of his *Operating System Utility Program Reliability – The Fuzz Generator project*) to reveal any security loopholes and coding errors in APIs, software, networks, and operating systems.

The primary purpose of API fuzzing is not to test the correct functionality of the API as such, but to explore and test the undefined region with the help of fuzzed data:

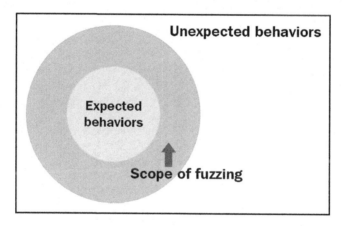

As shown in the preceding diagram, the scope of fuzzing is to expose any unexpected behaviors of the underlying API.

The life cycle of fuzz tests

The various stages in a typical life cycle of an API fuzz test start with identifying the target APIs and defining the inputs for the test, and end with the generation of logs showing vulnerabilities detected in the API. The following diagram depicts each phase of the fuzz testing lifecycle:

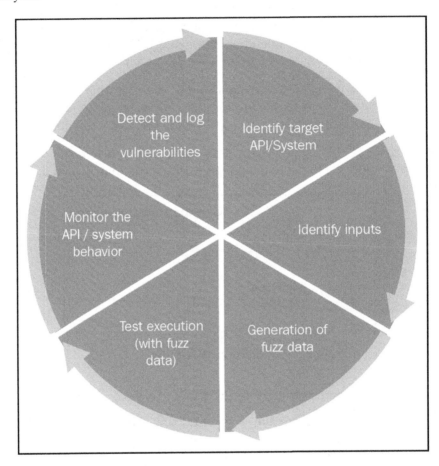

Fuzz testing strategy

Fuzz testing strategy varies depending on the attack vectors, fuzzing targets, fuzzing methods, and so forth. For an API, let's focus on fuzzing targets. Fuzz testing has two primary classifications—mutation based and generation based. We will look at the details of both classifications in the following section.

Mutation-based fuzz tests

Mutation or dumb fuzz tests are a simple approach, wherein we create new test data by altering existing data samples. Sample data generation starts with valid samples of protocols and altering the supplied inputs, to the extent of altering every bit of the inputs. The following diagrams illustrate two ways of going about mutation:

1. Bit flipping, where inputs are flipped in a sequence or in a random manner:

```
{                                              {
    "symbol": "EXc",                               "symbol": "EX-fu^zT@$c",
    "numberOfSharesHeld": 100,     ===>            "numberOfSharesHeld": 100,
    "tickerPrice": 19.9                            "tickerPrice": 19.9
}                                              }
```

2. Append a random string, where the end of the input has random strings appended:

```
{                                              {
    "symbol": "EXc",                               "symbol": "EXcccccccccccccc",
    "numberOfSharesHeld": 100,     ===>            "numberOfSharesHeld": 100,
    "tickerPrice": 19.9                            "tickerPrice": 19.9
}                                              }
```

Generation-based fuzz tests

Generation-based fuzz tests, also known as intelligent fuzzing, are tests based on an understanding of known formats, known protocols, and the generation of inputs from scratch according to the system/API specifications (RFC) and formats (for instance, the format from the API documentation).

Generation fuzz tests are capable of building test data based on the data model. Sometimes, these tests are as simple as injecting random bytes, and sometimes they can be much smarter, knowing good data values and combining them in multiple interesting ways (such as having regular expressions as part of the request body, having hostnames in the header, and changing intended response types to different types).

Before we conclude this section on fuzz-testing strategies, let's get to know another very successful fuzz testing method, known as protocol-based fuzz testing (also known as syntax testing, grammar testing, and robust testing). In protocol-based fuzz testing, the testers have detailed knowledge of the protocol format, and their understanding depends on the given specifications. Here, the specifications are intended as an array of stored specifications within a model-based testing tool, and it is also capable of generating test data. Then, the tool needs to go through all of the specifications and add irregularity to the sequence, data contents, and so on to expose vulnerabilities.

Please note that, as the mutation approach does not require you to understand the protocol, you may feel more comfortable using it compared to the generation-based approach at first glance. However, the generation-based approach is a thorough, better, and recommended process even though it takes more time because it involves several valid input combinations. It does, however, lead to better code coverage and code paths.

Advantages and disadvantages of fuzz tests

The following points intend to justify why fuzz tests are popular among the software professional community:

- They are extremely simple, easy, cost-effective, and quick to set up as they are free of preconceptions about system behavior
- Their one-time setup is easy to repeat for regression (automation)
- As it is a protocol-aware test, test results lead to finding precise, descriptive, and easy-to-debug errors
- They enables you to find bugs that are impossible to find with the human eye in defined testing or approach-based testing
- They yields the best results when used in conjunction with black-box testing, beta testing, and other debugging methods

While fuzz tests bring many advantages to the table, we also need to be aware of and understand a few disadvantages, which are listed here:

- Mutation-based fuzz tests can run indefinitely (generate numerous test cases and run indefinitely) and so determining the optimal number of tests, or determining whether time they run for is long enough, is a difficult in some cases
- Tests results may report no defects, even after running numerous test cases

- Test results may report the same defects for various test cases
- It is challenging to find which test case caused the fault
- It is difficult to find the vulnerability in the event of a system crash

To conclude this section, let's list a few tools that you can take advantage of when running fuzz tests for APIs without much pain.

Open source:

Mutational fuzzing	Fuzzing Frameworks	Domain Specific fuzzing
American fuzzy lop	Sulley	Microsoft SDL MiniFuzz File Fuzzer
Radamsa—a flock of fuzzers	Boofuzz	Microsoft SDL Regex Fuzzer
OWASP WebScarab	BFuzz	ABNF Fuzzer
OWASP WSFuzzer	-	-

The preceding table details open source fuzzing tools. The following list provides a few commercial tools you may want to make use of for fuzz tests:

- Codenomicon's product suite
- The Peach Fuzer Platform
- Spirent Avalanche NEXT
- Beyond Security's beSTORM product

And also, here are a few of the latest tools that readers might find exciting to run through their APIs:

Tool	Reference/Link
REST-ler	https://www.microsoft.com/en-us/research/uploads/prod/2018/04/restler.pdf
Burp	https://portswigger.net/burp
Fuzzapi	https://github.com/Fuzzapi/fuzzapi

Fuzz-rest-api	https://github.com/dubzzz/fuzz-rest-api
Big-list-of-naughty-strings	https://github.com/minimaxir/big-list-of-naughty-strings/

Back to API testing

We have taken a detour from API tests and looked at many aspects of security tests in the previous sections. Now, let's get our focus back and redirect our journey to a few more API testing aspects in the rest of the chapter.

API test cases

To begin with, let's say that test cases for APIs need to have a few parameters or placeholders, such as input parameters, expected results, the time taken to receive a response (from the API), parsing input, error handling, and response formats so that test results of an API are ascertained and certified.

Before we move on to a few aspects of test case preparation, let's get a glimpse of the possible types of bug that API tests help us to detect:

- Mishandled errors or disgraceful error conditions by the API
- Any unused flags
- Missing or duplicate functionality
- Multi-threading issues
- Incorrect handling of valid argument values
- Validation issues such as schema validations or structure issues
- Reliability issues and performance issues (such as timeout and connecting and getting a response time) of the API
- API vulnerabilities and any security issues

Essential aspects of API test cases and test case preparation

The following list covers a few essential aspects of test case preparation for API testing, as the test cases on API testing depend on their outputs:

- Assert a return value based on different input conditions and a combination of inputs.
- Assert the behavior of the API when there is no return value. Check for return codes.

- Assert the events and triggers of an API if the underlying/target API creates subsequent events.
- Assert not only the API results in case of update data structure but validate the effect on the system that it has updated.
- Assert by accessing impacted resources when the API is involved in modifying specific resources.

API testing challenges

If you are ready with the necessary test cases, is it sufficient to start testing the intended API? No, it is not—there are some more challenges one should be aware of, and we will look at a few common challenges you may face and also how to address those challenges when you want to start API testing in the following sections.

Initial setup

The testing infrastructure and its stability/availability, and uptime. Starting and practising API testing in the design phase and checking the APIs for 100% uptime is key.

API schema updates for testing

Request and response schema or formats are the lifelines of the API. However, frequent changes to schemas are inevitable (especially during the development phase) and so test cases for schema configuration too. Managing tests in alpha and beta environments may reduce the number of issues (due to schema updates) by up to 90%.

Testing parameter combinations

Adding additional parameters to the API increases the number of combinations exponentially, while it is necessary to test every possible combination of parameter requests to find issues specific to configurations. API releases and ensuring potential API release candidates are available for testing helps address these challenges effectively.

API call sequence

Calling APIs in a specific sequence to attain the desired result is inevitable in many cases, and for those scenarios, test cases also need to have the proper sequence implemented. However, this is challenging in major APIs, and becomes even more challenging when cases of multi threaded applications are involved. Along with enforcing release candidates, a visual representation of a sequence of API calls or a flow chart for the sequence of API calls will help not only the testing phase but also the development team as well (as part of development phase).

Validating parameters

Checking numbers and the number of digits in a phone number, length restrictions, data type validations, data-ranges modifications, and such validation criteria or tests are daunting tasks for the testing team especially with larger APIs that have a vast number of parameters to validate. Implementing synthetic and **application performance monitoring (APM)** tools will help to ensure catching any problems that arise due to parameter validations. Validating parameter is one of the crucial aspects of security testing as well.

Tracking system integration

A data tracking system helps to find the correct responses to the calls. However, it is a challenging task for the team to ensure that the API testing system is working correctly with the data tracking system and calls that the API is making are getting the right response. you can address this challenge by implementing and including load tests with **continuous delivery (CD)**.

API testing best practices

The following section lists a few API testing best practices you should know about. To start with, the following are test case best practices:

- Group API test cases by test category (unit tests, functional tests, security tests, and so on)
- Ensure test cases indicate the declarations of involved (called) APIs on top of each test case
- Ensure parameter selections are mentioned explicitly in the test case itself
- Executes test cases independently, that is, each test case is a self-contained and an independent entity
- prioritize API calls, which helps to simplify API testing

- Keep test cases free from *test chaining* (reusing test data objects created by other tests)
- Test cases deal with one-time call functions such as delete, close window, asynchronous calls, and so need special attention to avoid undesirable executions
- Ensure API call sequences are well planned and also have clear execution plans
- Create test cases for every possible known input combination of the API, as this leads to better test coverage of the underlying APIs

API testing tools

It may be a good idea to complete our API testing journey with some information about a few common API testing tools. The following screenshot of API testing tools gives brief details on each tool, their ease of use, and supporting platforms and may come in handy:

POSTMAN	Katalon	APACHE JMeter	TRICENTIS	apigee	REST-assured	SoapUI by SMARTBEAR	Karate
API	API Web & Mobile	API	API Web & Mobile	API	API	API Web & Mobile	API
Paid + Free	Free	Open Source	Paid + Free	Paid + Free	Open Source	Paid + Free	Open Source
Windows Linux MacOS	Windows Linux MacOS	Windows Linux MacOS	Windows	Windows Linux MacOS	Windows Linux MacOS	Windows Linux MacOS	Windows Linux MacOS
Easy to setup & use	Easy to setup & use	Advanced programming skills needed to setup & use	Easy to setup. Need training to properly use the tool	Require end-points management knowledge to use	Easy to setup & use	Easy to setup. Need training to properly use the tool	Easy to setup & use

CQRS

Command Query Responsibility Segregation (CQRS) is an architectural pattern, proposed by Greg Young. CQRS suggests the segregation of the reading operations (queries) and writing operations (commands) of a system to separate subsystems, as reads are eventually consistent and retrieved from de-normalized views and commands are usually asynchronous and stored in transactional storage, and reads are eventually consistent and retrieved from deformalized views.

So, segregating read and write operations with separate interfaces or subsystems doesn't only help to maximize the performance of APIs, it also helps in security and scalability aspects, as well as managing merge conflicts at the domain level, due to update commands, leading to more flexibility.

Before we delve further into CQRS, let's look at traditional patterns for **Data Access** in the following diagram:

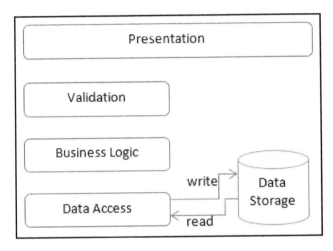

Traditional Data Source and DTO models (CRUD)

As depicted, the read and write operations of data (source) are from one data source or data storage, with updates or writes and Queries (read).

There are a few disadvantages with the CRUD approach, as listed here:

- The data that is being read and the data being updated may have different representations and managing that updated data in sync to serve both reads and writes is an overhead to the underlying system.
- Performance is affected by the high load on the data store and data access layers and depends on queries and the complexities involved in retrieving information. High volume transactions also increase the chances of data contention when records are locked in a data store and accessed by multiple domains.
- Managing security and roles for data access might be challenging as well.

The CQRS pattern addresses those disadvantages, as its implementation segregates queries (reads) from the update (**Commands**) operations with separate interfaces:

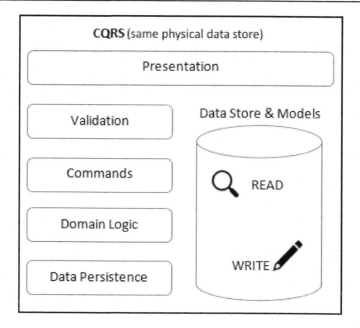

It also check the following instances:

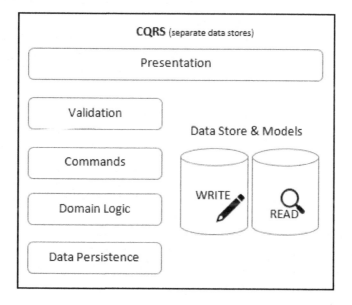

The preceding two diagrams depict two variations of CQRS implementation. The first one represents a simplified design and implementation of CQRS with read and write models within a single data source. Note that it is not a single data model (like CRUD), but read and write as a separate models. The downside of this version of CQRS implementation is that, unlike CRUD, the automatic code generation with scaffolding mechanism is not possible for CQRS based systems.

The diagram with a separate data source depicts another CQRS design, where we have two different physical data stores one for write or update operations (commands) and then another one exclusively for queries. Separate data store implementation maximizes performance, scalability, and security.

While CQRS brings higher performance, scalability, and security, it also brings increased complexity and maintenance overheads to manage consistency due to multiple data stores and also one would need to understand from the following list when to choose CQRS for your implementations:

- CQRS is suitable for systems in which number of writing (updates) and reading (queries) differ significantly
- It's ideal for systems in which reads and writes need individual scaling
- It's suitable for systems where the consistency of data is not critical (addressed eventual consistency) but the availability
- It 's ideal for systems that prefer fire-and-forget events (asynchronous events)
- It's suitable for the systems that have a data store access layer based on event sources
- It's ideal for systems that implement domain-driven designs and isolate the business or domain complexity, and having CRUD would make more complex

Summary

We are at the end of our API testing journey and, reflecting on of this journey, we have learned a few basics of API testing types and API testing approaches, starting from unit test cases, through to API validation tests, functional tests, load tests, and end-to-end tests, along with API monitoring. We have also touched on a few important API errors aspects such as execution errors, resource leaks, and error detection methodologies.

While we were looking at on API testing, we got to know a few critical security vulnerabilities in the REST API world, including sensitive data exposure, authentication attacks, XSS attacks, see-surf (CSRF), DoS attacks, and injection attacks. We did not just focus on attacks, as this chapter introduced the causes of those attacks (vulnerabilities), as well as methods and tools for detecting those API vulnerabilities by means of penetration and fuzz tests.

We continued on our API testing journey after understanding API security measures—we got to know a few of the basics of API test case creation, API testing challenges, and API testing best practices, and concluded our journey with a snapshot of API testing tools.

Further reading

Mastering Modern Web Penetration Testing (`https://www.packtpub.com/networking-and-servers/mastering-modern-web-penetration-testing`), Prakhar Prasad, Packt Publishing.

RESTful Service Composition for Smart Applications 7

Through the leverage of edge and digitization technologies and tools, all kinds of tangible elements in our personal, social, and professional environments are digitized. That is, these are becoming computational, communicative, sensitive, perceptive, responsive, and active. Digitized elements are also called smart objects or sentient materials. Further on, all sorts of embedded systems in everyday places (such as homes, hotels, and hospitals) are getting networked through a variety of communication and data-transmission protocols. Hence, the combination of digitized entities and networked embedded systems make our environments intelligent, which are typically self-, surrounding-, and situation-aware. Another noteworthy trend is that all of these empowered artifacts are increasingly integrated with remotely-held (cloud) applications, services, and data sources in order to be appropriately strengthened in their operations, output, and offerings. There are a number of integration and brokerage platforms, adapters, connectors, drivers, and plug-ins that enable **device-to-device (D2D)** and **device-to-cloud (D2C)** integration. This strategically-sound transition ultimately enables them to be innately smart in their actions and reactions. And this grandiose and technology-inspired transformation of everyday elements and entities in our daily environments leads to the timely formulation and delivery of service-oriented, event-driven, insight-filled, cloud-enabled, fault-tolerant, mission-critical, multifaceted, and people-centric services. The role of the powerful RESTful paradigm in building and providing these kinds of advanced and next-generation services is steadily growing.

This chapter is specially crafted to tell you all about the contributions of the RESTful services paradigm toward designing, developing, and deploying next-generation microservices-centric and enterprise-scale applications. It looks at how RESTful services that are capable of finding and binding with one another result in process-aware, business-critical, and people-centric composite services.

This chapter will cover the following topics:

- The need for service composition
- The various compositions methods (orchestration and choreography)
- The orchestration method
- The choreography method
- The hybrid version of orchestration and choreography towards smarter applications

Technical requirements

- This chapter is primarily a chapter with a lot of theoretical information
- Readers have to be familiar with the Java language and platform
- A simple service-composition example is fully developed and deployed in this book's GitHub repository

Briefing RESTful microservices

Without an iota of doubt, we're heading toward the promised knowledge era. Every common and casual thing in our everyday environment is being meticulously stuffed with the right and relevant intelligence in order to be adaptive, assistive, and adroit in its operations, output, and offerings. That is, all kinds of physical, mechanical, and electrical systems in our personal, professional, and social environments are systematically tuned to be digitized entities and elements. They gain the required knowledge through a host of noteworthy technological advancements, which are being brought in through the application of proven and potential digitization and edge technologies. The faster maturity and stability of information, communication, sensing, perception, vision, analytics, decision-enabling, and actuation technologies contribute immensely to the realization of intelligent solutions, systems, and services.

Fast-evolving digital technologies include state-of-the-art IT infrastructures, such as software-defined clouds, integrated platforms for big and fast data, streaming and IoT data analytics, the mobile-enablement of every enterprise system, the futuristic **Internet of Things (IoT)**, the mesmerizing blockchain technology, and the pervasive **software as a service (SaaS)** phenomenon. The well-known edge technologies include disappearing sensors, actuators, multifaceted micro- and nano-scale electronics, miniaturized stickers, pads, tags, barcodes, chips, controllers, specks, beacons, and LEDs.

The seamless combination of digital and edge technologies enables the mandated disruption, innovation, and transformation to dynamically and dexterously tend toward the IT vision, which is all about creating smarter homes, hotels, and hospitals.

The emergence of the **microservices architecture** (**MSA**) is being touted as the most interesting and inspiring thing for business and IT organizations across the globe. Currently-running web, cloud, and enterprise applications are being redesigned, refactored, and remedied using microservices in order to be flexible and futuristic. Further on, all kinds of devices, such as mobile devices (cellphones, smartphones, digital assistants, and tablets), handhelds, wearables, implantables (such as sensors and actuators), portables (laptops), fixed, nomadic, and edge/fog devices are also being empowered through microservices. That is, every digitized and connected device is being presented as microservices to the outside world. All of the device deficiencies and differences are being taken care of by this sort of service-enablement. As usual, every microservice is being stuffed with well-intended RESTful APIs. Hence, there's a separation between interfacing and implementation, which is technology-agnostic.

This chapter will look at how microservices enabled with RESTful interfaces are to be orchestrated and choreographed to formulate high-end and process-centric services.

Demystifying the MSA style

There are some crucial requirements to ensure business agility and automation through the smart leverage of the distinct advancements in the **Information and communication technologies** (**ICT**) space. The necessary IT requirements include maximizing team autonomy, optimizing development speed, providing flexibility without compromising on consistency, fulfilling resiliency, and easing up on maintenance. There are agile programming models and techniques to speed up the process of writing code for software applications, but designing and delineating application components in an elegant and extensible manner is vital to the intended success of software applications in the long run. There shouldn't be any vendor lock-in. Any technology and tool can be leveraged to produce and sustain application modules. Also, application components have to be modular in order to be right and relevant for enterprises, which are increasingly service-oriented, customer-centric, adaptive, and productive. Also, application components have to be publicly-discoverable, network-accessible, interoperable, and composable. Hence, the concept of MSA has started to flourish with the proper nourishment from worldwide IT experts. Microservices are fine-grained, horizontally-scalable, independently-deployable, API-driven, usable and reusable, portable, and technology-agnostic.

With the containerization movement picking up steadily, it's easy to have containerized microservices, the images of which can be downloaded and committed to be executable insight containers, which emerge as the most optimal runtime platform. As indicated earlier, microservices can be composed (orchestrated and choreographed) to create composite, process-aware, and business-critical applications. Container orchestration links multiple containerized microservices to create better and bigger containerized applications. Now, in order to manage containers—which are typically large in number in a typical IT environment—containerization orchestration platforms, such as Kubernetes, Swarm, and Mesos, are gaining popularity. With the availability of competent technologies and tools, containerized cloud environments are being set up by enterprises and cloud service providers to host, run, and manage microservices-centric containerized applications. Hence, legacy applications are being partitioned to be a collection of microservices, and there are platforms and infrastructures in order to run them. That is, large, monolithic applications are being cloud-enabled in order to reap the strategically-sound benefits of cloud environments and the powerful microservices architecture pattern.

The advantages of microservices

The surging popularity of microservices is due to multiple reasons. First of all, microservices strictly follow the single responsibility principle. That is, microservices do things one at a time but do it well. The MSA pattern mandates that different responsibilities need to be placed in different services. These fine-grained and self-contained microservices offer a number of unique benefits. The cost of developing, changing, and advancing is cheap, and the time to market is minimal. Each service runs in its own process space and is being stuffed with its own data store. Every service has to be bestowed with an easy-to-understand and should use APIs. RESTful APIs are the most popular for API-enabled microservices. The services talk to one another through API calls. To craft and sustain business-critical and enterprise-grade applications, multiple microservices have to be blended together. Microservices are modular (loosely coupled and highly cohesive). The lightly- or loosely-coupled microservices do away the dependency-associated risks and drawbacks. On the other hand, the closely-related responsibilities of a software module are kept together.

Each microservice implements a distinct business functionality and hence has a small code base. Therefore, it's easy and quick for service developers to bring in any desired changes. Also, microservices facilitate simplified and streamlined software design. Microservices can also be given to testers and users for initial verification and validation.

Microservices fulfill the varied goals of the agile design and development of software applications. Further on, as we've discussed legacy modernization in another chapter of this book, microservices emerge as the best fit for modernizing and migrating large, monolithic applications. Microservices easily leverage all of the innate competencies of cloud environments to produce and sustain next-generation applications, which are mandated to be agile, adaptive, and adroit.

Furthermore, the nimbleness, simplicity, and astuteness of microservices elevates them to be the most competent unit to build and deploy business-critical workloads. Also, because of its small size, there's a lower likelihood of introducing errors into the source code and it's easy to troubleshoot microservices and their combinations. Hence, there are a number of businesses, technical and user advantages of microservices architecture. Experts continuously publish a variety of best practices to leverage the unique capabilities of MSA in a highly beneficial manner. As software applications are becoming more integrated and hence complicated, the soothing experience of MSA is helpful in delegating the development, deployment, and operational complexities. MSA, if used intelligently, offers a litany of strategic advantages; the noteworthy ones include the agile design of applications, the support for both cloud-enabled and native software applications, and the enabling of the separation of concerns.

The emergence of cloud-native applications

The MSA pattern emerges as the most efficient tool for creating and sustaining software applications. In order to benefit in the long run, enterprises are strategizing on two things—empowering currently-running applications to be microservices-centric, and migrating those remedied applications to be hosted in cloud environments (private, public, and hybrid). That is, applications are becoming cloud-enabled through the leverage of MSA.

With the pervasiveness of cloud centers, software engineers and architects are designing, developing, and deploying microservices-centric applications in cloud environments. This scenario is being touted as cloud-native applications. Precisely speaking, in order to decisively reap all of the originally envisioned benefits (business, technical, and user), applications are being designed through microservices, developed using one of the integrated development platforms and frameworks, and deployed in cloud environments. The microservices-based software design is faster than the traditional, agile programming models, and methods are made available in plenty to speed up the process of software construction.

The continued adoption of enterprise DevOps tools and processes accelerates the continuous integration, delivery, and deployment of software applications, and the emergence of **site-reliability engineering** (**SRE**) concepts bring forth additional automation and acceleration for software engineering. Hence, the future belongs to cloud-native applications. That is, all kinds of enterprise, mobile, social, embedded, transactional, operational, and analytical applications are being built as cloud-native applications.

The growing ecosystem of IoT device services

We talked about business-specific and agnostic microservices, which are increasingly containerized. The container images of any software can be uniformly packaged, quickly shipped, and easily deployed across any software platforms to run and deliver their functionalities without any hitch or hurdle. With the rapid growth of a variety of purpose-specific and agnostic devices, there's a continued rise of device services, which are MSA-compliant. We have a variety of devices, such as medical instruments, robots, drones, wares, utensils, appliances, consumer electronics, and machines, which are gradually being connected in order to join in the mainstream computing arena. Leading market analysis and research reports forecast that there will be billions of connected devices in another one to two years.

The various functionalities of connected devices are being exposed via service interfaces. The service paradigm could fulfil the much-needed interoperability among different and distributed devices. That is, every device is being projected as a findable, flexible, and usable service. The robustness, versatility, and resiliency of microservices come in handy when presenting devices as services to the outside world, which eliminates all kinds of dependency-induced challenges.

The changing application ecosystem

Mainframe-era applications are typically monolithic and massive. They are centralized, inflexible, closed, and expensive to maintain. Then, we came across client-server and multi-tier distributed applications. There are business-domain-specific applications that solve specific problems. There are web, cloud, social, enterprise, mobile, wearable, and IoT applications. Then, there are operational, transactional, and analytical applications. With the solidity of microservices, all kinds of software applications get disintegrated into a number of microservices, which are very famous for facilitating easy integration, deployment, management, and manoeuvrability. Microservices are self-defined and hence autonomous.

They can be developed and deployed independently. Microservices are being stuffed with their own data stores. Microservices are decoupled, so dependency issues don't crop up. However, to create and sustain bigger and better applications, different and geographically-distributed microservices need to be found and fused systematically. That is, services should be matched and composed to realize composite applications, which are right and relevant for enterprise and cloud IT. Not only for enterprise applications but also for creating integrated and insightful applications, the act of composition acquires special significance.

Composition is being accomplished in two prominent ways—orchestration and choreography. As mentioned in the *The emergence of cloud-native applications* section, there are domain-specific and neutral applications that innately need the blending of multiple microservices to fulfil varying business requirements, market sentiments, and user expectations. In short, the composition of microservices deserves the highest recognition for producing smarter applications towards user-empowerment. Hence, to realize all kinds of smart applications, API-stuffed, extensible, configurable, interoperable, and composable microservices are the need of the hour. Composition tools and techniques are flourishing, and hence service composites are the best fit for constructing insight-driven, highly sophisticated, and integrated applications that can run on any runtime (bare-metal servers, virtual machines, containers, and functions). In addition, the future calls for device-centric cloud environments, which are aptly termed fog or device clouds. Microservice composites can run not only on resource-intensive servers but also on resource-constrained and networked devices, which is the real beauty of microservices.

Tending toward the API-driven world

Integration and collaboration are important needs for software to achieve business processes. Old and modern software applications run on multiple kinds of IT platforms and infrastructures. Software solutions automate most business processes. However, business applications have to spontaneously synchronize with other software packages in order to bear fruit. Processes, applications, and data have to be integrated to guarantee a comprehensive yet compact view for executives and end users. Communication is the key. APIs are the widely-recognized mechanism for software components to find one another to interact with in a systematic manner. APIs are being created and supplied with any kind of software, including web and cloud applications, databases, middleware, and platforms. The current internet paradigm is steadily expanding. Once upon a time, the internet was the network of networked computers. That is, all kinds of computers (both clients and servers) were networked to share their unique capabilities.

These days, not only computers but also our communicators and consumer electronics, such as smartphones, **personal digital assistants (PDAs)**, tablets, laptops, handhelds, and communication gateways, are also joining the internet. Precisely speaking, the **internet of devices (IoD)** paradigm is fast emerging and evolving.

All kinds of personal and professional devices, instruments, appliances, and machines are getting connected to the internet; all kinds of common and cheap things in our everyday environments are getting digitized with the help of scores of digitization and edge technologies and tools in order to be sufficiently empowered to join mainstream computing. Everyday items are becoming computational, communicative, sensitive, responsive, and active with the appropriate enablement of powerful and pioneering technologies. Now, with the faster stability of service-engineering techniques, we see the world as the **Internet of Services (IoS)**. That is, everything is expressed and exposed as a service for the outside world. All kinds of software and hardware systems, including embedded systems, are being presented as a collection of publicly-addressable and-available services. This is ultimately helping to hide systems' complexities and deficiencies.

At one end, we see an increased number of hardware systems (IT infrastructures), software applications and services, data sources, and scores of platforms in the internet space. However, creating and sustaining APIs for these kinds of internet-attached systems, applications, and services isn't an easy task. At the other end, we have a variety of digitized, embedded, networked, handy, trendy, slim, and sleek I/O devices. Hence, in order to establish a beneficial link between the ground-level systems and the faraway internet-hosted systems, APIs are the way forward. In short, the RESTful service paradigm comes as a solace by simplifying and streamlining API creation and usage for systems integration and collaboration.

The Representational State Transfer service paradigm

RESTful services assist in establishing a beneficial relationship between computers and other I/O devices with internet-based systems, applications, and data sources. The RESTful API uses the pervasive HTTP methods to perform the most common actions (GET, PUT, POST, and DELETE). **Representation State Transfer (REST)** is a promising and potential architectural style for designing loosely-coupled applications over HTTP. RESTful services are the simplest and most sought-after services that blend well to result in web, mobile, cloud, and IoT applications.

API design best practices

When creating APIs, the following **non-functional requirements (NFRs)** and the **quality of service (QoS)** attributes need to be given utmost importance in order to develop flexible APIs. The most popular ones include performance/throughput, scalability, simplicity, modifiability, portability, and reliability. These qualities can be achieved if APIs are being prepared based on the constraints. Here is a list of the most crucial constraints:

- **Client-server architecture**: This essentially prescribes that the client and server applications should be able to evolve independently. A client has to know only resource URIs. There shouldn't be any other dependency between the client and the server systems. Therefore, the design of the client and server interfaces can be done separately. This constraint gives developers much-needed flexibility as the same API can be leveraged across multiple backend server and database systems. The APIs can be easily changed to accommodate special requirements without making any destructive impact on others.
- **Cache-ability**: As we all know, caching is the age-old practice of storing copies of frequently-accessed data in multiple locations along the request-response path. When a client asks for a resource representation, the request typically goes first to the nearest cache to get the data. If the desired data is not found in the local cache, the next destination for the client request is the proxy cache or the reverse cache of the requested resource. If none of the caches have the latest data/fresh copy, there's no other option but to knock the resource itself. Optimizing the network using caching reduces latency, optimizes bandwidth usage, reduces the load on servers, and hides any network failure.

There are other constraints, which are explained in other chapters in detail.

Learning about service-composition methods

Orchestration and choreography are the well-known and widely-used ways of accomplishing composite services. With the containerization movement picking up, microservices are being containerized and run in cloud environments. With the adoption of container-orchestration platforms, multi-container applications are being easily and quickly realized. Hence, composite applications are being realized at the service level and at the container level. Microservices are, for getting composed, having to find and bind with other microservices in order to accomplish greater goals and reach bigger targets. A simple example is that, when a new service gets registered in the service registry, it has to call a couple of other services, such as authentication and authorization services. Depending on use cases, services may need to interact with more services in order to be relevant to their stakeholders and subscribers.

As indicated elsewhere, every microservice is stuffed with its own data source. Every microservice is enabled with its own one or many interfaces. Due to the surging popularity and simplicity exhibited by the RESTful service paradigm, the majority of APIs are RESTful APIs. The following diagram vividly illustrates the following. There are several microservices in the server side and a client is accessing one or more services. For the idea of microservices to flourish, services need to be dynamically integrated in order to facilitate service interactions purposefully:

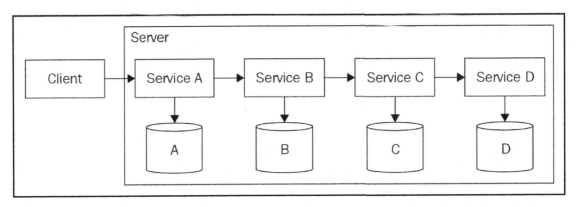

There are a few important challenges here. The calling service doesn't know whether the serving services are doing well. The services being requested can be overburdened due to an unprecedented number of service requests. The service performance, health condition, and security information are not known to calling services. Also, there are no failure-handling and compensation mechanisms here. When multiple services are being involved for business processes and transactions, it's important to know which part of the data and control flow faces the problem. The root of the problem has to be identified in order to streamline troubleshooting.

Further on, these kinds of interactions happen through tight coupling, but tight coupling can lead to dependency issues. This is why lightly- and loosely-coupled services are preferred: so that the development and deployment can be done independently. Also, service interactions don't produce any issues. RESTful APIs are the method for service collaboration.

Any change being made on one service has cascading implications; the operational complexities of service environments are bound to escalate as more services join. Hence, experts have come out with competent alternatives that solve these bad implications by invoking tightly-coupled services.

Service orchestration and choreography

Orchestration microservices have to be composed through an orchestration engine. The composition has to happen through predefined patterns, which are typically described using an orchestration language. Orchestration is more suitable and relevant for implementing business process flows. A competent and standards-compliant orchestration engine immensely contributes as a central brain to guide and guarantee the control flows and their execution. The policies/business rules are being managed and manipulated through the orchestration engine in a centralized manner. The 360-degree view of an application flow is delivered through the orchestration engine. The service and operational-level agreements (SLAs/OLA) are estimated and codified through the centralized engine. Simplistically speaking, all of the centrally-managed and commonly-used functionalities are being abstracted out of participating services and are being incorporated in the orchestration engine, which also has a business process flow and management engine.

Service chaining and workflows, widely termed as service orchestration, are helping out in legacy and enterprise application integrations:

- **Short-running orchestrations**: These are stateless and synchronous besides dealing with momentary data and sessions. They are a kind of request and response type. They talk to multiple services in a sequenced manner. Based on the output of the first service, the orchestrator forms an appropriate message for the second service, and so on.
- **Long-running orchestrations**: These are typically stateful and asynchronous. These involve human involvement, interpretation, and instruction and are made to run for longer by leveraging persistent data storage.

There are a few drawbacks too. There's a kind of tight coupling being established between the orchestrator and all of the associated application components/services. Adding new services and states mandates for an update in the central business logic. The central coordinator sometimes emerges as a single point of failure.

Choreography, on the other hand, implements a data flow between multiple decoupled services. Each service knows what sort of data it can expect and provide. There is no need for a centralized conductor to run the flows. This is all about peer-to-peer service composition. Each service is stuffed with the required intelligence to act and react. Each microservice is a self-defined and contained service, and each microservice communicates and completes the assignment via messages and events. **Event-driven architecture (EDA)** is emerging as the core architectural style and pattern for the increasingly event-driven world. Choreography is more suitable for implementing event-driven applications. Due to their decoupled nature, microservices can be replaced and substituted with better service implementations.

Additional services and their instances can be incorporated without affecting the system. New technologies and algorithms can be leveraged easily. All kinds of service dependencies and their negative implications are getting eliminated. The single point of failure is not there in the choreography-based service composition. However, there are a few drawbacks. Without a central conductor or coordinator, the monitoring, measuring, and management of service interactions and collaborations remain a challenge. That is, looking at a sequenced view of services that talk to one another is problematic. Empowering every microservice to be self-reliant and intelligent in their actions and reactions is tough, and bringing forth business-mandated and technology-enabled advancements across the participating services is a bit difficult. Choreography facilitates scalability and a shared-nothing architecture. Hence, experts and exponents are of the view that, by combining these two architectural styles, most of the emerging application scenarios can be elegantly tackled.

As we all know, business processes are becoming complex due to various reasons as days go by. Though a process consolidation toward optimization happens on one side, business processes continuously grow to become complicated and long-running. Processes also have to involve geographically-distributed and different microservices. Hence, process governance and management become painful. As the number of contributing microservices is growing rapidly, the number of fine-grained interactions among microservices is bound to increase exponentially. Hence, there are technology-sponsored solutions and best practices that surmount the lingering issues of microservices and their interactions. The main methods are orchestration and choreography. The subsequent sections describe their needs, key drivers, capabilities, and how to use them.

Beginning with service orchestration

Business processes are being accomplished through a variety of service implementations. However, there's a sequence for involving services. Typically, a business process indicates the sequence of services to be leveraged. Orchestration is a way for service composition through a centralized coordinator. This coordinator/brain guides and fulfils the business process requirements, just like a conductor in an orchestra—he/she leads the team as the central authority. By employing such an intermediary among different microservices, the issues that come from tight coupling go off once for all. That is, we get loosely-coupled microservices and they don't need to know each other. They also don't need to know whether other services are running. The communication can be mainly synchronous. That is, the requesting services should wait until they get the response from the requested services.

There is one controller or coordinator that acts as the service orchestrator. That is, all of the service interactions happen via the orchestrator. This follows the well-known interaction:

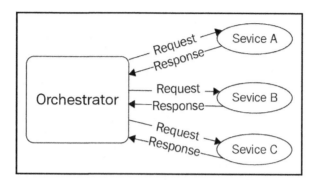

For example, we need two or more services to be involved and invoked to accomplish a business process. The sequence of calling is also important here. The orchestrator makes a call to each one and waits for a response from the requested service. Once the response reaches the orchestrator, the next service in the sequence has to be called out, and so on. Check out `https://medium.com/capital-one-developers/microservices-when-to-react-vs-orchestrate-c6b18308a14c` for more information.

The shortcomings of service orchestration

This is a good way to have tighter flow control when there's a need for synchronous communication and processing. There are a few drawbacks with this—if the first service isn't responding, the other services can't be called. That is, it creates a kind of coupling that results in unwanted dependency issues. The orchestrator becomes the single point of failure, and hence the recommendation is to go for clustered orchestration. Synchronous communication blocks other service requests.

The following diagram illustrates how the orchestration process gets accomplished through the participation of disparate and geographically-distributed microservices:

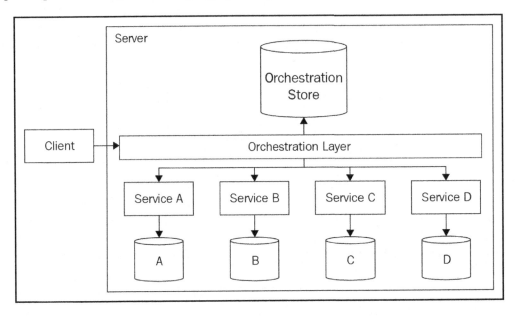

This composition model typically doesn't address failure cases. Most of the time, the service request is being attended. The failure rate is mostly one percent. The best practice is that if there is a failure, one or other viable counter measures, such as compensation, has to be initiated immediately in order to wriggle out of the chaos. The retry and repair activities are the other mechanisms to ensure business continuity. Data and disaster-recovery capabilities have to be in place to reduce the data loss in order to maximize business profits. Considering the drawbacks of service orchestration, the service choreography (this is explained in detail in the subsequent sections) is gaining a lot of attention.

Applying orchestration-based composition

If most of the works have to be done in a sequential manner (if there is zero possibility for parallel execution), orchestration is the way to go. If there's a need to keep the control flow logic centralized, orchestration is the way forward. If there are hundreds of microservices participating with different control flows, centralization is preferred. The mantra of distributed deployment and centralized management is getting fulfilled through orchestration. If the decoupling is not a strict mandate, the orchestration method is the widely-used one.

Beginning with service choreography

When building a microservices-centric applications, the service dependencies have to be nipped in the budding stage itself. Orchestration leads to dependencies, which are bad in the long run. Hence, all kinds of dependencies have to be avoided to fulfil the strategic vision of self-defined and autonomous microservices. Experts contend that EDA is the way forward for solving some of the challenges previously quoted. That is, the controlling logic is being stuffed in the orchestrator module, whereas in this case, the logic is inscribed in each of the participating services; the logic is distributed and these empowered services (smart services) know beforehand how to react to various events. The communication is asynchronous and an event bus (dumb pipe) is being leveraged to route events. This means multiple services can consume the same events and then initiate their ordained tasks. The results are then packaged and transmitted as events back to the event bus at the same time. As previously noted, these microservices are called **smart entities** and the event bus is just a dumb pipe. No intelligence is embedded in the event bus, which is the primary communication infrastructure for event-driven microservices.

The asynchronous nature removes the blocking or waiting, which is the main drawback of orchestration. Services, on receiving events, can produce other events, which are looped back to the event bus to be consumed by other services to do their assigned works. This sort of decoupling is demanded in the microservices world.

The following diagram shows how the event-driven architecture pattern functions:

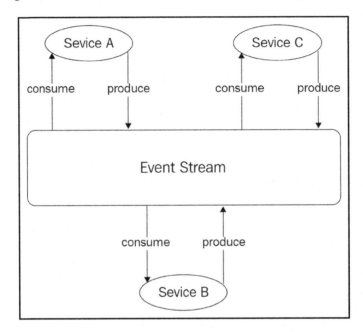

Hence, event producers and consumers, without knowing anything about others, collaborate in a purpose-driven manner. Due to parallel processing (many services receive the event and go ahead with their processing), faster processing by services is ensured. Newer services can easily join and contribute without impacting others. The existing services can be easily manipulated to accommodate business, technology, and user changes, which are, without an ounce of doubt, the new normal. Microservices can be independently developed and deployed, and this empowers different and distributed development teams to focus on their core activities toward the faster realization and deployment of microservice-centric applications. An event stream stores all of the events. Suppose a service goes down while events are still being produced; after some time, the service comes back to life, gets back all of the missed events, and acts upon them. Also, this EDA, a kind of reactive architecture, enables us to separate out the read and write activities. That is, both of these activities can be independently accomplished. The advantage of this segregation is that they can be independently scaled based on the evolving requirements. The application is read-heavy, then that part can be scaled alone without any impact on the write part.

With choreography, the services are accordingly empowered to act and react as per the evolving situation. Services behave like dancers—performing their assigned movements to appropriately react to other dancers, so as to finish the process in an organized way.

Primarily, the choreography concept depends on the popular EDA. The choreographed services typically react to events and put their output onto the queue of the event bus, and from there, other authorized services pick up and start to showcase their unique capabilities. **Event Bus** is the primary intermediary and communication infrastructure. This is illustrated in the following diagram:

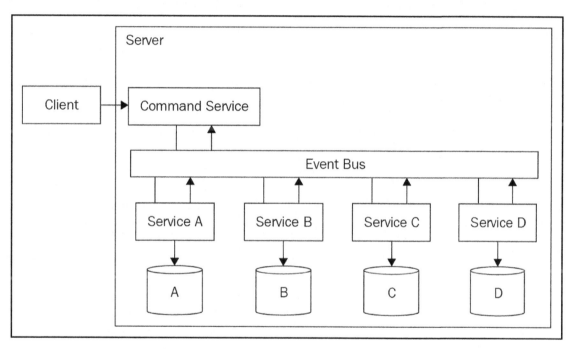

Services don't need to talk to other services in order to initiate and implement an action. Services are waiting for some events to get initiated somewhere and get forwarded to them through the event bus, which is the primary messaging middleware/broker/bus.

The shortcomings of service choreography

Systems that are choreographed are loosely coupled, highly flexible, and easily amenable to changes (internal as well as external). As an example, let's consider an order application. Using the reactive architecture (event-driven choreography), the flow can be represented as follows (this is taken from `https://blog.bernd-ruecker.com/why-service-collaboration-needs-choreography-and-orchestration-239c4f9700fa`):

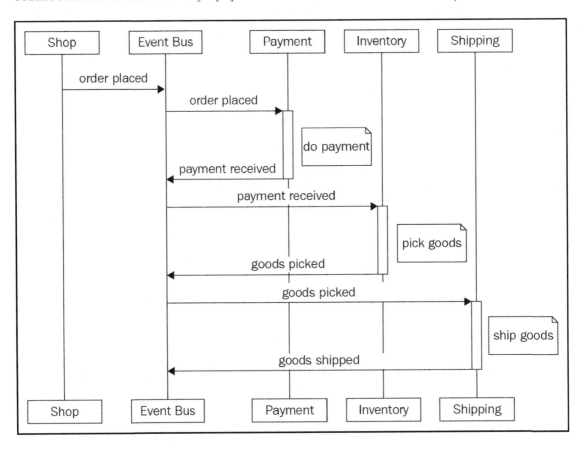

The payment service is destined to react to the order-placed event. The issue here is that the payment service has to know its consumer. If any other service needs the payment service, we need to make the changes in the payment service. Now, there's a new addition in the business requirement. The addition is that VIP customers can pay later by invoice. This change is to affect multiple components. The payment service has to execute payments for non-VIP customers only.

The inventory service also has to react on the order-placed event, but only for VIP customers. The following diagram explains this process:

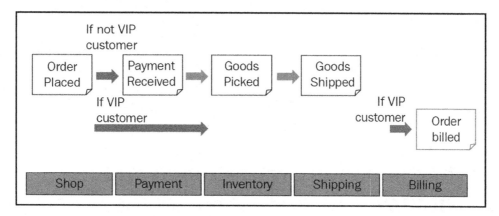

This requires the introduction of an additional component that brings in a clear separation between **Service A** and its users. This is called the **event-command-transformation pattern**:

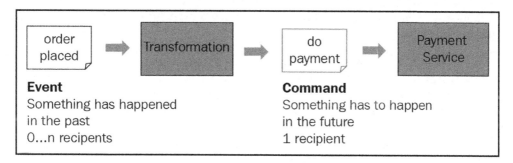

The event-command-transformation pattern is ultimately helping to realize decoupled event-based systems.

The second hurdle is that the payment service might take longer to complete. Customers have to clear their payments and this may take days or weeks. This is a long-running process flow and it's mandatory to track the state. It clearly bats for an orchestrated style of collaboration. Hence, the blending of orchestration and choreography is the best way for pitching in highly flexible architecture for composite applications.

Applying choreography-based composition

Choreography helps to accomplish business processes in a parallel manner. It's possible to change the process by adding, relegating, replacing, substituting, and decommissioning process components. If all or most of our processing can be performed in an asynchronous manner, this composition method is the best fit. Parallel execution is the main motivation of the reactive architecture. As previously indicated, the flow logic is typically distributed in this method. And if this decentralization is manageable, the choreography method is good. To create a centralized and consolidated view for monitoring, measurement, and management, the best option is to use correlation IDs.

The hybridization of orchestration and choreography

We've seen that both of the composition methods have pros and cons. That is, with software platforms and packages becoming more distributed, integrated, and complicated, there's no one architectural style that is a perfect fit in all situations. Therefore, IT professionals have come out with the hybrid versions of orchestration and choreography to overcome these limitations.

The first hybrid pattern uses reactive (event-driven) between services (choreography for inter-service communication) and orchestration within a service (intra-service communication). In the following diagram, we have three services: A, B, and C. These are event-driven and reactive to one another via the event bus. **Service A** consumes an event and gets triggered to orchestrate calls to the services D, E, and F. These calls can be synchronous or asynchronous. Then, on getting the result from the services, **Service A** produces an event:

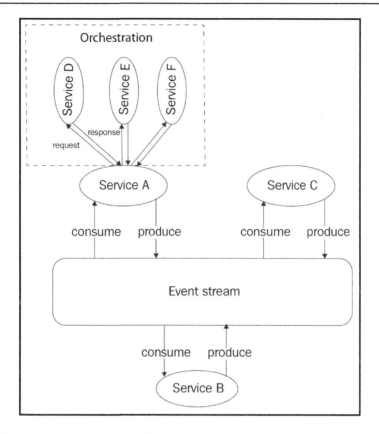

The A, B, and C services are decoupled. However, the D, E, and F services within **Service A** are coupled. This means if these services are doing synchronous processing, the blocking surfaces here. The event bus facilitates asynchronous processing among the A, B, and C services. Each service (A, B, and C) is stuffed with the control logic to exhibit an independent behavior. That is, the logic is typically distributed across multiple services, whereas the control, flow, and other horizontal capabilities are being centralized in the case of the orchestrator.

The second hybrid pattern uses reactive (event-driven) between services and a coordinator (reactive orchestrator) to assist the flow. In this example, it leverages the concepts of commands and events. As shown in the following diagram, the coordinator produces commands to the event stream, and the microservices that are empowered to act for the particular commands receive the command, do the desired processing, and then create and pass on the events to the event stream.

In this example, services A and C start at the same time, and the coordinator consumes the generated events from the event stream and reacts to the events accordingly:

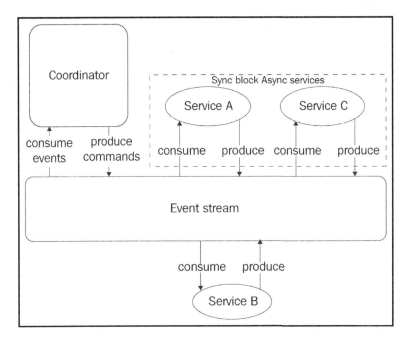

The services are generally decoupled, yet still there's a kind of coupling between the services and the coordinator. That is, the coordinator has to know what commands a service needs to get in order to react correctly. Events between services lead to asynchronous processing. The overall flow logic is stuffed in the reactive coordinator. The coordinator, as usual, is a single point of failure.

Another example of the hybridization of orchestration and choreography

Here is another interesting example, taken from https://dzone.com/articles/event-driven-orchestration-an-effective-microservi.

Choreography

As shown in the following diagram, a process is getting initiated by an event from a user. The process is then accomplished by the respective microservices collectively in a choreography mode. This method ensures light coupling and high cohesiveness:

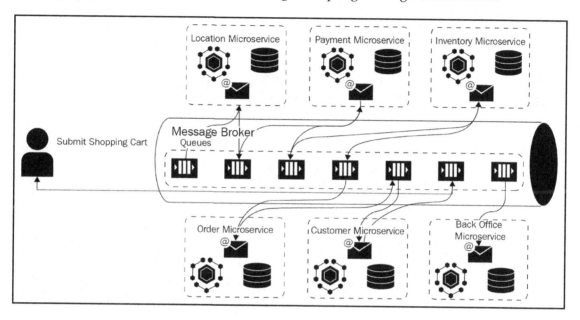

Service choreography using the message broker

There are a few important drawbacks with this approach. Choreography typically enables a decentralized approach and hence all the participating services need to be embedded with the relevant business-processing logic. Any business- and communication-logic changes have to be shared across all the microservices, and the state information of the process has to be stored separately. There is no centralized service to take care of all of the services. Finally, the strict implementation of the ACID properties isn't possible because of multiple distributed services participate towards the process fulfillment.

Service orchestration

There is another approach found in the web. This is to implement a centralized service orchestration through by integrating the **business process model and notation (BPMN)** workflow and REST. The following diagram clearly depicts how a complex **Shopping Cart Microservice** is realized:

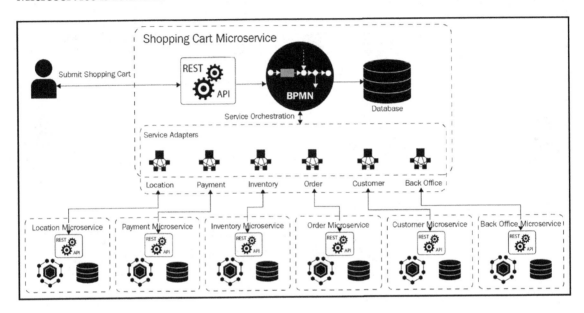

Service orchestration using BPMN and REST

As you can see, there are three primitive resource types. The corresponding path details for those resources are also etched in the preceding image. For a monolithic application, the central server would have handled requests for all the resource destinations. Further on, there is a shared datastore that stocks the resources as distinct tables. For complex queries, the much-discussed concept of complex joins comes to the rescue.

The hybridization – event-driven service orchestration

As shown in the following diagram , the shopping cart service is implemented as an orchestration service using the BPMN workflow. However, all of the various service adapters are being replaced through an out-of-the-box AMQP, but the service adapters are eliminated through a common out-of-the-box AMQP adapter, which is one of the prime components of the AMQP event bus, which is the message broker to decouple the services:

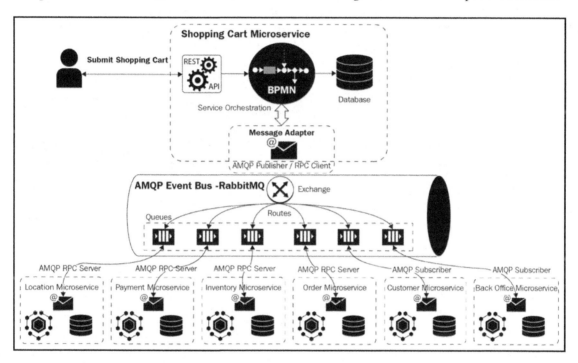

Data management

The core philosophy of MSA is the decentralization of software design and development. The decentralization not only guides the organization of business logic but also how data has to be persisted.

In a monolithic architecture, application components and data are traditionally centralized. One of the SQL databases, such as SQL server, is used as a single database with multiple tables. This is the way data gets persisted in the previous era. Some portions of the application logic even get delegated to the SQL server database in the form of stored procedures, complex joins, and so on.

Thinking in REST

To correctly and concisely organize data in a decentralized fashion, the RESTful service paradigm comes in handy. That is, the REST concept introduces a new way to model data. There are multiple resources in any application. REST gives each participating resource a URL. Then, the recommendation is to use the standard HTTP verbs to interact with the resource. The author of the article at `https://medium.com/@nathankpeck/` `microservice-principles-decentralized-data-management-4adaceea173f` has come out with a sample API for a small social-messaging application:

HTTP Request	Intent of request
GET /users/	Fetch a list of users
POST /users/	Create a new user
GET /users/1	Fetch user with ID 1
DELETE /users/1	Delete user with ID 1
PUT /users/1	Update user with ID 1
GET /messages/	Fetch a list of messages
POST /messages/	Create a new message
GET /messages/1	Fetch message with ID 1
DELETE /messages/1	Delete message with ID 1
GET /users/1/messages	Fetch list of messages written by user with ID 1
GET /users/1/friends	Fetch list of friends for user with ID 1
PUT /users/1/friends/2	Add user with ID 2 to the list of friends for user with ID 1
DELETE /users/1/friends/2	Delete user with ID 2 from the friend list of user with ID 1

There are three primitive resource types—user, message, and friend. There is a set of paths for the resource types, as illustrated in the following diagram. In the case of a monolith application, the central server would handle requests for all of the resource paths and there is a single database that stores all of the resource types as tables:

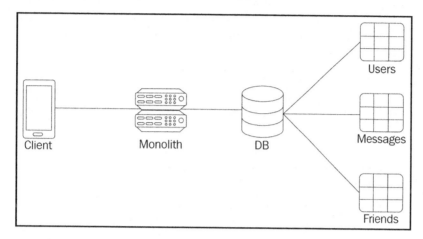

However, for a microservices-centric application, every microservice has its own database.

This arrangement ensures tighter security for data. That is, every data request, access, and manipulation has to be accomplished through microservice APIs. The philosophy here is that there's a one-to-one mapping between microservices and resource types:

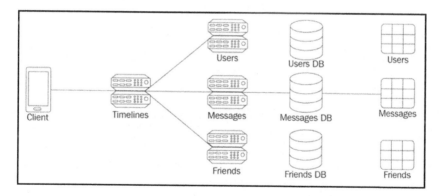

Having a unique database/database instance for each microservice brings forth a number of advantages.

Discarding SQL join

A noteworthy tip for better data management is to avoid the SQL join operation. As every database is logically separated in the MSA world, doing SQL join function is very tedious and time-consuming. It's going to be a technical and security nightmare. However, there can be different application requirements. For example, suppose the messaging application mandates for timeline view. That is, the timeline view has to show the most recent message from each friend of the authenticated user. Also, this new view has to show the friend's name and other details along with the message sent.

It's still possible to implement this complicated view using the basic REST API. That is, the client has to employ several API calls to different resources to fulfill this specialized view requirement:

```
GET /users/1/friends

├─GET /users/2

├─GET /users/3

├─GET /users/2/messages?order=latest&limit=1

└─GET /users/3/messages?order=latest&limit=1
```

That means there is a total of five requests. This is to degrade the performance. A workaround is to bring forth a new route to the API:

HTTP Request	Intent of request
GET /users/1/timeline	Fetch timeline of messages from friends of user with ID 1

The **Client** can then fetch this single timeline resource to get all the data it requires to render the timeline view. That is, it creates an additional timeline microservice that lives on top of the three data microservices. This new microservice treats each underlying microservice as a resource. This top-level microservice joins the data from the underlying microservices and exposes the joined result to the client.

In the microservice era, the localized database operations are being accomplished through a composite microservice:

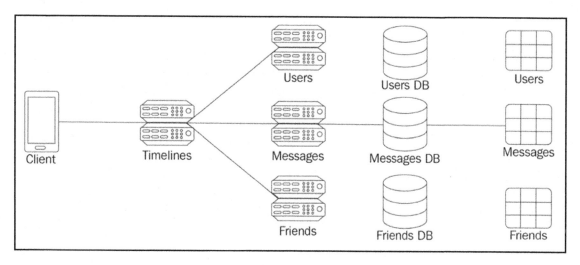

The much-discussed performance issue does not creep in here as the timeline service is predominantly hosted in containers along with the other three services. All of these are in the same physical machine or within nearby machines. To further reduce round-trip network penalties, the timeline service could leverage the advantages of *bulk fetch* endpoints. The user microservice could have an endpoint that accepts a list of user IDs and returns all of the matching user objects. The advantage here is that the newly-carved-out timeline service only has to make one request to the friends service, one request to the user service, and one request to the message service. The timeline service functions as a centralized place to define the logic and this separation facilitates to accommodate any business, technology, and user-inspired changes at later point in time.

Eventual consistency

This is a well-known characteristic of NoSQL databases. This isn't an issue for transactional databases, which are the primary data-persistence mechanism for the centralized architecture. However, when data gets separated into many logical or physical databases, the consistency feature can't be attained easily.

For example, consider what would happen if a user fetched their timeline at the same time that one of their friends deleted their account:

1. The timeline service fetches the list of friends from the friend service and sees a friend ID that it needs to resolve
2. Friend deletes the account, which deletes the user object from the user service, as well as all of the friend references in the friend service
3. Timeline service attempts to turn the friend ID into user details by making a request to the user service, but receives a `404 Not Found` response instead

It's clear that decentralized data modeling requires extra conditional handling to detect and handle race conditions where underlying data has changed between requests. For complex applications, it becomes necessary to have some tables together in the same database to fulfill the database transaction. The idea is that these linked tables have to be handled by a single microservice. If related data needs strong consistency, the option is to use the proven *two-phase commit* mechanism.

Polyglot persistence

Decentralized data management helps to take advantage of polyglot persistence. Different types of data have different storage requirements. We have multi-structured and massive amount that needs batch and real-time processing. For streaming data, there are the following streaming-analytics platforms:

- **Read/write balance**: Some types of data have a very high write volume. This needs a different type of data store.
- **Data structure**: Some types of highly-structured data, such as JSON documents, may be better stored and served via a document-oriented NoSQL database.
- **Data querying**: Some data may be easily accessible using a simple key-value database, whereas other types of data mandate for advanced querying based on the values of multiple columns.
- **Data life cycle**: Some data is needed for a short time and can be stored in a fast and in-memory database, such as Redis or Memcached, while other data has to be retained for all time and hence stored using durable disk storage.
- **Data size**: Data size is varies considerably these days. There are object-storage options that accommodate staggering amounts of data.

Hence, data management in the ensuring microservices era is quite different and challenging too. However, data professionals have come out with competent data persistence, representation, interchange, masking, wrangling, management, analytics, and security solutions.

Summary

Microservices have to be composed through the orchestration engine. The composition has to happen through predefined patterns, which are typically described using an orchestration language. Orchestration is relevant for implementing business-process flows. A competent and standards-compliant orchestration engine acts as a central brain to guide and guarantee the control flows and their execution. The policies/business rules are being managed and manipulated through the orchestration engine in a centralized manner. The 360-degree view of an application flow is delivered through the orchestration engine. The service and operational-level agreements (SLAs/OLA) are estimated and codified through the centralized engine. Simplistically speaking, all of the centrally-managed and commonly-used functionalities are being abstracted out of participating services and are being incorporated into the orchestration engine, which also has a business-process flow and management engine.

Service chaining and workflows, widely termed as service orchestration, are helping out in legacy and enterprise application integrations.

Divide and conquer has been the mantra for moderating the design, development, deployment, and operational complexities of complicated systems. MSA is being positioned as the most efficient and agile design technique. Then there are agile development processes to speed up the realization of microservices. With the faster stability of DevOps concepts and the scores of automated tools accelerate the integration, delivery, and deployment of microservices in cloud environments.

To craft process-centric, business-aware, production-ready, and enterprise-grade applications, microservices should be identified, matched for their competencies and capacities, and composed. There are two composition methods—orchestration and choreography. In the next chapter, we'll explain the best practices for producing effective and extensible RESTful service APIs.

8
RESTful API Design Tips

Enterprise-scale applications across industry verticals are being increasingly built as a collection of polyglot microservices. Due to the surging popularity of the **microservices architecture (MSA)** as the most optimized and organized application architecture, most business-critical applications are being meticulously designed, developed, and deployed as a set of independent, yet interactive, microservices. Another noteworthy trend is the tremendous success of REST APIs for services and applications. All kinds of applications (operational, transactional, and analytical) are being fitted with REST APIs in order to simplify application integration. Further down the line, web, cloud, mobile, and IoT applications are being stuffed with REST APIs.

Modern application platforms for design, development, debugging, delivery, deployment, and decommissioning purposes are also attached to REST APIs. Integration, orchestration, governance, brokerage, compliance, and management platforms are being exposed to the outside world through REST APIs. Because of its simplicity and lightweight nature, the REST paradigm has captured both minds and market share in large quantities. Precisely speaking, every worthwhile microservice, application, and platform is being frontended with a REST interface. Without a shred of doubt, RESTful APIs have become penetrative, pervasive, and persuasive. That is, RESTful APIs play a vital role in building and integrating applications.

This chapter is dedicated to discussing the design patterns and best practices to build competent and compatible REST APIs that can easily cope with technological and business changes.

This chapter will deal with the following topics:

- Articulating the importance of APIs
- Accentuating API design patterns and best practices
- Enumerating API security guidelines
- Explaining the various tools and platforms associated with API design, development, integration, security, and management
- Tending toward the API-driven digital world

Technical requirements

This chapter details the various best practices for designing efficient RESTful APIs. Readers are expected to have some knowledge of, and basic programming experience in, the REST architectural style in order to fully grasp and implement the best practices discussed in this chapter.

Beginning with APIs

The concept of the **application programming interface** (**API**) is gaining dominance due to its significant contribution toward exposing any application or service to the outside world to find and use its unique business and technical competencies. To enable application, service, and data integration, APIs are being widely recognized as the way forward. Data gets exchanged between different applications and services. There are mandates for bringing forth highly integrated systems. This means that a variety of third-party applications and backend systems have to be systematically integrated. The middleware solutions, in the form of enterprise application hubs, enterprise service buses, message brokers and queues, API gateways and management suites, and service meshes, are seeing significant utilization toward local as well as remote application integration. All these integration engines are being fitted with well-intended and -designed APIs.

As we all know, the device ecosystem grows rapidly with the availability of scores of slim and sleek, handy and trendy, and purpose-agnostic, as well as specific, devices in large quantities; that is, connected devices are increasingly participating in mainstream computing. Here, too, the contributions of APIs for enabling devices, data sources, and services toward data and logic exchange are growing steadily. APIs hide the heterogeneity and multiplicity of devices to the outside world. That is, every device is expressed and exposed as a service, and every service is getting partitioned into an interface and implementation. This segregation goes a long way in maintaining up devices for longer periods of time. When it comes to dynamically equipping devices with additional capabilities, APIs are indispensable.

In short, an API is a kind of a messenger that receives and processes requests and ensures it runs enterprise systems successfully. Social networking sites, such as Facebook and Twitter, are a few of the companies that use open or public APIs for the benefit of their business. A start-up can open its APIs in order to enable third-party software to use its software. For an integrated world, setting up, composing, securing, controlling, and enhancing APIs becomes paramount for global enterprises in showcasing their distinct capabilities to their customers, partners, and employees. With digital technologies taking center stage in the IT world, the elegance of APIs is assuming top spot.

Learning about application programming interfaces

According to accomplished experts, an API is a set of rules and tools for initiating and governing how business workloads interact. Now, with the faster proliferation of the cloud, the interaction level has gone up and beyond business applications. That is, scores of IT optimization and automation services also have to interact with one another in order to simplify and streamline business-process automation. APIs have to uniquely and uniformly find one another, initiate data interchange, and verify information for software applications to leverage one another for their business benefits. Let's use a few comparisons to explain APIs and their roles and responsibilities in our increasingly connected world.

If applications were vehicles on the road, APIs would be the traffic rules. The rules prescribe how vehicles must behave on the road.

If applications were food items, APIs would be recipes. APIs specify and govern how various ingredients fuse together to create tasty and trendy meals.

If applications were houses, APIs would be the blueprint, which articulate how different construction artifacts blend to form a house.

Why have APIs become a mainstream concept?

Having understood the crucial roles of APIs in our increasingly software-defined and - designed world, faster API production becomes a crucial task for API developers. That is, forming appropriate rules for the intended success of the APIs is vital. API designers create and publish APIs, which allow other applications to find and interact with them.

Suppose you are exposing one or more customer-facing web and mobile applications that run on cloud environments. These applications are diligently being fitted with one or more APIs. Now, having API-attached applications enables other developers to build their own applications that can easily be integrated with the web and mobile applications. This integration makes applications bigger and better. Implementing business processes becomes easier, faster, risk-free, and rewarding. The customer experience with the omni-channel aggregation capability goes up significantly. There's no need for a web-scale company to devise and design APIs. Even for an idea, an application gets built and decorated with a simple API. Application developers are becoming accustomed to creating and sustaining APIs in order to expose their applications to a larger audience.

As we've emphasized several times, application integration becomes simpler with APIs. There were other options for enterprise integration, but they were insufficient in many ways. APIs have emerged as the standard for process integration. When an API designer releases an officially accepted and clearly defined set of rules, others can confidently embark on API-inspired application and platform integration. Thus, APIs provide fresh possibilities and opportunities. APIs grant developers the requisite power to control not only what others can do with their applications, but also prescribe what others can't do with their applications.

APIs have become indispensable

Path-breaking technologies are emerging and evolving fast toward digital innovation, disruption, and transformation. A variety of breakthroughs are being unearthed and popularized in order to bring in a variety of acceleration, automation, and augmentation in IT and business spaces. We are being bombarded with a number of application architectures, ranging from **service-oriented architecture (SOA)**, **event-driven architecture (EDA)**, and **resource-oriented architecture (ROA)** to MSA. Containers have become the default runtime for services. Cloud servers are being expressed and exposed as a collection of containers. With the surging popularity of container-orchestration platforms, creating container clusters and using them to run software applications and services has become the most prominent way to develop, deploy, and manage software. The cool convergence, as explained elsewhere in this book, between containers and microservices has propelled the next generation of application delivery. Each microservice is being fitted with one or more APIs. Further on, each microservice has its own data store. For data security and effective data management, each database is also being given an API to perform data operations with confidence and clarity.

The other prominent advancements are the faster proliferation of cloud environments and the fact that each cloud center is being stuffed with thousands of applications and platforms. Cloud-hosted platforms enable third-party application developers not only to develop newer applications, but also facilitate a seamless and spontaneous integration with their applications. As we are heading toward federated cloud environments to create composite applications, APIs emerge as the most crucial entity toward fulfilling the fast-emerging multi-cloud idea. **Device-to-device (D2D)**, **device-to-cloud (D2C)**, and **cloud-to-cloud (C2C)** integration gets facilitated through APIs.

Learning about the major types of APIs

There are a few API types. **Remote procedure call (RPC)** is the one that enables applications to call one or more functions in other applications remotely. XML and JSON are the content types and there are RPC APIs for both XML and JSON. In the web services world, SOAP has been ruling the world with a number of standard specifications for different purposes. But then, due to the extreme complexity, the adoption rate has come down sharply. Now, with the lightweight REST architectural style, every service, application, platform, middleware, and database is exposing RESTful APIs.

Describing API platforms

Considering the importance of APIs for the forthcoming digital era, tool and product vendors have come out with a variety of integrated platforms to enable API life cycle activities. The following sections discuss different platform solutions that empower the API world.

Creating API development platforms

There are several ways to produce high-quality APIs. Creating new APIs from the ground up, refurbishing the existing ones, and automatically generating APIs out of currently-running integration are the well-known ways. Here, we need platform support to create APIs in other ways. There are API design and integration platforms available for accomplishing this need. We now have thousands of **software as a service (SaaS)** applications being delivered through cloud environments. These services are generally API-attached. These APIs can be reused across. However, these APIs could be limited in their functionality. Thus, APIs have to be customized and enhanced in order to fulfill our requirements. Building fresh APIs from scratch is time-consuming and error-prone. Freshly-built APIs have to go through several iterations in order to be categorized as reasonably stable and mature.

However, with high-end API design and integration platforms, it's possible to speed up the creation of APIs from an existing integration with a few clicks. This way, we aren't discarding the functioning applications and can save a lot of time by leveraging the existing investments. That is, API platforms enhance the **return on investment (RoI)**.

Typically, the client-side team designs and develops the application, the server-side team readies the backend IT infrastructure for application deployment, and the testing team is mandated to test client as well as server-side output. These teams should work in a collaborative manner to develop a REST API for the project:

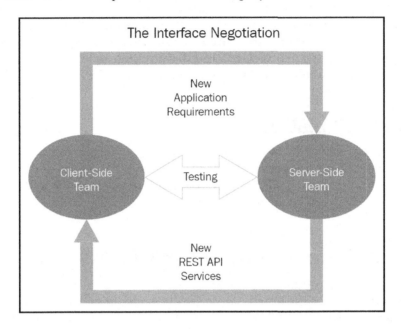

REST APIs are changing frequently with the insights being put forward by business consumers, partners, and employees. These changes have to be incorporated into the APIs and their mapped services. This definitely takes up time and, hence, the time-to-market is bound to increase. In order to accelerate and augment the REST API design, development, documentation, and testing, a number of automated solutions are available that enhance team collaboration substantially.

RestCase is a cloud-based API development platform. This unique platform empowers developers to collaboratively create REST APIs. This enablement is being achieved through a number of distinct platform modules. The key modules include an intuitive browser-based interface, which automatically generates documentation, tests, and mocks. This platform enables rapid iterations and testing by creating a mock of the API.

In order for development teams to work with QA and operation teams, the API development platform comes to the rescue. This platform helps development teams to build better APIs with ease. Developers' productivity goes up significantly when they are being empowered through an API-development platform. The development time and costs will come down. The API platform increases innovation through sharing and collaboration with the distributed research and development teams.

API-integration platforms

We are steadily moving toward the digital era. Everyday objects are being empowered with digitization and edge technologies in order to become digital. That is, everything in our everyday environments becomes computational, communicative, sensitive, responsive, and active. Every digital artifact is being fitted with an appropriate API to be publicly found, network-accessible, and easily usable. For simplifying API integration, the most competent solution is API integration platforms. There are several use cases being mentioned by integration experts and architects as to why enterprises should adopt API-integration platforms.

With the emergence of cloud environments as the one-stop IT solution for all kinds of business offerings and operations, it's projected that in the years ahead, most enterprise, personal, mobile, and web applications will reside in clouds (public, private, hybrid, and edge). The popular enterprise-grade applications are **enterprise resource planning (ERP)**, **supply chain management (SCM)**, knowledge and content management, HR, finance and facility management, and asset management. Besides, all kinds of operational, transactional, and analytical applications are also being modernized and migrated to cloud environments in order to reap the benefits (user, technical, and business) of the cloud.

Thus, it's becoming mandatory for IoT devices, desktop, wearable, and smartphone applications to connect with cloud applications and databases. Cloud applications, platforms, and infrastructures are predominantly API-enabled. That is, D2D, D2C, and C2C integration requirements grow sharply in the extremely connected world. To gain best-in-class applications, the role of API integration platforms is simply awe-inspiring.

Legacy integration

We've inherited a lot from the mainframe era. We have a number of legacy applications running in various industry verticals. Banking applications are still running legacy code. No one can dispute that the mainframe computer gives the highest performance. Typically, legacy applications follow the monolithic architecture. Also, legacy applications are massive. There are several other drawbacks associated with the legacy era. Still, due to their unique capabilities, enterprises are pretty slow to modernize their legacy investments. This encourages to bring an integration pipeline between modern and legacy applications. Legacy systems carry and store a lot of business transaction data. The API-integration platform enables data integration. That is, data can be extracted, transformed, and loaded into databases and warehouses associated with, and attached to, new applications. To produce and sustain integrated systems, it's mandatory to get and use legacy data. API-integration platforms are handy for this persisting need.

API integration platforms facilitate the formation of composite applications. With MSA becoming the shrewdest choice of application architectures, composing (through orchestration, choreography, or hybrid methods) is an important job for producing process-aware and business-critical applications. As we all know, every microservice exposes an API. Thus, to combine multiple microservices to produce composite applications, the contributions of API integration platforms are manifold.

API integration platforms ensure faster cloud adoption and future-proof enterprise integration. You need an API-integration platform to future-proof enterprise integration. The following is forecast in years to come:

- Millions of software services
- Billions of connected devices
- Trillions of digitized artifacts

As every physical, mechanical, electrical, and electronic system is fitted with APIs and presented as services, the adoption of API integration platform solutions is bound to escalate in the years to come.

API management platforms

As businesses build enterprise and mobile applications for their end users, partners, and employees, APIs are becoming indispensable. Applications have to perform well over any kind of network. APIs provide design time and runtime access to data services hosted in cloud infrastructures. Enterprises are predominantly transactional. Increasingly, mobile commerce and business applications are transactional. Thus, we need API management platforms in order to precisely manage APIs.

We have discussed the various features and needs for API development and integration platforms, and how they assist software developers and integrators in arriving at integrated systems with confidence and clarity. Now, we are moving toward API management and its automation through management platforms. Generally, API management is all about designing high-quality APIs, and then publishing and analyzing them in order to continuously track their usage. There can be both internal as well as external-looking APIs, which have to be search-friendly and consumable. As the world is tending toward embracing the API economy, there are several products and platforms that simplify and streamline API-management activities. The primary purposes of an API-management solution are as follows:

- **API design**: API-management solutions empower developers and external parties with all the requisite knowledge and capability to design, produce, and deploy APIs. Further down the line, it helps in making API documents, and setting security policies, service levels, and runtime capabilities.

- **API gateway**: We have allocated a separate chapter to describe the various functionalities of API gateways and how microservices benefit through the leveraging of API gateway solutions. These days, API-management solutions are also empowered to contribute as an API gateway, which is a centralized and clustered frontend for any service user to leverage distributed microservices. API gateways function as a gatekeeper for all downstream APIs and regulate service interactions in a secure manner.

- **API store**: APIs should be stored in a centralized place so that internal and external users can leverage them. Thus, as service marketplaces, API marketplaces are evolving fast.

- **API analytics**: With the heightened usage of APIs, it's important to track key metrics, such as API usage, transactions, and performance. Capturing this decision-enabling and value-adding data, and processing it, helps to extract useful insights to improve service quality.

The end-to-end API life cycle activities (authentication, provisioning roles for users, policy establishment and enforcement, rate limiting of user requests, API data analytics, and monitoring) are being taken care of by management platform solutions. These solutions also enable and enhance API consumption by developers, external parties, and employees. API documentation is also being automated. The API-management suite uses caching to lessen the load on services. API log, operational, performance, scalability, and security data gets collected and subjected to a variety of investigations through the API analytics feature in order to understand the service state so we can perform tuning. Almost all enterprises are embracing APIs in order to be online and strive for improved market reach. Further on, the API catalogue is being published in the company portal. The versatile solution is to deploy API-management platforms to substantially increase business agility and adaptability.

APIs have to be artistically architected. APIs aren't just to enable every software package to have a frontend toward integration, they have to be extremely user-friendly. API endpoints have to be easy to understand and use for performing basic tasks. APIs are expected to remarkably enhance developers' productivity. Learning design patterns has to be fast and easy in order to empower developers to create well-designed APIs. APIs have to be designed to be long-lasting. That is, API consistency has to be ensured. API quality also has to be seriously verified and validated, otherwise, defective APIs waste a lot of time for developers. Both API providers and consumers demand top-quality APIs. With automated tools for API design, deployment, and management, better and more consistent results are being realized by enterprises across the globe.

APIs have shown glimpses of successes and are used to fulfil application integration, which has been a hassle for business-enterprise IT teams. APIs are positioned as the proven way forward for all kinds of integration requirements. Besides web and cloud enablement, the process of mobile enablement is gaining a lot of mind and market shares in order to provide any time, anywhere, any device, and any network information and service access. APIs have to be designed not only to tackle currently available devices, but also futuristic devices. There are a number of artistically designed I/O devices hitting the market consistently. Every connected device and clustered infrastructure, besides software systems, is being enabled by attaching efficient and extensible APIs in order to be found and bound to create business value.

There are a multitude of techniques and tools you can use to speed up API-based integration in a risk-free and rewarding manner. As previously discussed, we have integrated platform solutions (open source as well as commercial-grade) aplenty toward the API economy. These platforms intrinsically guarantee the quality of the APIs being produced and used. The quality is mandated to attain the benefits of the API phenomenon.

Demystifying the RESTful services paradigm

This book takes a deep dive into RESTful services and APIs. Despite being simple, REST is a fully-featured architectural style. Producing, exposing, and sustaining high-quality RESTful APIs to achieve smooth functional integration is a crucial yet challenging job for IT professionals. Predominantly, REST is implemented with the HTTP protocol. However, REST is not tied to HTTP alone. REST APIs are implemented for a *resource*, and the resource can be an entity or a service. These APIs provide a way to identify a resource by its URI. URIs can be used to transfer the current state of a resource representation. APIs can be represented as a set of endpoints stuffed with verbs and nouns. A verb typically represents an action, such as get, put, or delete, while the nouns indicate arguments appropriate to the action. It's always a good practice to have a mechanism to communicate error messages and successful execution. APIs have to clearly articulate their services and parameters in order to lessen developer errors. The error messages also have to be comprehensive in order to unambiguously convey what's happening to the end users.

With the widespread usage of the service paradigm, there has been a surge popularity for RESTful services, which are quite lightweight compared to SOAP services. Service-oriented application development and assembly have become the *de facto* standard in software engineering. For developing and deploying internet applications, leveraging RESTful services as application components has grown sharply. RESTful applications and services are fitted with compatible and competent APIs. RESTful services bring up the much-needed agility, adaptability, and simplicity for application development. APIs have become so common across IT services and business workloads. In addition, APIs are the most common elements for software infrastructure, middleware solutions, integration servers, containerization platforms, and backend database systems. APIs come as a standardization mechanism for enterprise applications to interact in a consistent and cognitive manner.

Due to the phenomenal growth of cloud-native and enabled applications, there is a need to establish a seamless and spontaneous link between enterprise and personal applications with cloud-hosted applications and data sources. Here, the REST paradigm scores well over other options. We have a bevy of programming and scripting languages for the client- and server-side applications. Not only desktop and laptop computers, but also handhelds, wearable, portables, nomadic, wireless, and mobile devices are becoming integrated with web applications. The environments become highly complicated and heterogeneous. Also, many devices and services have to collaborate to fulfill business processes. The REST paradigm comes to the rescue here. The REST concept is an abstraction for running web applications on different environments, such as Windows or Linux.

RESTful services guarantee the much-needed flexibility to host and run applications coded using different programming languages and platforms. Heterogeneous applications are being enabled to interoperate with one another through the power of RESTful services. Devices are being exposed as device services, which are being frontended with a RESTful API. Another widespread trend is that cloud applications are REST API-driven. Not only resource-intensive systems, but also resource-constraint embedded devices, are benefitting from the RESTful services paradigm in order to be connected. There are several device-centric communication and data transmission protocols, and the REST phenomenon is using them to become the favorite of service developers and users. There are several constraints imposed on this service implementation concept in order to be hugely benevolent for a number of usage scenarios.

Characterizing the REST architecture style

First and foremost, the REST paradigm is an architectural pattern. There were a number of design patterns published by experts in order to design and develop RESTful services. There are integration and deployment patterns for the quick realization of the pioneering REST paradigm.

The REST paradigm is compliant with the famous RoA pattern. The application state and functionality are methodically divided into distributed resources. These resources are available online and, hence, each resource can be accessed and used with the ubiquitous HTTP commands (GET, PUT, POST, and Delete). If we want to put a file in a file server, we need to use PUT or POST. If we want to get a file from the server, we can use the GET command. If we want to delete the file, the DELETE command is our go-to option. The REST architecture, is as usual, client-server and layered. It supports caching on the client side. Also, REST applications are stateless. This means they don't store the state of the application. The distinct characteristics are explained as follows:

- **Client-server**: The client can be anything that sends a service request to the server. The server side will host a RESTful service, which provides the business functionality to the client.
- **Stateless**: The server doesn't store the client session information. Clients have to share all the required details with the server to get the appropriate answer. That is, RESTful services are self-defined, self-contained, autonomous, highly scalable, and performing.

- **Cache**: As the server doesn't store the client information, it's the responsibility of clients to keep all the relevant information. Thus, the concept of the cache has emerged and become popular. Sometimes, the client sends the same request to the server again. As REST services are independent, the client would get the same response. In order to reduce network traffic, the idea of a cache got introduced on the client side. The speed of getting the service response is quicker here as the cache is storing the previous response and the cache is positioned on the client side.

> **Caching** is all about storing copies of frequently-accessed data in several locations along the client and server route. Typically, a client request gets passed to the server on the other side of the world. However, a series of caches are being incorporated between client and server components. That is, the request first knocks the local cache at the client side, and then the reverse proxy at the server side. If any of the caches have the latest resource representation, it can be used by the client. If not, the request will be sent to the server component to fetch the latest information.

- **Layered system**: Due to the growing complexity of enterprise applications, layering was introduced. This means it's possible to incorporate additional modules between the client and server. We're comfortable with three-tier and multi-tier applications. This is a complexity-mitigation technique.

REST Resource Representation Compression

REST APIs can return the resource representations in a variety of formats (XML, JSON, HTML, and text). Resource representations can be compressed to save network bandwidth and storage requirements. There are different transmission protocols that enable compression, and clients are accordingly notified about the compression algorithm used.

Hypermedia as the Engine of Application State (HATEOAS) is an important constraint of the REST paradigm. The term *hypermedia* refers to the links that point to various types of multimedia content (images, videos, audios, or text). This architectural style helps to use hypermedia links in the response message so that clients can dynamically go to the correct resource.

Idempotent REST APIs

If we make multiple identical requests and receive the same response every time, the APIs are generally called **idempotent**. Some API consumers knowingly or unknowingly make the same request twice or thrice. The APIs have to understand this and reply with the same response.

The point is that we have to build and deploy *intelligent APIs. One trait of them is the idempotent APIs.* We have to have *idempotent REST APIs* for all the standard HTTP operations, such as GET, PUT, and DELETE. Only POST APIs will not be idempotent.

As previously mentioned, RESTful communication takes place on the HTTP protocol, and the HTTP commands are being used by the REST client to interact with the REST server. This uniformity and simplicity works wonders for the faster and easier adoption of the REST paradigm, which becomes an important concept in the increasingly connected world.

REST API design considerations

With the usage of APIs increasing rapidly, the API design process is getting a lot of attention from a variety of sources these days. Not only is it important to insightfully blueprint and implement highly-optimized and -organized APIs, but we also need to empower them to be resilient, robust, and versatile for the web, mobile, and cloud worlds. The availability of APIs for the continued function of applications is essential. The high performance and throughput of APIs is vital. The number of user requests, the number of transactions, and the amount of data getting processed are critical for APIs to contribute their might to the application world. APIs have to scale well in order to tackle extra user and data loads automatically in order to be relevant for their consumers and stakeholders. There shouldn't be any API-induced application slowdown and breakdown. We discussed the importance of API security in a separate section. Any kinds of internal errors, security holes, or vulnerabilities in APIs have to be weeded out through testing procedures and tools. Any kind of outsider attack also needs to be given sufficient consideration.

Applications have to fully comply with all the stated API requirements. That is, applications have to send correct data and protocols, as etched in the API rulebook. If there's any deliberate deviation, the result can be irreparable damage. Thus, API monitoring, log collection, and adept management are necessary for success. When designing APIs, service architects and API developers have to take the following into serious consideration. APIs play a crucial role in fulfilling the **non-functional requirements (NFRs)/quality of service (QoS)** attributes for RESTful services. As we all know, RESTful services guarantee simplicity and ubiquity. Thus, when designing REST APIs, architects and designers have to give special importance to the following NFRs:

- **Performance**: This is an important parameter when designing APIs for RESTful services to interact and collaborate.
- **Scalability**: RESTful APIs have to be designed to support a large number of application components. The number of interactions among those components should also be on the higher side.
- **Modifiability**: Newer technologies keep coming up, business sentiments keep being chopped and changed, and user expectations are also evolving. Since *change is the only constant*, APIs have to be built to be adaptive to changing requirements.
- **Portability**: APIs are being used, tested, refined, and deployed in API stores. APIs have to be made portable to work across systems.
- **Reliability**: APIs have to be reliable to withstand any kind of failures and faults at the system level. There may be failures at the component and data levels, but the system should still continue to function and deliver its obligations.

As we struggle to build and deploy highly-scalable, -available, and -reliable systems with high performance, the arrival of APIs as a soothing element toward fulfilling the previous NFRs is being viewed and welcomed with appreciation.

Enumerating RESTful API design patterns

API design is turning out to be a core pillar for any API product strategy to attain the desired success for software products. Any software package has to be attached with appropriate APIs in order to be found and bound remotely. Exposing APIs helps any third-party service or software provider to get linked and used. Therefore, producing easy-to-use, forward-looking, and sustainable APIs is vital for the API-driven world. Good API design considerably enhances the **developer experience** (**DX**) and can improve performance and long-term maintainability. The API implementation is typically hidden from API clients. Such a separation brings much-needed flexibility for any kind of advancements to be brought to the API implementation without affecting any API client. A well-designed API has to have the following properties:

- APIs have to support all standard and mutually-agreed platforms
- With the growing device ecosystem, any client can call and use APIs
- Nothing is going to be static
- API changes are mandated then and there, as applications and services are bound to be constantly modernized
- API design and modification has to be done in such a way that clients aren't negatively impacted

Media types

As everyone knows, clients and servers normally exchange resource representations. Typically, in a `POST` request, the request body contains a representation for a resource to be created. On the reverse side, in a `GET` request, the response body contains a representation of the received resource. Generally, formats are specified through the use of *media types* (alternatively termed MIME types). For non-binary data, it's JSON (`media type = application/json`) and XML (`media type = application/xml`). The **Content-Type** header in a request or response specifies the format of the representation.

Having understood the relevance of APIs for creating composite enterprises, IT professionals have unearthed a number of API design patterns, which are easy for API designers and developers to understand and use:

- **Statelessness**: For web-scale applications, the number of users employing a variety of client devices to get served through REST services is in the millions at any point in time. Web applications made through RESTful services have to be internally and externally scalable. Thus, storing client session information in an application server can degrade application performance. That is, application servers have to be stateless. APIs have to be designed to support the statelessness property.
- **Content-negotiation**: We know that a resource can have multiple representations in order to fulfill the varied needs of different client devices. Requesting a suitable presentation by a client is termed content-negotiation. Another option is that different representation can be referred to using different URLs.
- **Uniform resource identifier (URI) templates**: The URIs with placeholders in them. By using named substitution variables, the templates can be used to create URIs for specific resources. The templates are used in specification documents to describe where resources reside. Clients should be aware of these templates to generate the full URI for any resource. This is due to the fact that resources are not typically linked to other resources. It's the responsibility of clients to decide on a resource's URI manually. The proper solution to this predicament is to link those resources from a known place. Individual product offerings have to be linked from a centralized product listing resource. Thus, URI templates come in handy for unambiguously identifying the URI for any resource.

- **Versioning**: This is an important practice. APIs keep changing to accommodate business and technology changes. API compatibility is a serious stuff. Developers are being continuously pressed to bring in verified changes on APIs. Occasionally, backward compatibility is being required in order to enable work with older versions of APIs. The idea is that if the version number is attached with an API, there's no conflict and it makes light of users' tasks. API versioning also helps to precisely track the API's evolution.

- **Bulk operations**: Services are being decorated with fine-grained and coarse-grained methods. Bulk operations are being typically implemented through coarse-grained methods. API designers have to take care of this thing. Fine-grained methods typically demand multiple requests and responses, which wastes a lot of network bandwidth resources. With a few requests, bigger and better operations can be accomplished.

- **Pagination**: Exposing a variety of resources through a single URI can lead to applications fetching a large amount of data for the client. It's not possible to show all the representation details in a single page. Pagination comes to the rescue here in reducing the amount of data that will be communicated to the client, so the network bandwidth can be conserved. This pattern also avoids any unnecessary processing at the server side. During the API design phase, though it's a challenging task to foresee the amount of data that will be returned as part of response, its necessary for API designers to anticipate and planned for the paging resources requirements

- **Sorting**: Sorting is an important feature for any API endpoint that returns a large quantity of data to the client. To facilitate the sorting functionality, many APIs add a *sort* or *sort_by* URL parameter, which can take a field name as the value. Good API designs let you specify *ascending* or *descending* order when sorting. A sort parameter should contain the names of the attributes on which the sorting is performed, separated by a comma.

- **Filtering**: It's an accepted statement that URL parameters is the way to go for embedding basic filtering to REST APIs. If we have a `/products` endpoint, which is products for sale, we can filter via the property name, such as `GET /products?state=active` or `GET /products?state=active&seller_id=1234`. The problem here is that this only works for exact matches. If we want to filter for a range (price, or date), there is a challenge. URL parameters typically have a key and a value, but for performing advanced filtering, we need a minimum of three components: the property/field name, the operator, and the filter value.

There are ways to encode these components into URL parameter keys/values. You can find more details on the options here: `https://www.moesif.com/blog/technical/api-design/REST-API-Design-Filtering-Sorting-and-Pagination/`. Restricting resources or responses by restricting number of queries (resources) with specific and limited attributes along with their expected values is called filtering. So it would be possible that one can apply filters in a collection on multiple attributes or allowing several values for one filtered attribute.:

- **Unicode**: Modern-day APIs have to support more than English characters. If Unicode characters are embedded in a URL, the API has to be developed accordingly.
- **Error logging**: All kinds of error messages have to be meticulously collected and subjected to a variety of investigations to extract any useful insights from logs. The client request may have errors. There may be errors being caused by the API itself. Thus, log collection is an important process for error analytics.
- **Stateless authentication and authorization**: As mentioned many times, REST APIs have to be designed to be stateless. Each request has to be self-contained to fulfill user requests without the knowledge of clients. If the primary service fails to transact, its various instances have to come to life to implement requests in time. Not just for service requests, but also for authenticating and authorizing users, stateless services need to be involved and invoked. Typically, user information gets stored on the server side so that the subsequent requests don't need to go to the authentication service. However, this approach fails the scalability test, and hence, every request has to carry all the relevant information in order to be authenticated and authorized. This isn't restricted to users—service-to-service authorization is also being facilitated through this approach.

The expert recommendation is to use JWT with OAuth2 for user authentication. For service-to-service communication, it's paramount to have the encrypted API key in the header component of the request message:

- **Swagger for documentation**: API documentation is very important for developers to gain a deeper understanding of APIs and their unique capabilities. The accuracy of API documents is far more important for the envisioned success. Instead of using human resources to generate API documents, it's easier and faster to employ automation techniques and tools to create API documents. APIs, along with the annotations and metadata, contribute to producing documents in an automated manner. Swagger is a widely-used tool for documenting REST APIs. The document generated contains the details regarding the usage of a specific API. It also provides the relevant details of the input and output information for a method in the API.

- **HTTP status codes**: There are many articles and blogs in the web that table HTTP status codes. These help clients to understand the real situation facing servers. That is, when a client request reaches server-side services, the server will generate a litany of responses back to the client. There may be a failure or success. The status codes sheds some light on what happened at the server side.

- **HATEOAS**: Each HTTP GET request has to supply all the information in the response message. These details help to find the various resources related directly to the requested object through hyperlinks, which are embedded in the response. Also, it has to have all the details that describe the pertinent operations being made available on each of those resources. This is termed HATEOAS. HATEOAS simplifies the navigation through a resource and its available actions. This facilitates clients interaction with an application for different actions. All the metadata is getting embedded in responses from the server.

We have discussed most of the API design patterns, which are sourced from multiple sources, such as blogs written by experienced practitioners. There are design patterns, best practices, metrics, and other knowledge guides for risk-free and rewarding experiences in relation to application, service, device, middleware, and database APIs.

API security design patterns

API security is essential. If there's any manipulation allowed on APIs, the results may be catastrophic. Here's an article that enumerates all the things an API developer has to minutely make in order to arrive at impenetrable and unbreakable APIs: `https://dzone. com/articles/top-5-rest-api-security-guidelines`. First, the identification and authentication are being performed in order to empower users to access RESTful APIs. Next in line is none other than authorization. The RESTful API design has to be done in such a way that it's possible to establish and enforce authorization rights. Also, bringing the correct changes into authorization policies/rules also has to be part of the API design. The rights-based access of resources has to be made mandatory.

It's API designer/developer responsibility to ensure the design is mandating the API key or session token validation for the specific resource collection and action. For an example, if there is an API exposed for a book, then allowing any user to delete the entries is not prudent.. But it's OK to allow anyone to get a book catalogue entry. Further down the line, the session token or API key has to be embedded in the message body or sent as a cookie to diligently protect privileged collections or actions from any unauthorized use.

Whitelist allowable methods

We all know that REST services allow multiple methods for performing different operations on a resource. To avoid any kind of conflicts, RESTful services have to be developed and deployed to ensure that only correct methods are accepted for processing. Other methods automatically are made to get an appropriate error message. The key security attacks are detailed as follows:

- **Cross-site request forgery**: Resources are being exposed by REST services to the outside, along with a well-designed API. It is crucial to protect PUT, POST, and DELETE request **cross-site request forgery (CSRF)**. The standard protection approach is to use one of the token-based approaches. If there's any **cross-site scripting (XSS)** in our application, CSRF can still be easily done even if we use random tokens, hence, experts recommend leveraging viable mechanisms to prevent XSS.
- **Input validation**: We execute validation both on the client and the server side. The client- and server-side script languages have innate capabilities to properly validate requests and responses. If there's an incorrect user input, it's better to reject that. Also, it's better to log input validation failures. If there are more failed input validations, the option to consider is rate limiting the API.

- **URL validations**: It's possible for attackers to tamper with any part of an HTTP request to break into the employed security methods. The key parts making up an HTTP request include the URL, query string, headers, cookies, form, and hidden fields.
- **Secure parsing**: All incoming messages have to be systematically parsed for any security violations. It's true that REST can accept messages being framed through multiple mechanisms, including XML and JSON.
- **Validate incoming content types**: When we use the POST and PUT methods for submitting new data, the client is expected to clearly specify the content-type (such as XML or Java).
- **The servers never assume the content type**: Servers always have to verify whether the content type and the content are the same. If they don't match, an appropriate error message has to be communicated back.
- **Validate response types**: This is another validation. REST services allow multiple response types and, hence, the client has to articulate the preferred order of response types in the **Accept** header, which is part of the request message. Also, there are many MIME types for the typical response types, so clients have to specify which MIME types should be used in the reply message.
- **XML input validation**: There are XML-specific attacks (XML External Entity and XML signature wrapping) and hence, XML-based services have to securely parse XML messages to be protected against attacks.
- **Security headers**: To correctly interpret server messages, the server has to embed the content-type header with the correct content type.
- **XML encoding**: XML messages should be constructed using an XML serializer. Then, only the XML content can be parsed by the browser and be devoid of any XML injection errors.
- **Cryptography**: When data is getting transmitted, it gets encrypted. That is, the **transport-level security (TLS)** has to be enabled. TLS is important when credentials, updates, deletions, and any other value-added information get transmitted across. Even experts recommend using mutually-authenticated client-side certificates to guarantee the utmost security to RESTful web services. Similarly, when data gets persisted, the data has to be encrypted, and when data is being used by any application, appropriate security measures have to be in place.

- **Message integrity**: Cryptography ensures confidentiality, but we need message integrity. That is, we leverage the message digest/hashing algorithms toward message integrity. A **JSON web token (JWT)** is a standardized, optionally validated, and/or encrypted container format. This is used to securely transfer information between two parties.

> JWT defines the structure of the information that's being communicated across the network and it comes in two forms: serialized and deserialized. The serialized form is used to transfer data through the network with each request and response. The deserialized form is used to read and write data to the token. JWT is useful for the following scenarios:
>
> **Authorization:** JWT (Jason Web Tokens) enables logged in user to access routes, services and resources as the JWT tokens would be part of subsequent incoming requests (after the initial request), and JWT is a popular adoption for SSO (Single Sign On) implementations as well.
>
> **Information Exchange**: JWT is emerging as a way to securely transmit information across parties. JWTs can be signed using public and private keys, so it's easy to understand who the senders are. Also, through message digest, it's proved that the message wasn't tampered with along the way.

API security is an important phenomenon. There is a growing array of best practices and patterns for securing APIs. Collecting error logs comes in handy when visualizing any kind of security implications, In time, this is the surest way forward to guarantee fool-proof security for APIs being designed, published, and maintained.

In conclusion, developers should try to understand the prevailing context and the future. It's not easy to come out with a strategically sound API off the bat. APIs can make or mark the whole scenario if done with passion and discussion. API designers have to start thinking in terms of user perspectives. A robust design is a key factor in producing and sustaining state-of-the-art and multifaceted APIs. A poorly designed API may lead to failure or the customer may not be satisfied with the applications and services.

Summary

The microservices architecture is the prime architectural pattern and style for producing multifaceted and enterprise-scale applications to be elegantly hosted and run on cloud environments (local and remote). Microservices are lightweight, simple to build and deploy, self-defined, fine-grained, and network accessible. They also follow the single functionality principle.

Nowadays, everything that communicates over HTTP and uses JSON- or XML-formatted messages or the HTTP methods (GET, POST, PUT, or DELETE) gets called a RESTful API. RESTful APIs are easy to design and build. The seamless and spontaneous combination of microservices and RESTful APIs opens up fresh possibilities and opportunities. Hence, designing high-quality RESTful APIs acquires special significance in our increasingly connected and services-oriented world. This chapter provided the relevant patterns, best practices, and general guidelines to come up with top-quality RESTful APIs.

Further reading

- https://www.packtpub.com/application-development/hands-restful-python-web-services-second-edition
- https://www.packtpub.com/application-development/building-restful-apis-go-video
- https://www.packtpub.com/web-development/restful-web-services-scala

9
A More In-depth View of the RESTful Services Paradigm

With the grand arrival of a bevy of futuristic and flexible information technologies, automated tools, optimized infrastructures, integrated platforms, and multifaceted devices, the world is bound to experiment and experience hitherto unknown software applications and services toward empowering businesses and people. With the faster proliferation of slim and sleek, handy and trendy smartphones, we are destined to have a dazzling array of easy-to-use and eye-catching mobile applications and services. With wearables, portables, fixed devices, handhelds, and wireless gadgets joining in mainstream computing, the application scope, size, speed, and structure are bound to escalate appreciably. To fit applications into every segment of devices, software developers across the world are expected to bring forth customizable, composable, and configurable applications by leveraging the potential and promising programming languages, platforms, toolkits, software-development methodologies, design patterns, and best practices. The software landscape is, therefore, expanding continuously with the utmost confidence and clarity. Hence, the rollout and the impact of pioneering software packages, homegrown applications, turnkey solutions, insightful platforms, and process-aware composite software are running on expected lines. That is, we are tending toward the software-defined world—software is the vital cog in humanity's bright future.

This book, especially this chapter, is dedicated to explaining the emerging techniques and tips to produce RESTful services and their corresponding APIs quickly and easily. This chapter has the following objectives:

- Software-defined and driven world
- Describing the emerging application types
- The REST paradigm for application modernization and integration
- The RESTful services for digital transformation and intelligence
- Best practices for REST-based microservices

Technical requirements

There are no special technical requirements for this chapter as it doesn't talk about designing, developing, or deploying a software package. Other chapters describe how RESTful APIs for microservices are being designed and used. Further on, a few chapters explain the nitty-gritty of producing standalone and utility-like RESTful services for application and data integration. API design techniques and best practices are also covered in detail in this book. This chapter throws more light on how the enigmatic RESTful paradigm is going to be a trendsetter for the forthcoming era of a software-defined world. The RESTful techniques, tools, and tips presented in the other chapters come good for this chapter. Precisely speaking, the role and responsibility of the path-breaking RESTful idea is bound to escalate, with the world tending toward the one fully enriched, enabled, and empowered by adaptive and adroit software.

Tending toward the software-defined and software-driven world

Every common and casual thing in our mid gets digitized in a systematic manner to be extremely computational, communicative, responsive, and active. With a variety of network options, every kind of embedded system (small and large) becomes interlinked with one another in order to be purposefully discoverable, accessible, assessable, interoperable, and collaborative. That is, all kinds of heterogeneities and complexities that constitute a significant barrier in terms of enabling digitized objects and connected devices to talk to one another in a sensible fashion are being immediately decimated through software-enabled abstraction techniques and tips. It is a well-known and indisputable truth that software eats the world. Every device, consumer electronics, industry machine, flying drone, humanoid robot, medical instrument, home utensil and ware, enabling toolkit, handheld, networkable wearable, portable, fixed system, network solution, automobile, and engine in our everyday environment is getting empowered by embedded software adapters, connectors, and drivers. That is, software enablement is the most vital process and target for everyday objects to be empowered accordingly to decisively join in the mainstream IT. Anything stuffed with some relevant software snippets can become digitally important. That is, ordinary things are getting readied to be extraordinary for the ensuing era of the digital economy. Advanced cars and vehicles are being stuffed with a lot of software modules in order to establish and ensure high-level automation.

Similarly, home, building, and industrial automation is accomplished through the embedding of software libraries. Flights, drones, robots, SCADA systems, sensors, actuators, industrial machinery, boilers, and oil rigs, are being enriched with software agents in order to be software-enabled. Thus, software enablement has become a mandatory assignment for **original equipment manufacturers (OEMs)**. The next question is how to enable software-defined and -driven systems to find one another in order to initiate fruitful collaborations. APIs have emerged as the mechanism to assist in facilitating seamless and spontaneous device integration.

RESTful services and APIs are the prominent and dominant method for enabling **device-to-device (D2D)** and **device-to-cloud (D2C)** integration capabilities. The grandiose vision of **cyber-physical systems (CPS)** is to get nourished and then flourish with the smart application of RESTful methods.

Software-enabled clouds for the digital intelligence era

As outlined previously, the role and responsibility of software is on the climb. The software is participative, pervasive, and persuasive, too. All business establishments embrace software engineering technologies and tools to bring in deeper and more decisive automation. Industry verticals are keen on strategizing and strengthening their software portfolio in order to get ahead of their competitors. Software developers across the globe build, curate, refine, and deposit their software applications in publicly available software registries/repositories to facilitate overwhelming usage. Therefore, with the faster proliferation of software modules, the application of software packages, products, and programs is growing steadily. The application landscape is expanding its horizon constantly. The application types are also expanding correspondingly to tackle more complex requirements, since there is a widespread realization that software decides the automation journey. In the following sections, we'll discuss the principal application types.

The IoT applications and services

With the faster maturity and stability of scores of connectivity and integration technologies, the mesmerizing IoT era has started to unfold and supply its unique contributions for society as a whole. Without an ounce of doubt, the IoT paradigm will bring forth a variety of innovations, disruptions, and transformations for all kinds of business enterprises and organizations. If leveraged appropriately and aggressively, every business vertical is bound to enjoy the distinct benefits of the flourishing IoT model for a long time. Not only businesses, but also every individual, institution, and innovator will benefit immensely from the growing IoT power. The short-term and long-term implications of the IoT domain are undoubtedly tremendous and trend setting as per the reports of worldwide market research and analyst groups. The IT discipline, which is being widely recognized as the greatest business enabler, is receiving a massive boost with the arrival and articulation of the IoT concept. The IoT idea is permeating quickly and becoming pervasive and persuasive too.

With the continued spread and adoption of the IoT paradigm, the business and IT worlds are going to be bombarded with a number of premium IoT applications and services. The various industry domains, including manufacturing, retail, energy, healthcare, smart cities, government, defense, utility, and logistics, are meticulously exploring, and experimenting with, various IoT technologies and tools in order to get ahead of their competitors. A dazzling array of pioneering IoT use cases are being illustrated by the various industry segments in order to be correct and relevant to their loyal consumers.

The first and foremost implication of the IoT concept is the grandiose and voluminous realization of digitized entities and elements (alternatively touted as smart objects). With the systematic leveraging of edge technologies, all kinds of everyday things are being transitioned to be self-, surrounding-, and situation-aware. The second noteworthy output arising from the advancements in the IoT space is the faster proliferation of connected devices. All kinds of embedded systems are being networked and made to join in the mainstream computing. The third and final result is the growing array of device services, which are typically microservices. With the speedier adoption of the **microservices architecture (MSA)**, we will be bombarded with a large number of microservices to produce next-generation enterprise, cloud, web, and mobile applications. It's anticipated that by the year 2020, we will have the following:

- Millions of microservices
- Billions of connected devices
- Trillions of digitized entities

We have massive cloud centers for large-scale data storage and processing. We have both shared and dedicated network infrastructures in order to quickly carry data to faraway cloud environments. There are persistent and transient storage options. The costs of cloud storage capacities are coming down steadily. The faster proliferation of cloud centers across the world takes away the worry of setting up and sustaining massive IT infrastructures locally. There are insightful and integrated big, fast, streaming and IoT data analytics platforms. There are many enabling frameworks, automated tools, and powerful engines that are emerging and evolving to accelerate the process of transitioning data to information to knowledge, and then to wisdom. Thus, the emergence and convergence of several proven and potential technologies and tools simplifies and speeds up data analytics and mining for the purpose of extracting actionable insights. In short, the communication and collaboration of IoT devices results in a huge amount of poly-structured data, which has to be consciously captured, cleansed, and crunched in order to unearth hidden patterns, useful associations, bigger possibilities, newer opportunities, avoidable risks, and real-world intelligence. The knowledge discovered gets disseminated to the correct systems, devices, applications, data sources, and storages in order to empower them to determine their next course of action.

Cloud-enabled applications

As articulated in the preceding section, we will look at a variety of IoT applications and services in the days ahead. Besides, we will also see enterprise-scale, distributed applications running on cloud servers. With the overwhelming success of MSA, all kinds of legacy (monolithic) applications are methodically being enabled to be cloud-ready and microservices-centric applications, which are famous for scalability, availability, and flexibility. That is, massive applications are being partitioned into a number of fine-grained, publicly-discoverable, network-accessible, interoperable, API enabled, composable, portable, horizontally-scalable, and independently-deployable microservices. There are application-modernization and -migration toolkits to move refactored and remedied applications to cloud environments in order to reap all the originally envisaged benefits of the cloud conundrum. There are best practices, integrated platforms, and patterns (architecture, design, integration, orchestration, security, and deployment) aplenty to quickly undertake legacy modernization to produce cloud-enabled applications.

Cloud-native applications

Newer applications are being designed, developed, debugged, and deployed directly in cloud environments. There are production, execution, and orchestration platforms made available on cloud environments (private, public, and hybrid). These applications are intelligent enough to accrue all the benefits of cloud computing. Microservices are the basic and optimal building block for building enterprise-scale and business-critical applications to be delivered through cloud environments. Microservices are formally containerized and deployed multiple times per day in order to meet the varying expectations of businesses and customers. There are a number of automated tools that eliminate all sorts of friction between development and operation teams so as to ensure the faster delivery of updated and upgraded applications to their users and subscribers.

Mobile, handheld, and wearable applications

Today, there are billions of smartphones acting as the main device to connect, access, and assess software applications any time, anywhere, and on any network. That is, all kinds of cloud, web, and enterprise applications are being stuffed with mobile interfaces. This mobility enablement has become the norm for application developers and providers. Not only applications, but also software and hardware infrastructures, are being fitted with mobile interfaces to enable remote monitoring, management, diagnosing, and repairs. In our everyday life, we encounter millions of mobile apps being developed and stocked in mobile stores. Smartphone users can download and install them with ease. Thus, these days, mobile, handheld, and wearable applications are receiving a lot of attention and affection from users and developers alike. We need competent mechanisms to attach APIs to these applications so that other applications/services can easily find and bind to come out with business-centric applications. There are several easy-to-understand and -use methods and mechanisms for producing technology-agnostic RESTful services and their APIs.

Transactional, operational, and analytical applications

Enterprise applications vary in their capabilities. They not only have to fulfill their functional requirements well, but should also fulfil a number of **non-functional requirements (NFRs)**, which are known as the **quality of service (QoS)** and **quality of experience (QoE)** attributes. Performance, scalability, sustainability, modifiability, extensibility, availability, resiliency, security, reliability, and adaptability requirements are being categorized as the important NFRs. As for the public, open and cheap internet emerges as the prime communication infrastructure, since most of the applications are web-enabled. That is, web interfaces are the widely-used mechanism for accessing web-scale applications.

Business-to-business (B2B) and **business-to-consumer (B2C)** applications are typically transactional in nature. There are viable techniques for ensuring complex transactions. With the spread of geographically distributed systems, the need for distributed transactions becomes more important. As we all know, the web is the dominant and decisive way of accessing information, content, applications, services, and data sources. Therefore, a number of **online transaction processing (OLTP)** systems have arisen in order to natively support different transaction requirements.

Like transactions, data analytics occupies the central part of next-generation, enterprise-scale systems. Data gets carefully collected, cleansed, and crunched in order to extract actionable insights from growing data heaps. Extracted insights are used to make intelligent and real-time decisions. Precisely speaking, these are going to be data-driven insights and insight-driven decisions. There is no place for intuition-based decisions any more. There are analytical platforms and data warehouses/marts/cubes that facilitate data mining, analytics, and investigations. Analytics is the core of any business application, IT platform, and infrastructure to deliver their unique services. All of the next-generation applications are innately empowered to be analytic. Existing applications are being enabled to be analytic by incorporating analytical applications, such as **online analytical processing (OLAP)** applications. Thus, analytical applications are going to be the prime component of mainstream IT.

Finally, with the seamless linkage of operational technology and information technology environments, software applications hosted in enterprise and cloud servers have to be able to receive real-time operational data and event messages to be right and relevant for their consumers. A variety of operational applications and databases are emerging to meet the evolving needs of operational environments. Ground-level operational systems emit a lot of time-series data and event data, and they get streamed to enterprise systems (transactional and analytical data stores). There are data analytics platforms that make sense of the data streaming into them. Smarter environments, such as smarter hotels, homes, hospitals, manufacturing floors, and **cloud-enabled data centers (CeDCs)**, are going to be empowered when they get seamlessly integrated with nearby or faraway transactional and analytical systems.

Knowledge visualization applications

The ensuing era is definitely knowledge-centric. Knowledge discovery and dissemination are going to be the prime activity for knowledge workers. Software services, personal as well as professional devices, IT systems, and business applications have to be supplied with real-time and real-world knowledge in order to be adaptive terms of in their actions and reactions. There are 360-degree dashboards, visualization platforms, and report generation tools available in order to graphically and illustratively display and convey the results. Let's look at these applications in more detail.

Social applications

This set of applications is currently very popular among young people. Typically, web 1.0 applications are simple and one-way, whereas web 2.0 applications are social and facilitate two-way communication. That is, users not only read, but also write back. To facilitate outside-in thinking, social applications are the way forward. There are several social and professional applications that empower society as a whole. Digital communities are being formulated and employed to equip people with their skills and knowledge sharing. Social applications, because of their large number of subscribers and followers, produce a lot of useful data. When social- and people-related data gets consistently collected and subjected to a variety of investigations, individuals and institutions are bound to find a lot of actionable insights. There are new types of analytical capabilities, such as social network analytics, behavioral analytics, and sales promotion and marketing campaign analytics, that have emerged due to the widespread proliferation of social applications.

Scientific and technical applications

Software plays a vital role in shaping various scientific and technical applications. Scientific experiments generate a lot of data, which can be captured and crunched to generate usable results. Similarly, there are technical applications that leverage the software capabilities. These two disciplines require the unique contributions of software platforms, products, patterns, and processes in order to be highly relevant to their users. There are mathematics-specific software packages aplenty to help mathematicians with their research activities; other science, technology, engineering, and art disciplines are benefiting immensely and immeasurably from the advancements and developments in the software space. There are innumerable innovations in the **information and communication technology** (ICT) landscape toward software deployment and execution.

Centralized and distributed applications

There has been a swing between centralized and distributed computing models. Clouds typically are centralized, consolidated, and converged environments that host applications. Recently, clouds have been federated in order to host and run distributed applications. Considering the exponential growth of data and the complexity of applications, the onset of distributed computing can't be stopped. With the cloud paradigm, leveraging commodity servers for large-scale application and data processing is gaining momentum. Horizontal scalability is preferred over vertical scalability and, hence, distributed systems are enjoying a surge in popularity. Applications are also being methodically partitioned to be distributed. Data gets distributed across thousands of worker/slave nodes. The computation moves to the place where data resides. There are a number of paradigm shifts with the explosion in distributed computing. The issue of network latency comes into the picture. Server virtualization has also spread to network and storage virtualization with the greater acceptance and adoption of distributed computing. The arrival and articulation of MSA lead to the realization of distributed applications. In short: distributed computing and applications are inevitable. They have to be welcome in order to meet fast-evolving business and IT requirements.

There are certain limitations associated with centralized environments and applications. The overarching views are that distributed systems ensure high availability, affordability, and scalability. That is, the motto of future IT is distributed deployment and centralized monitoring, measurement, and management.

Decentralized and intelligent applications with blockchain technology

As noted in the preceding section, centralized applications are well-suited to certain situations. However, in the recent past, there has been an increased market for decentralized applications, with the faster adoption and adaptation of the blockchain technology. The blockchain paradigm promises a bevy of disruptions and transformations when realizing and running decentralized applications across multiple industry verticals. The issues that face centralized systems and applications are nullified in decentralized services and solutions. Typically, decentralized systems are owned and operated by different organizations and, hence, the security of decentralized software is technologically tightened. The much-touted unbreakable and impenetrable security of software systems is guaranteed through the decentralized approach. The **peer-to-peer (P2P)** interactions facilitated by the decentralized approach is turning out to be a silver bullet for many recent use cases. The faster maturity and stability of blockchain technology is clearly driving IT professionals and organizations toward the production of decentralized systems. The blockchain paradigm also resulted in the new concept of smart contracts, which leads to the realization of adaptive applications.

Composite and multi-container applications

Decomposition and composition techniques have been extensively used to achieve breakthroughs in software engineering. Monolithic applications are being dismantled through decomposition tips, whereas decomposed application modules are being combined with one another in a sequenced manner in order to create smarter and more sophisticated applications. With containers emerging as the most appropriate runtime environment for microservices, we need to produce enterprise-scale, mission-critical, and adaptive applications out of containerized microservices. There are composition (orchestration and choreography) platforms and engines to simplify and speed up the act of building process-aware and people-centric applications. There are process-enabling languages that help us to develop process-optimized and -integrated applications.

Event-driven applications

We still have scores of monolithic and mainframe applications, especially in the financial sector. Today, most of the applications are following the client/server style. There are cloud (online, on demand, and off-premise) applications. With a variety of additional and third-party systems joining, the application architecture moves to *n*-tier distributed computing. With blockchain, the P2P architectural pattern is getting a lot of attention from various stakeholders. There are other variants, such as **service-oriented architecture (SOA)** and **resource-oriented architecture (ROA)**, that inherently support request/response, and fire and forget. And also, there are ways to achieve light and loose coupling between participating components.

But the future undoubtedly belongs to **event-driven architecture** (**EDA**), which is the way forward to realize sensitive and responsive (S and R) applications. With the unprecedented explosion of independent, yet connected, devices, the EDA style facilitates decoupled applications. Any noteworthy event or state change triggers other devices and applications to jump into action. There are event stores and processing platforms (open source as well as commercial-grade solutions). Simple/atomic events get accumulated and aggregated to form complex events. Event messages are streamed to be subjected to a variety of investigations, which are greatly simplified through leveraging streaming analytics solutions and solutions. There are enabling frameworks for event and stream processing. Applications are being innately empowered to be adaptive, based on any insights extracted from event messages. Applications are going to be people-centric and proactive, while delivering their unique services. EDA is one of the prescribed ways to build intelligent systems.

High-quality applications

As discussed, there are I/O device-specific, server-centric, language-oriented, architecture-inspired, and technology-agnostic applications aplenty. Today, most applications are being coded to fulfil the functional requirements identified. With IT being pronounced as the greater business-enabler, evolving business requirements are insisting that IT professionals and professors devise workable ways of incorporating NFRs into the source code. The prominent NFRs include performance, scalability, availability, resiliency, reliability, security, extensibility, accessibility, and modifiability. These QoS and QoE attributes are being mandated to be elegantly embedded in our everyday software applications. There is a new discipline that is emerging and grasping the attention and affection of software engineers and architects—**site reliability engineering** (**SRE**); that is, not only business applications and IT systems produced in an agile fashion, but also they have to be designed, developed, debugged, delivered, and deployed in a highly reliable manner. The written goal is to ensure application resiliency and reliable IT infrastructures. Future challenges for IT experts are many and diverse. Building high-quality applications is beset with innumerable difficulties. Scholars and scientists are working overtime to bring forth best practices, knowledge guides, optimized processes, architectural and design patterns, integrated platforms, competent infrastructures, and easy-to-understand and -use procedures to simplify and streamline the production of high-quality software systems.

Resilient applications

As mentioned elsewhere, microservices is positioned as the preferred element for building and deploying next-generation applications. Different and distributed microservices, when composed, form flexible applications. With the widespread insistence of reliable IT systems and business applications, there are viable methods emerging and evolving fast for embedding precisely the much-needed reliability competency into software systems. Generally speaking, system reliability is the application's resiliency and the system's elasticity. That is, when faced with any internal or external attack, the application has to survive in order to continuously deliver its obligations. Applications have to be innately empowered to proactively detect any issues, and then contain them to stop them from cascading into other system components. Thus, systems have to be technologically fault-tolerant in order to be highly available. In short, the resiliency capability is to identify and avoid issues without bringing down the whole system. The deployment of additional instances for each service comes in handy when fulfilling user requests. The second aspect is the elasticity feature; that is, when systems are under heavy load, they have to scale up or out accordingly to tackle the extra rush of users and data messages. Thus, besides ensuring the utmost security for the application and data, guaranteeing reliability is gaining importance.

The REST paradigm for application modernization and integration

Monolithic and massive applications are being modernized and migrated to cloud environments in order to reap all the originally envisaged benefits of the cloud computing model. Microservices are emerging as the most optimized building block to produce enterprise-scale applications. Not only for development but also for application modernization, microservices are being touted as the most suitable approach. That is, legacy applications are being systematically partitioned into multiple interoperable, portable, publicly discoverable, network accessible, reusable, composable, fine grained, technology-agnostic, containerized, horizontally scalable, and independently deployable microservices. The point here is that every microservice exposes one or more interfaces. RESTful interfaces are the most popular ones for microservices to connect and compose bigger and better services. Microservices are therefore typically RESTful services. Thus, application refactoring and remediation are being sped up and streamlined through RESTful services and their APIs. Service, application and data integration, and orchestration happen through RESTful APIs.

In short, new technologies and toolkits, programming and script languages, architecture and design patterns, integrated platforms, pioneering algorithms, enabling frameworks, composable and clustered infrastructures, optimized processes, fresh building blocks, data formats, and protocols are constantly emerging and impacting the discipline of software engineering. Agile software development methodologies are getting the importance to build applications quickly. Besides, the role and responsibility of microservices is increasingly felt in realizing enterprise-scale applications. That is, besides agile techniques, microservices contribute immensely to the rapid development of applications. In other words, applications are being readied instantaneously by compositing multiple microservices.

Applications are mainly interdependent. They can't work in isolation. They have to be integrated dynamically to offer users an integrated experience. Applications also have to be linked up with other applications, data sources and stores, data processing and data analytics platforms, and messaging and middleware systems. Thus, the inescapable integration has to happen via well-intended and designed APIs. Finally, legacy applications have to be dismantled into easily manageable and loosely coupled modules. These modular components, in conjunction with management solutions, will significantly enhance their utilization, efficiency, visibility, and controllability. Further on, on a per-need basis, several modules can be picked up and combined to create bigger and better applications.

Application programming interfaces

We are heading toward everything as a service. **Application programming interfaces** (**APIs**) have become the technology of choice for enterprises to express and expose their capabilities as services. Every service has to have one or more interfaces and backend implementations. Companies around the world are plunging into the usage of APIs. A few unique usage models have emerged to assist business enterprises in meeting changing business needs with all alacrity and adaptivity. Enterprises that are strategizing for digital transformation are expediting the task of leveraging multiple channels and RESTful APIs to get ahead of their competitors. APIs have become the strategic asset for organizations to be easily connected with their business partners, suppliers, retailers, distributors, warehouse providers, logistics and supply chain experts, and consumers. It's simply the API economy. They are enabling design patterns and usage models as ambitious businesses across the world embrace the concept of APIs.

This section looks at the following four APIs usage models that can address business needs with all the requisite agility and efficiency:

- Public APIs
- Internal and private APIs
- APIs for IoT sensors and actuators
- APIs for integration

Public APIs for external integration and innovation

We're being bombarded with a number of next-generation and novelty-attached I/O devices. With miniaturization technologies flourishing consistently, we're being supplied with a slew of slim and sleek, multifaceted, and powerful smartphones, tablets, wearables, portables, and other IoT devices. That is, the digital device ecosystem is expanding continuously. On the other side, the rapidly accumulating digital content, information, and services are being made available to be found, accessed, and consumed anywhere, at any time, on any network, and on any device. That is, there are fresh channels to connect with enterprise and cloud servers to acquire and aggregate the various services, such as information, commercial, transaction, analytical, and other online services. In order to standardize service discovery, matching, and leveraging, the widely recommended approach is to leverage APIs. APIs are emerging as the next-generation channel for enterprises to share their services and information in a controlled manner. With the steadily growing digital ecosystem, APIs have emerged as the way forward for multinational corporations to deliver their offerings to a wider market. With the explosion in digital assets, APIs are being established as the prime method for accessing, assessing, and using digital assets. There is a rush of digital service providers. To create enhanced business value, geographically distributed service providers need to be identified and integrated with one another on-demand through APIs. Every service is being blessed with one or more APIs. There are API management and gateway solutions from the open source community as commercial-grade solution providers to reduce the API development, operational, and management complexities.

Private APIs for internal purposes

Internal APIs improve utilization and enhance efficiency within and across an enterprise. Internal APIs makes it easy for internal developers to discover and consume internal services in a free-flowing fashion. The emerging trend is that every worthwhile application meticulous being service and API-enabled. Typically, every enterprise is blessed with a variety of backend systems, such as database management systems, **message-oriented middleware (MoM)** solutions, message brokers and queues, data processing and data analytics systems, and knowledge visualization tools, which are service enabled to expose their own interfaces (APIs) to facilitate the goals of service connectivity, integration, and orchestration. When an organization wants to create fresh APIs for internal use, it has to add them on top of the service APIs of existing systems.

There are a few public APIs, but there are many APIs for internal use because there may be hundreds of internal services that leverage multiple data formats and transmission protocols. To strongly foster reuse, speed, efficiency, and agile application development, enterprises should publish their internal APIs in a searchable catalogue.

APIs for IoT devices

We discussed IoT devices and their services to humankind at the beginning of this chapter. It's anticipated that there will be 50,000,000,000 connected devices in the years ahead. Disposable, yet indispensable, devices are being produced in large quantities to automate everyday activities. Embedded devices are networked to team up with one another in a collaborative manner in order to develop and deliver situation-aware services to people. There are novel use cases being unearthed and rolled out to enhance the proliferation and penetration of the IoT paradigm. Due to the multiplicity and heterogeneity of IoT devices, the operational, management, and security complexities of IoT devices are being deployed in homes, hotels, hospitals, retail stores, manufacturing floors, railway stations, restaurants, and self-driving cars. Nowadays, sensors and actuators have become the eyes and ears of every digital application these days. Every device is becoming computational, communicative, perceptive, and active.

There are edge and fog devices with sufficient power to form ad hoc clouds to capture, store, process, and analyze real-time, time-series, and streaming data to extract actionable insights that can be looped back to devices and people to make intelligent decisions in time and to engage in correct and relevant activities with all the clarity and confidence. Futuristic IoT applications and services need to be exposed via RESTful APIs in order to perform device integration and service orchestration.

APIs for application integration

APIs are bound to play a vital role in fulfilling the complicated tasks of process, data, and application integration. SOA has laid down a stimulating platform for service-oriented applications and integration. The faster maturity and stability of **enterprise service bus (ESB)** products has expedited the setting up and sustenance of service-oriented, integrated, and insight-driven enterprises. The API-driven integration of disengaged services for producing integrated systems is attracting a lot of attention.

In short, worldwide enterprises are embracing APIs as a strategic path to achieve the much-touted digital disruption, innovation, and transformation. External APIs opens the way for clients' developers to implement and involve the exposed APIs to connect and collaborate with the software application. The remote monitoring, measuring, and managing of applications is being made possible by means of externally exposed APIs.

Describing the RESTful services paradigm

The developing trend in the software engineering space is that applications are now being made out of multiple services through integration, orchestration, and choreography. Workflows are the prominent unifying factor. That is, they help to identify the relevant services, and the chosen services get integrated into proper sequencing to arrive at competent composite services and applications. The challenge is to service discovery, access, assess, and use. There are communication and data transmission protocols to facilitate service-to-service interactions and collaborations. The REST approach is becoming easy to understand and use. This section will describe how REST is streamlined and how interactive services lead to powerful applications.

A resource, which is the primary architectural component of the ROA, is similar to an object in the popular **object-oriented programming (OOP)** concept. As objects, there are methods that work on the resource directly. The key difference between OOP and ROA is that only a few standard methods are defined for the resource. However, for an object, there can be one or more methods. Further on, resources in ROA can be consolidated into collections of resources. The condition is that each such collection created has to be homogeneous. Resources can be blessed with data. The richness of data that gets associated with a resource comes handy in leveraging the resource in an efficient and effective manner. JSON is the most appropriate and popular data model to appropriately enrich resources. Resources are increasingly represented using JSON objects. The special _type key-value pair is used overwhelmingly to store the type of any resource. The JSON data types such as string, number, Boolean, null, or arrays are the values of any key-value pairs.

The REST paradigm comprises three prominent classes of architectural elements: connectors, components, and data elements.

A **connector** is a thing that connects the point of your reference to a destination system. Connectors are responsible for identifying and accessing various web resources and changing the current representations of those identified resources. Roles are the interface for various components that get implemented by different programming languages:

- **Client connector**: REST is for the request-and-response paradigm. Clients send requests and get appropriate responses from resources.
- **Server connector**: RESTful servers continuously listen for requests from clients. Servers deliver responses for requests.
- **Cacheable responses**: Can be stocked in clients or servers in order to speed up the response for subsequent requests. Several clients can concurrently get cached information.
- **Resolver**: Translates resource identifiers into network addresses.
- **Tunnel**: Relays service requests. Sometimes, components deviate from their primary obligations to do tunneling.

In the REST paradigm, the various pieces of software that interact with one another are called **components**:

- **Server software**: This software solution uses a server connector to receive the request from the client software. The server is the source for resources and their representations.
- **Client software**: Clients use a client connector to formulate and convey a request to the server and it receives the response.
- **Gateway software**: This is a kind of middleware solution that intelligently translates the requests and responses that happen between clients and servers.

Data elements are an important ingredient of the powerful RESTful service paradigm. The previously indicated REST components communicate the state representations of data elements. There are six data elements in the REST paradigm:

- **Resource**: As per the REST specification, the ROA is the core architectural style and pattern. Resources are the main element of the RESTful paradigm. A resource is a conceptual mapping to a variety of physical or logical/digital/cyber/virtual entities. The mappings change over time. Every RESTful resource is uniquely represented and identified through an appropriate address. Resources include images from Instagram, movie titles, and so on.

- **Resource identifier**: Resources need to be uniquely identified in order to be found, accessed, and used. The **uniform resource identifier (URI)** identifies every resource. URI is the way forward for clients and servers to communicate in an unambiguous manner. A resource can have multiple URIs. This becomes necessary for indicating the varying location details of the resource. URIs are used to exchange resource representations.
- **Resource metadata**: Metadata is important for resource utilization and management; it provides additional details regarding the resource. The added information, such as location information and alternative resource identifiers for resources, enables resource manipulation and management. That is, resources also include the RESTful API-specific information, such as URLs and relationships.
- **Representation**: We have talked about resources and indicated that JSON is the preferred data model for defining the data associated with resources. However, for resources to communicate to a client over an HTTP connection, their representation have to be converted into a textual representation. This representation has to be formally embedded as an entity in an HTTP message body. Precisely speaking, the resource representation is the state of the resource at that point in time, and bound to change. The state value is transmitted between clients and servers. A representation typically captures and conveys the current or desired state of a resource. A particular resource can have multiple representations.
- **Representation metadata**: This metadata gives extra details regarding the representation in order to simplify representation.
- **Control data**: This defines the action being requested on resources.

REST architectural constraints

The REST architectural constraints are primarily the design rules that clearly convey the distinct characteristics of the REST paradigm. These constraints aren't there to dictate what kind of technologies and tools to use; they just indicate how data gets transferred between the various components, such as clients and servers:

- **Separation of concerns between clients and servers**: There is a clear disconnect between clients and servers. This unique separation enables the development and deployment of client-server applications independently. Any advancement and alteration of one thing doesn't affect the functioning of another. The decoupled nature guarantees the elimination of dependency-induced issues.

- **Stateless communication**: Server machines don't need to store any session information about the contexts of clients' calls. This means that any new requests can be handled by any server instance. However, the authentication details of clients in a session can be stocked so that new requests within the session don't need to be authenticated by the identification and access management system.
- **Clients to cache responses**: Clients can cache server responses, since every server response comes with the decision enabling, cache-related details.
- **Connections may be direct or indirect**: Clients can talk to servers directly or through intermediaries, which can be a proxy or other brokers. This separation increases system flexibility. The need for scalability is fulfilled easily with this intermediary.
- **Uniform interface**: The interactions between the various web application components (clients, servers, and intermediaries) get simplified due to the uniformity of their interfaces. If any of the components deviate from the established standards, there is a possibility that the web applications will break down. The four basic HTTP operations, GET, POST, PUT, and DELETE, provide the much-needed uniformity for all the contributing components to find, interact with, and accomplish tasks with clarity and confidence. The other operations, HEAD and OPTIONS, primarily deal with metadata management.
- **Layered system**: Layered and tiered systems mitigate development and operational complexities. Increasingly, there are many layers between the client and the server. These layers act as intermediaries, such as gateways and proxies, to automate some of the aspects of interactions. A proxy typically is an intermediary that's been selected by a client. The proxy provides interfaces to services, such as data translation, performance enhancement, and security protection. On the other hand, the gateway is another intermediary imposed by the network or server to provide an interface for specific services.

Leveraging intermediary components leads to a substantial reduction in the interaction latency, security enforcement, and encapsulation of legacy systems. Thus, for the faster development of web applications and to make legacy applications more modern, modular, and web-enabled, the RESTful services paradigm contributes immensely.

The **simple object-access protocol (SOAP)** mechanism is the original approach to access and use services. It's an XML-based messaging protocol that exchanges information among computers. There are a few perpetual issues with SOAP, and hence the origin and the dissemination of the REST paradigm, which is a comparatively lightweight and service-oriented application protocol, is widely appreciated. Due to the explosion in web applications and services, the creation and the sustenance of competent web architectures has become an important task.

The REST method is a famous architectural style that is closely aligned with the concepts used in the ubiquitous HTTP protocol. REST doesn't prescribe the details of component implementation and protocol syntax. However, it includes the fundamental constraints upon connectors, components, and data. This outlines the basis of the web architecture and, so the essence of its behavior as a network-based application. The REST paradigm illustrates a simple web application design and development through a set of architectural constraints. These architectural considerations ensure the scalability of component interactions, the standard interface, and the independent deployment of components.

Precisely speaking, REST itself doesn't define where or how the state of various resources should be stored. REST specifies how the state can be retrieved using the ubiquitous GET operation. The state can also be provided through the PUT and POST operations. It's also possible to have read-only resources that just support the GET method. As discussed elsewhere, the resource state could be provided by any means, such as a filesystem, a dynamic combination of other resources, or physical sensors. The REST paradigm is an approach or design pattern for designing resource-oriented application services. That is, REST is an architectural style for networked applications.

REST improves the performance, scalability, simplicity, and visibility of network-based applications. REST naturally encourages correct and efficient developer-computer and developer-developer communication. So, REST can be described as a way of building services and applications (we described a variety of software applications in the beginning of this chapter) by following a set of specific constraints between consumers and providers.

The advantages of REST

Typically, there could be many interactions between requesting and serving services to fulfill a business process and, hence, the communication among different and distributed microservices has to happen fast with less overhead. REST is mandated to have less latency networks for speedier service requests and fulfillment, which makes REST APIs a good fit. REST APIs not only support XML and JSON, but also support more optimized binary representation formats, such as a protocol buffer or Avro. Further on, it can upgrade to HTTP/2.0. Billions of people across the globe use the web for a variety of purposes. There are millions of developers creating a variety of web applications. Thus, a competent web architecture is needed to fulfill the varying requirements of businesses and people. In short, the powerful REST paradigm helps to build software architectures and applications that implicitly inherit all the praiseworthy qualities of the web. RESTful services bring forth a few important capabilities, such as greater scalability, efficient network use, and the independent functioning of clients and servers.

The REST paradigm inherently supports the ROA. Everything, as per the REST specifications, is a resource. Software architectures are typically a combination of several configurable architectural elements. In the case of REST, the principal architectural elements are components, connectors, resources, representations, and a few data elements. Resources are the building blocks of RESTful APIs. A resource can be anything that an application wants to expose on the network for other applications to find and operate through various HTTP methods. It can be text content, images, video and audio, a white paper, or a bank account. These resources are linked together by embedding the respective hyperlinks in HTML documents. Note that the resources can be retrieved, updated, and deleted by both humans and software programs. The following diagram illustrates this and shows the potential relationships between distributed and different resources via hyperlinks:

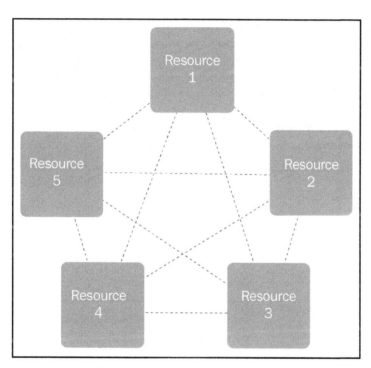

To unambiguously find and use them, each resource has to be given a unique name, which is called a URI. A sample URI is `http://www.paris.fr/weather`. As indicated in the preceding diagram, a resource can expose its state through the concept of representation. A representation typically contains both metadata (such as resource size, media type, or character set) and content (binary image or text document). The representation varies significantly. For example, the representation of a confirmation of purchase on an e-commerce site could be an HTML document. For a wedding picture, the representation could be a JPEG image streaming. For a contact in an address book web service, it could be an XML file. Thus, it starts with the resource identification and there's a corresponding representation for each resource identified.

Self-descriptive messages

Clients should express their preferred state through a host of request messages. A resource's current state gets communicated by the server to any client through a response message. For example, a wiki page editor can send a message to the server requesting to transfer a representation. The representation change may suggest a page update, which is the new state for the server-hosted and -managed web page. However, the server takes the call to accept or deny the client's request. As indicated in the previous paragraph, the self-descriptive messages may include metadata to carry and convey the additional details regarding the resource state, the representation format and size, and the message itself:

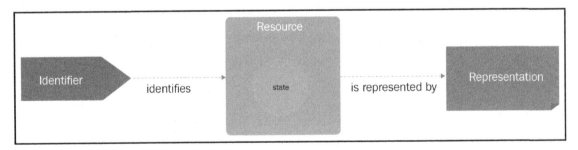

The core operations (GET, PUT, DELETE, and POST) performed on the current state of the resource are pictorially indicated in the following diagram. The state gets modified and updated by those operations. The diagram also indicates that the resource is delimited from its external environment, which interacts with it. That is, multiple parties can interact with the resource without any problem:

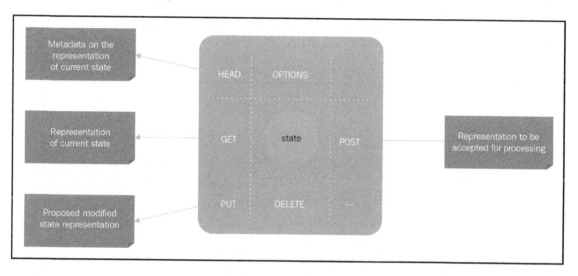

The resource is initiated with a state, which is in the middle of the previous diagram. The state is managed in any way that makes sense. Writing or reading from a database or file is one thing, but without any backend database, the business logic can't do any dynamic computation. The result is sent back to the requesting client. The previously mentioned core operations define its uniform interface.

Establishing and providing a REST API isn't an easy thing to do. An application, as per the REST paradigm, comprises multiple and distributed resources that provide useful capabilities to the application's consumers. API developers have to understand the problem domain, analyze the business, technology, and user requirements, and accordingly have to design the various participating and contributing resources. The resource selection finally leads to the formation of the APIs, which need to be found and used for business automation. The following diagram illustrates how we define a REST API as a set of hyperlinked resources. The resources are being exposed by a web service, websites, and microservices:

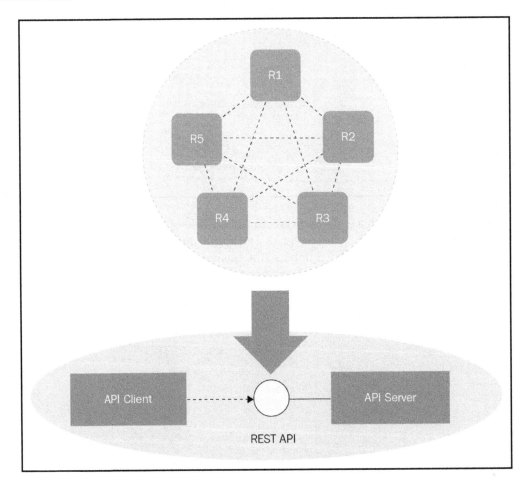

We are heading toward the software-defined world, and every tangible thing gets enabled through appropriate APIs. Thus, the much-touted API economy is beginning to shine. Corporations are keen to embrace this strategically sound transition. APIs have become the interesting and inspiring component for our business and IT systems:

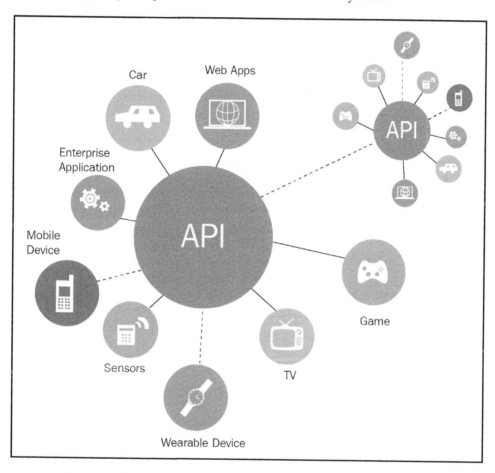

Precisely speaking, the ROA facilitated by the REST paradigm is being pronounced as the major contributor for enacting the envisioned digital transformation, not only for business enterprises, government organizations, and IT companies, but also for humanity. With technologies permeating everyday life, people are going to be the smartest in decision making and in deeds. SOAP is the first industry-wide approach for the goal of service-enablement. Due to various complexity factors, REST is gaining market and mind shares, as illustrated in the following section.

SOAP versus REST

SOAP is a matured and stabilized protocol with a number of standard specifications, and these specifications are simplifying and streamlining the development, deployment, management, governance, and composition of services. There are standardized markup languages to represent the interfaces of services. In order to be unambiguously understood, SOAP predominantly uses XML rather than HTTP to define message content. **Web services description language (WSDL)** can enforce the use of formal contracts between the service API and consumers. SOAP has a built-in WS-reliable messaging standard to increase service security during asynchronous execution and processing. SOAP has a built-in stateful operation capability for conversational state management.

As indicated in the preceding section, REST is easy to understand as it uses HTTP as the data transmission protocol and the basic CRUD operations. This ease of use simplifies work for software developers. REST also consumes less network bandwidth as it isn't as verbose/bulky as SOAP. Unlike SOAP, REST is designed to be stateless, and REST responses can be cached at clients to guarantee better performance and scalability. REST intrinsically supports many data formats. The overwhelmingly used data format is JSON, which is capable of providing better support for web browsers and mini-clients. JSON's association with JavaScript simplifies the consumption of API payloads. RESTful services are becoming pervasive due to their lightweight nature. All kinds of cloud, mobile, embedded, and IoT applications are leveraging the REST paradigm, which is increasingly paramount for application, data, and UI integration requirements.

When to use REST versus SOAP

REST is superior to SOAP in many respects, including the following:

- **Developing a public API**: REST, which is famous for ROA, invariably focuses on resource-based or data-based operations. Its core operations (`GET`, `PUT`, `POST`, and `DELETE`) are inherited from the ubiquitous HTTP. This minimalist approach makes the REST paradigm easy to understand and use across application and industry domains. Application and service developers find it easy to play around with the RESTful approach. The response gets easily consumed by web browsers. Precisely speaking, the simplicity innately provided by REST is one of the key reasons for its unprecedented support and success. Realizing its potential, there is a consistent transition from SOAP to REST.

- **Performance, flexibility, and scalability**: APIs are the entry point for applications to be identified, integrated, and used. There are event messages and procedure/method calls between applications' APIs. A widely circulated tip is that applications that require a lot of back-and-forth messaging have to choose the REST way in order to be successful. If there's a networking issue, the RESTful service approach allows the application/process to retry once the connection is re-established. REST makes it easy to do so without any major interruption. With SOAP stateful operations, the retry aspect seems to be a difficult affair as it involves more initialization at multiple levels, including the state code. Since REST is stateless, the session information isn't stored on the server machine, and this enables REST services to be independently retried and horizontally scalable.

The RESTful service paradigm enables us to perform easy and fast calls to a URL and get an immediate response. SOAP services require the keeping of a stateful connection with a complex client. REST, on the other hand, bats for stateless connection. The cache isn't stored in server applications. Therefore, testing RESTful applications is quite easy compared to SOAP applications.

SOAP provides ways of remotely accessing and manipulating objects (nouns) through procedure/method requests; REST focuses on the operations (verbs) that can be executed on resources. REST, therefore, has been widely adopted by public API practitioners. REST is always better than SOAP in situations that don't mandate for the full map for a set of objects to the client. Transmitting object details back and forth will waste a lot of expensive network bandwidth. Also, network latency comes into the picture. Especially in bandwidth-starved environments, this multiple-call requirement can be a huge barrier. APIs consumed mostly by mobile applications relate to those scenarios where we don't need to leverage SOAP at all costs. Public APIs frequently change because the expectations of consumers and businesses vary. In this world of start-ups and APIs without specific contractual agreements, REST is a natural and universal choice.

Best practices for REST-based microservices

In this section, we'll discuss a few best practices that make your MSA developer-friendly, so they can manage and track errors easily:

- **Meaningful names**: It's always important to provide a meaningful name in the request header, so if any problem, such as performance degradation, memory wastage, or a spike in user load, occurs, developers and performance engineers can easily understand from which microservice this request was originated and cascaded. It's therefore a best practice to provide the logical `name/{service id}` in the `User-Agent` property in the request header, for example, `User-Agent:EmployeeSearchService`.

- **API management**: In the REST-based microservice architecture, one microservice accesses another microservice via an API. The API acts as a facade to other microservices. Therefore, it's mandatory to build APIs carefully, and changing APIs entails additional problems. That is, APIs have to be designed with future demands in mind. Any changes in the API method signature aren't good because many microservices depend on the APIs to access and assess the microservice. Therefore, the tasks, such as API usage, versioning, and management, acquire special significance in our increasingly API-centric world.

- **Correlate ID**: Microservices, for the sake of guaranteeing high availability, are typically spread across multiple servers. That is, there can be multiple instances of the same microservice. With containers emerging as the most optimized runtime for microservices, running multiple instances of a microservice has become the new normal. To fulfill one client request, the control has to go through multiple microservices and instances. If one service isn't doing OK in the pipeline due to a problem, we need to understand the real situation of the service to determine our course of action. The aspects of service tracking and distributed tracing gain importance for the microservices architecture to be successful and smart in the connected and cloud era. The widely-recommended mechanism is always to generate a random UUID for every client request and pass that UUID to every internal service request. Then, by capturing the log files, it becomes easy for service operators to pinpoint the problematic service.

- **ELK implementation**: Microservices are small and simple. In any IT environment, there can be hundreds of microservices, and each microservice has multiple redundant instances in order to ensure the much-wanted fault tolerance. Each instance generates a log file, and administrators find that visiting each log file to locate something useful is not an easy affair. So, capturing and stocking log files, implementing a powerful search engine on the log file store, and applying appropriate **machine learning** (**ML**) algorithms to that log data in order to extract and emit any useful patterns, noteworthy information, or beneficial associations are vital in order to make sense of the log data. ELK, which is an open source software, fulfills these differing requirements in a tightly-integrated manner. E stands for Elasticsearch, L for Logstash, and K for Kibana. Elasticsearch just dumps the logs and provides a fuzzy search capability, Logstash is used to collect logs from different sources and transform them, and Kibana is a **graphical user interface** (**GUI**) that helps data scientists, testers, developers, and even businesspeople to insightfully search the logs as per their evolving requirements. Considering the significance of log analytics, there are open source as well as commercial-grade solutions to extract log, operational, performance, scalability, and security insights from microservice interaction log data.
- **Resiliency implementation**: There are frameworks and solutions that guarantee reliability (resiliency + elasticity) when services interact with one another.

REST-based microservices are popular not only due to their extreme simplicity, but also due to the fact that services communicate directly (synchronously) with each other over HTTP. This direct communication means that there's no need for any kind of intermediary, such as a hub, bus, broker, or gateway. For example, consider a B2C e-commerce system that instantly notifies customers when a particular product is back in stock. This notification could be implemented via RESTful microservices:

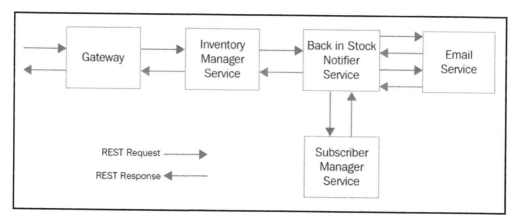

It should be noted that the communication is point-to-point. Still, hardcoding services' addresses isn't a good thing to do. Therefore, the prominent workaround is to leverage a service discovery mechanism, such as Eureka or Consul. These are highly available centralized servers where services register their API addresses. The availability status of services for instantaneous serving is registered with the centralized servers. Client services can request a specific API address from this centralized server in order to identify and leverage the appropriate services. Still, there are several shortcomings, which are listed as follows:

- **Blocking**: Due to the synchronous nature of the REST approach, the update stock operation won't do anything until the notification service completes its task of notifying all relevant customers. If there are thousands of customers wishing to be notified of the additional stock, the system's performance is bound to degrade sharply. This performance issue happens due to the tight-coupling approach. One way to overcome these issues is to embrace the pipeline pattern. The architecture diagram then gets modified as follows:

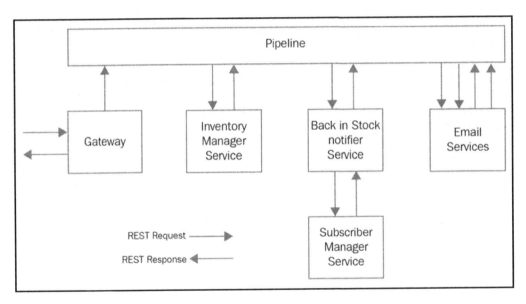

Here, the communication is still REST-based, but the real shift is that the point-to-point communication is eliminated forever. The **Pipeline** entity is entirely responsible for orchestrating control and data flows. The services are totally decoupled, and this decoupling makes microservices autonomous. However, with this approach, the services must rely on the pipeline orchestration in order to contribute to the cause and, hence, services are self-defined, yet not self-sufficient.

- **Asynchronous messaging**: Consider a typical messaging-based system. Here, both the services—input and output—can be defined as commands or events. Each of these subscribes to the events that it's interested in consuming. Further, these events are received reliably through a mechanism, such as a messaging queue/broker, when the events are placed on the queue by other services. With this approach, the stock notification subsystem could now be remodeled as follows:

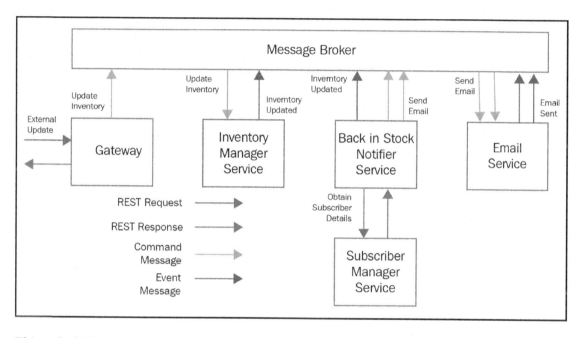

This refurbished architecture brings forth a number of crucial advantages, such as enhanced flexibility, service isolation, and autonomy. This shift eases the addition, removal, or modification of services without affecting the operation or code of other services. Any kind of service failure can be gracefully handled. These need to be carefully considered when designing and developing microservices-based enterprise applications.

As technologies become increasingly complex, best practices and procedures sourced through various experimentation come in handy for architects and developers to create strategically sound software systems. As microservices emerge as the most optimal building block for production-grade and extensible business and IT systems, our focus gets turned toward the ways of leveraging the matured and stabilized REST paradigm to create and sustain business-critical and microservices-centric software applications.

The API-first approach

We are going to have a dazzling array of IoT devices, data, services, and applications. Data analytics shall assume a greater proportion due to the uninhibited explosion of IoT sensors and actuators, which make any physical, mechanical, and electrical system to be digitized and connected. Also, web, enterprise, and cloud applications are mobile-enabled. Thus, there are multiple channels for application, device, and information access and usage. The domain of enterprise mobility is very popular. There are performance-hungry legacy applications. Application dismantling takes a lot of time and talent. Therefore, the popular approach is to attach extra APIs to existing applications in order to make them available to the external world. However, this isn't a strategically sound approach. On the other side, considering the optimal and organized nature of cloud infrastructures, new-generation applications are being directly designed, developed, and deployed on cloud servers.

Therefore, the prescribed approach is to build the API first and then to have cloud applications on top of that API. The idea behind the widely circulated API-first development (https://www.restcase.com/) strategy is to arrive at a futuristic API. This approach enables software developers to accomplish their work with clarity and confidence. The implementations can be highly advanced and efficient. This separation between interface and implementation facilitates the incorporation of modified code at a later point in time without affecting access to the application and service.

With clouds positioned as the one-stop IT solution for all kinds of software systems, monolithic and massive applications are being cloud-enabled to become open for innovation, disruption, and transformation. Greenfield applications are predominantly initiated and implemented as cloud-native applications. There are code repositories (public and private). Cloud-native code, once finished, gets checked into a repository. Thus, code is built and integrated with all the necessary code segments to create an integrated application. Vital tests are performed on the application to check whether its code passes through all the gates successfully. Then, there are continuous delivery and deployment tools to deliver the curated and refined code to provisioned IT resources to start the deployment process.

Developing API-first

This is an interesting strategy. Development works are happening in a sequence. The requirements elicitation, service design, development, debugging, delivery, deployment, and decommissioning typically happen in a synchronous manner. The quality control and assurance team is waiting for the code to be fully developed and integrated. Once the prototype is ready, the documentation team starts preparing the APIs. If any improvement, correction, or addition requirement arises, the design and development teams start working on them. This is a waste of talent and time. If the API for the proposed service is finalized in consultation with the project sponsor and the end users, the software construction and deployment time is reduced sharply. This is depicted in the following diagram:

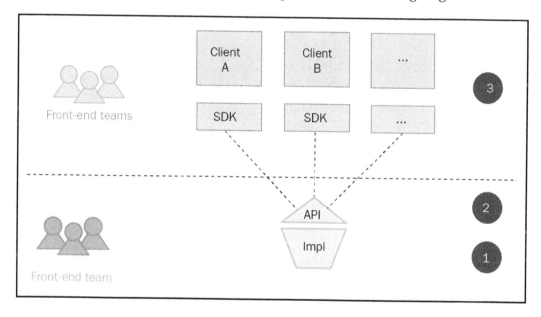

Therefore the API-first development process is being recommended because it facilitates a kind of parallel development by all teams. The software can be released independently. The dependency on other teams is substantially less in this case:

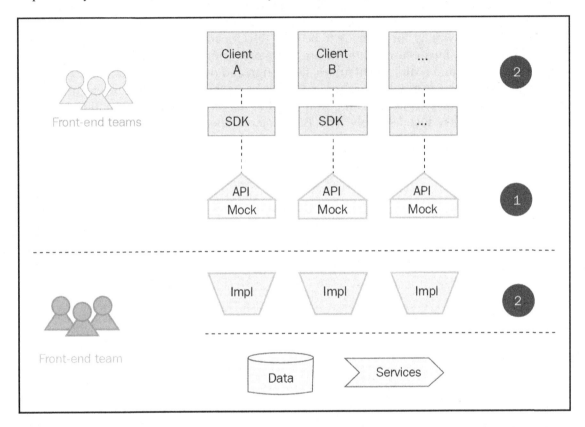

Here, the APIs are first created and mocked. Then backend, frontend, and test teams start to work with the mocked APIs. Once the **API** is finalized, all teams can easily switch to the production or staging API. This procedure saves a lot of development time.

 RestCase is a cloud-based API development platform. The platform allows developers to collaboratively create REST APIs using an intuitive browser-based interface, which automatically generates documentation, tests, and mocks. RestCase further enables rapid iteration and testing by creating a mock of the API that developers can make calls against immediately, without waiting for the actual development and deployment of the API, thereby eliminating impediments from various development teams.

Building services API-first

This is a best practice that's wisely and widely recommended by experts. By defining and designing the APIs first, a variety of things can be done properly. Project sponsors get an overall view of the system under development. Incorporating changes is quite easy in this case. The software developers can proceed with their development and testing tasks with confidence. Salespeople can explain the nitty-gritty of the software system to any prospective customers and consumers. API testing can be done first. API management is made easy in the increasingly API world. Everything is being fitted with one or more APIs in order to be found, bound, and used according to evolving needs.

Summary

In this chapter, we discussed the salient features of the RESTful services and APIs in making the road toward digitally transformed businesses and societies easier to navigate. The simplicity and modularity of the REST paradigm leads to the production of highly flexible and futuristic software applications. As the web and cloud enablement of digital assets assume a more prominent role, the role and responsibility of the REST idea are bound to increase in the days to come. We tend toward deeply connecting our everyday environments. The dream of having many cognitive environments is consistently on the rise. Hence, it's clear that the unique and innate capabilities of the mesmerizing RESTful services should be reaped in order to achieve the things described in this chapter. This chapter has given you a lot of useful information on the REST concept and how it's going to be a trendsetter in the IT world. This book will cover the various aspects of the RESTful paradigm.

Further reading

- https://www.packtpub.com/application-development/restful-java-web-services-third-edition
- https://www.packtpub.com/application-development/building-restful-web-services-go
- https://www.packtpub.com/application-development/building-restful-web-services-net-core

10
Frameworks, Standard Languages, and Toolkits

Software frameworks are the lifeline of software applications. They provide extended capabilities and offer many out-of-the-box implementations so that application developers don't need to handle every coding aspect of software and can focus on building faster and smarter business capabilities by using out-of-the-box capabilities, libraries, APIs, and models provided by the frameworks.

We'll provide a short introduction to few popular frameworks along with a little bit of information about their supported programming languages, capabilities, standards, and characteristics, such as footprints, adaptability, cloud deployment friendliness, and ease of development.

The aim of this chapter is to introduce readers to a few prominent frameworks that can come in handy when choosing the right framework for their API-development needs. Please note that the list of discussed frameworks isn't exhaustive, and there's no intention to provide a comparison between them.

The following are the chapter objectives:

- This chapter is all about introducing a few prominent frameworks to app developers who want to jump-start their RESTful APIs and microservices with their acquainted programming languages
- It's an attempt to provide readers with an introduction, guidelines, and advantages and disadvantages for few programming language-friendly frameworks so that they can pick and play with a more suitable framework for their RESTful API development needs

Technical requirements

As we'll discuss a few prominent frameworks based on the Java, Python, and Go (programming) languages, having a basic understanding in one or more programming languages would enable readers of this chapter to jumpstart their RESTful API development with one or more of their favorite frameworks. This chapter serves as reference material as well as a technical guide for those who have a minimum understanding of any of these three programming languages.

Core features of a framework

As we are aware, frameworks are software libraries, APIs, scaffoldings, AJAX, caching, security, compilers and much more. It's imperative that we refresh our memory with the following core qualities of any framework, as our selection of framework relies on these qualities:

- Simple, consistent, easy to adapt, and faster to implement
- Layered architecture, well-designed and -documented
- Built with genuine trade-offs
- Built with reusable libraries and reused libraries (borrowed from the past)
- Integrated and designed to evolve

Let's look at a few Java-based frameworks to understand their capabilities regarding their design, footprint, documentation, and adaptability, along with their advantages and disadvantages.

Spring Boot

One of the most popular open source, Java-based frameworks is **Spring Boot**. It offers an excellent platform for many Java developers to build and deploy REST-based applications with a rapid turnaround time.

The fundamental design principles of Spring Boot is as follows:

- Provide radically faster and widely-accessible code, reusable libraries, and boilerplates for all Spring development

- Be opinionated (certain, strong, and expressive), think outside the box, and provide a way for developers to customize as per their requirements, and challenge the defaults

- Provide non-functional requirement features variations that are common to classes of the project that can be used for instrumentation (such as security, embedded servers, health checks, metrics and externalized configuration))

- No code-generation mechanism and no need for XML configurations

 Boilerplate code or boilerplate represents a code or code library incorporated in a software application, and we can reuse those libraries with little or no alteration.

Let's see what makes Spring Framework a popular choice for app developers for their RESTful API development.

Core features of Spring

Spring's application, external configuration, profiles, and logging are the constituents of Spring's core features. Let's look at each constituent and its values:

- The Spring application provides a convenient way to bootstrap our applications
- External configuration helps us to work with same application code in different environments by using YAML, environment variables, or even with command-line arguments
- Profiles segregate parts of an application's configuration and make it available only to certain environments
- It provides out-of-the-box Apache Commons Logging capabilities, however, it doesn't stop us from use different logging frameworks

Database integration with Spring data

Database integration is an important part of any production software applications, and we'll observe how Spring makes the lives of developers better by providing exciting capabilities to integration for traditional SQL databases and NoSQL technologies:

- **SQL**: Spring provides far-reaching support to work with SQL databases. JdbcTemplate for ORM, with Spring data, provides an additional level of functionality called **repository creations**.
- **NO-SQL**: A Spring-based programming model for data access, called **Spring data**, powers the Spring Framework and provides a quick-and-easy access mechanism to connect to a variety of NoSQL technologies.

Messaging integration

Integration with messaging systems is super simplified with the Spring message framework. Be it simple messaging with JmsTemplate for JMS or ActiveMQ support or be it an AMQP for advanced messaging or for Apache Kafka integration the Spring-framework, it provides simple methods for messaging integration.

Extending Spring with auto-configuration

In many practical scenarios, we need to develop shared libraries (within an organization or as a contribution to open source) and in such cases create specific configuration classes—as modules (JAR). Making it available in the application's classpath makes the development faster and easier by eliminating the need to define specific beans that are included in the auto-configuration classes. The configuration examples could be LDAP, different DB sources configurations, or security configurations.

Writing unit tests and integration test cases

Writing unit test cases and integration tests are essential practices for any developers. Spring provides better capabilities to write unit tests, tests in isolation scripts, and integration tests. Spring Framework comes up with a few utilities and annotations for testing our applications. Spring-boot-starter-test is the favorite test utility for most of developers as its starter tool imports Junit, AssertJ, Hamcrest, and Mockito. Spring-test and Spring-boot-test for integration tests are common libraries and come in handy when writing integration tests. What's exciting about the spring test framework is that we can add some additional test dependencies of our own as well.

Benefits of Spring Boot

Before we move to another popular framework, let's look at some advantages of Spring Boot:

- Quick setup, rapid development, and push to production (enterprise ready)
- Effortless and quick integration with security, ORM, and JDBC
- Embedded lightweight HTTP servers
- Along with Java, it also supports Groovy
- Supports Maven and Gradle build tools
- Modular and plays well with other libraries
- Quick learning, broad, and in-depth documentation
- Very active community (of development and documentation) online and offline

Drawbacks of Spring Boot

While Spring has many advantages, we should also be aware of its drawbacks:

- Frequent breaking changes (by introducing new capabilities and defect fixes) between versions
- May create an obligation to use latest versions
- Too much information and documentation may be overkill
- Vast framework finding specifics may be hard for few (may affect rapid prototyping)

The author's choice for all of the code in this book is also Spring Boot, and from examples in `Chapter 2`, *Design Strategy, Guidelines, and Best Practices*, and `Chapter 3`, *Essential RESTful API patterns*, we've seen how easy it was to bring up RESTful APIs with Spring Boot. Numerous capabilities are built-in with Spring Boot, and it's one of the matured frameworks of the software industry.

Beginning about Light 4j

Light is a cloud-native micro-services platform developed with Jave SE, with design goals of high throughput, low latency, and a small footprint. Light 4j is a general-purpose web/API framework with different frameworks, such as OAUTH2, Portal, Logging, Messaging, and Metrics, built in.

Core features of Light 4j

The light-4j platform aims at containerized microservices and supports a design-driven approach from the OpenAPI specification for the RESTful API and the GraphQL IDL for GraphQL services and has code-generation and runtime models (for validation and security).

As a platform or a framework, it's good that it addresses a few technical cross-cutting concerns, such as auditing, load-balancing, authentication, and health checks, so that service or API developers can focus on business logic without worrying too much about those technical concerns, also called **non-functional requirements**. Light 4j provides various handler logic and separates those non-functional requirements from the business context, to help the API developers to focus on developing business logic.

Learning about Light Rest 4j

Light Rest 4j is a framework that is built on top of Light 4j, and designed to speed up RESTful API development and deployment. It has many middleware handlers designed around Swagger 2.0 and open API 3.0 specifications. Light-rest-4j comes with open API metadata, open API security, an open API validator, Swagger meta, Swagger security, and Swagger validator.

Light-code-gen

We can build RESTful APIs or services with the OpenAPI 3.0 specification-ready light-rest-4j provided frameworks and scaffold a project with a command-line tool called **light-code-gen** tool. It enables JWT scope-verification and schema-validation for any service requests.

The light-code-gen tool helps us to scaffold a project with a specification file and a config JSON file. The command-line tool can be as simple as a Java command-line tool, docker command line, or even a script that can be part of the DevOps pipeline. light-code-gen works with our favorite Maven build tool as well.

Choosing Light 4j over the rest

Let's conclude this section with the following facts about Light 4j, as it may help you determine whether to choose Light 4j for RESTful API development:

- Java-SE-based framework

- Scalable design

- Low latency

- Small memory footprint

- Several handlers as plugins

- Out-of-the-box OAuth2 integration (security-first design)

- Easy integration with other frameworks

- A built-in dependency-injection framework

- Benchmarks indicate as this the fastest RESTful framework

- May involve a steep learning curve due to poor documentation

- New to market/industry, so not much feedback yet on production systems

Light-rest-4j, built on top of the light4j framework, is very promising and gaining popularity due to various features—lightweight, very low latency, designed for scalability, not J2EE-based but J2SE-based, and its security-first design.

Spark Framework

Spark is a micro-framework founded by Per Wendel for creating web applications in Java with minimal effort, and it's a free and open source Java Web Framework, released under the Apache 2 license.

The Spark Framework is a rapid-development web framework built with Java 8 Lambda Expression (based on the lambda philosophy), so it can help to build a web application with fewer verbose, in fact you can build a REST API with a JSON response in less than 10 lines of code and provide Node.js-like experience when developing a web API. Cool, isn't it?

Core features of Spark Framework

Let's get a glimpse of some of the core characteristics of Spark:

- Designed to create APIs faster and more easily

- It's a lightweight library

- Provides simple interfaces through which we can define routes and dispatch them to functions for the paths we requested

- Follows the Java 8 lambda philosophy (create web APIs with fewer lines)

Creating an API with fewer lines

Typically, we would write the following few lines to bring up a hello world API with Spark:

```
1 import static spark.Spark.*;
2
3 public class MyHelloWorld {
4 public static void main(String[] args) {
5 get("/sayhello", (request, response) -> "Hello Reader");
6 }
7 }
```

That's it! Line one, `spark.Spark.*`, as indicated in the preceding code snippet, does the magic. By using CURL (curl `http://localhost:4567/sayhello`), we would visualize the following request and response as output for the previous code:

```
Request:

GET http://localhost:4567/sayhello

Response:

Hello Reader
```

As we can see in the preceding snippet, curl hits the application, so the lambda function of `Spark.*` fires and the client (curl in this case) gets the output of the static lambda function. It's not just a simple hello world API; we can write complex RESTful APIs with Spark as it supports a variety of functions, such as query maps, cookies and sessions, filters, redirects, exception and error handlings, and views and templates.

Benefits of Spark

Now it's time to review the advantages of Spark (and then we'll review another exciting framework called **Dropwizard**):

- Java-8-EE-based and based on the lambda philosophy (less verbose)
- Facilitates rapid development
- Enables App developers to create scalable REST APIs
- Fast and lightweight
- Best suited and excellent fit for rapid prototyping purposes
- Scores high on the speed factor as Spark is a thin wrapper around Java EE's servlet API
- Simplified and effective routing
- Brings better productivity by providing a simple **domain-specific language (DSL)** for routing API endpoints to handlers
- Maven and Gradle support

Drawbacks of Spark

Any popular framework may have drawbacks, and Spark is no exception:

- Not as popular as other frameworks (small community)
- May not be suitable for huge projects (SQL and NoSQL plug-and-play aspects)

Dropwizard

In this section, we'll review another popular Java-based framework licensed under Apache, called Dropwizard. This framework is named for a character from a K.C. Green webcomic (http://gunshowcomic.com/316) series.

Overview

Dropwizard is a stable, mature framework, assembled with several Java libraries, yet lightweight and intended to help API developers by providing features that one can quickly develop and deploy web applications to production servers. Dropwizard's principal design goal is to provide reliable, reusable, and high-performance implementations of everything that a web application needs and provide out-of-the-box capabilities that the application is deployable in production servers. Framework's reusable libraries make the core application lean and focused, hence reducing both time-to-market and maintenance burdens:

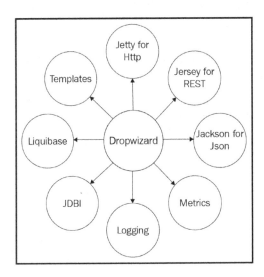

As we can see in the previous diagram, **Dropwizard** supports several powerful libraries, and we'll see some details about each in the following sections.

Core features of Dropwizard

Dropwizard tailors several high-performance Java-library implementations, such as Jetty, Jersy, Jackson, and Metrics. Let's take a quick glimpse at a few of these libraries.

Jetty for HTTP

Dropwizard uses the Jetty HTTP library and spins up an HTTP web server with its `main` method, and so facilitates running your web application as a simple Unix process and piggybacking on existing Unix process management tool. By having this `main` method as a way of spinning up, the process leads to the following:

- No need to manage the traditionally-burdensome Java production process
- Gets rid of PermGen issues
- No need to customize the application server's configuration
- No need for separate deployment tools
- No classloader issues

Jersey for REST

As we know, the JAX-RS reference implementation Jersey is open source; it comes with its native API toolkit to simplify the development of RESTful web services and their clients in Java. Jersey also exposes numerous extension SPIs (software platform infrastructure as a services model). Dropwizard bundles Jersey as its RESTful web app framework and helps developers to write clean code, providing testable classes that gracefully map HTTP requests to simple Java objects that streaming output, matrix URI parameters, conditional `GET` requests, and so on.

Jackson

A critical need for app developers is having the object mapper from JSON and allowing the domain model to export directly to those Java objects. Dropwizard gratifies those app-developer needs by having Jackson as its primary core feature along with many others.

Metrics

This Java library acts as a powerful toolkit and offers ways to measure the behavior of components that are deployed in production. Combined with other prominent libraries, such as Ehcache and Graphite, Metrics stands as it provides full-stack visibility to our RESTful API and web applications.

Liquibase

Dropwizard includes the open source solution for managing revisions of database-schema scripts. Liquibase supports various types of database, and various file formats for defining the DB structure. The highlight of Liquibase is its ability to roll back changes (forward and backward) from a specific point.

Other noteworthy features

Before we get into its advantages and disadvantages, let's take a glimpse at other noteworthy libraries in Dropwizard:

- **Logging**: Logback and slf4j for performant and flexible logging

- **Hibernate validator**: Offers easy ways for user input validation, along with capabilities of generating i18n-friendly error messages

- **Http interactions**: Bundled with Apache HttpClient and Jersey client libraries, it helps low-level and high-level HTTP interactions with other web services

- **JDBI**: Provides a simple, comfortable, and straightforward way to establish Relational database connectivity with Java backends

- **Templates**: Dropwizard supports Freemarker and Mustache, the simplest templating systems for consumer or user-facing applications

Benefits of Dropwizard

As we are covering the advantages and disadvantages of each framework, let's touch upon them for Dropwizard as well, so that you can decide why or why not to use Dropwizard. The following are its merits:

- A Java framework
- Out-of-the-box support for configuration, application metrics, logging, operational tools, templating, and much more
- You can do rapid prototyping
- Ops-friendly
- Very modular
- Develops high-performance RESTful web services
- Supports many open source and independent libraries
- Implementation of monitoring at its best with Metrics
- Supports integration and the use of several third-party frameworks

Drawbacks of Dropwizard

A few factors that you may consider drawbacks of Dropwizard are as follows:

- Maintaining applications with third-party frameworks and libraries may bring debugging nightmares
- Though there are several powerful libraries, there may be situations where you need a specific library, but it isn't supported by Dropwizard (restriction of using only what Dropwizard provides)
- It may incur a steep learning curve

Understanding Go framework for the RESTful API

Go is one of the friendlier programming languages for microservices and RESTful APIs. Go is a general-purpose, procedural programming language with advanced features and clean syntax. It influences the efficient management of dependencies using package-assembly and supports environment adopting patterns alike to dynamic languages.

An overview

There are many powerful frameworks that Gophers (Go lang programmers) can employ to reuse proven, extensible, production-grade external packages out of the box for their app's development. This section intends to cover some details and functions for two Go-language-based frameworks—Gin-gonic and Revel – that you can use to jump-start your RESTful API development.

Gin-gonic

Gin is an HTTP web framework written in Go. Gin design is much out of Martini, another Go framework, however, with better performance than Martini. The Gin framework claims: *If you need smashing performance, get yourself some gin*. Gin-gonic helps developers to write less boilerplate code and build a request-handling pipeline.

 Martini (`https://github.com/go-martini/martini`) is a framework developed with the Go language. Its modular and non-intrusive design makes the framework simple to use. However, please be aware that it's no longer maintained or supported.

Core features

Gin is a very lean framework and supports essential and much-needed features and functionalities for you to design and develop a RESTful web service. The trimmed-down version has essential libraries as well, and you can create your own reusable and extensible pieces of code.

HttpRouter

HttpRouter is a lightweight and a high-performance HTTP request router for Go; it's also called **multiplexer** (or mux, for short). Unlike the default mux of Go's net/HTTP package, this customized mux helps to bind the routing variables in the routing pattern and matches against the request method. The best part of this router is its small memory footprint, optimized for high performance. As this custom router employs a compressing radix tree structure for efficient matching of the long paths, a large number of routes is possible with the custom router.

Http2 server push

Gin supports Http2 server push capabilities out of the box. Server push helps the server to utilize its network resources fully and so improves the page-load time. HTTP/2 introduced a concept called **server push**, which allows the server to push the additional required resources to the browser even before they are explicitly requested.

Multi-template

Gin allows by default the use of only one HTML template. However, there's a custom HTML rendering to support multiple templates, that is, more than one `*template.` template.

Upload files

By using `multipart.write`, we can write files into the cache and send them to the server through the `POST` method.

Other noteworthy features

Though *Gin-Gonic* has many libraries and supports several features, here are some of its best features:

- Groups routes
- Writes into log files
- Custom validator
- Custom middleware
- Builds with *jsoniter*

Benefits of Gin-Gonic

Let's see a few pros of *Gin*-Gonic:

- Lean and lightweight
- Zero-allocation router
- Complete set of unit tests
- Backward-compatible, new releases will not break the old code
- High performance and highly scalable

Drawbacks of Gin-Gonic

Let's be aware of a few disadvantages of this framework:

- May not be suitable for large, enterprise-based implementations
- Low server processing capabilities, which forces clients to handle the workloads
- May incur a steep learning curve

Revel

In our list of frameworks, one of the most promising is Revel. It's fully-featured, designed to provide out-of-the-box asynchronous, stateless, and modular capabilities to our web APIs. Let's learn a bit about Revel and its abilities in the following sections.

Core features

Revel is a self-contained, almost full-stack web framework, with customizable middleware and an externally-configurable framework that Gophers would develop and stand up their RESTful APIs really quickly. Let's get to know some of the fundamental features of Revel in the following sections.

Router

URLs and routes definitions are configurable in the file, as shown:

```
[METHOD] [URL Pattern] [Controller.Method]
GET / MyGoSite.Hello
```

We can route the URLs with Revel in different ways. The following are a few routing methods with examples:

- **Fixed-path routing**: Fixed-path or exact-match routing of the HTTP method and the path to invoke specific methods and controllers
- `GET/About App.About`
- Use exact match/About as path and `App.About` as method on the `App` controller
- **URL**: *Parameters* routing - segments of the path extracted *with*—prefix
- `GET /user/:id User.Details`

A few other methods that Revel supports for routing (that we aren't covering in this section) are auto-routing, reverse-routing, static serving, and purge.

Server engine

The best part of Revel's server engine is that app developers are free to implement their favorite HTTP engines. Revel uses the Go HTTP engine by default, but it allows us to configure any other server engine, such as fastHttp, New Relic HTTP, or our custom developed HTTP engine. How cool is that?

Controllers

Controllers in the Revel framework are the logic containers responsible for executing the API logic. The controller holds the incoming HTTP requests information, such as query parameters, path parameters, JSON body, and form data, to the handlers.

Handlers

HTTP request routers are responsible for comparing the incoming requests against a list of predefined URL paths and calling the respective handlers. Handlers are responsible for writing response headers and bodies. Any Go object that satisfies the `http.Handler` interface can be a handler. Interestingly, Go's HTTP package is distributed with functions that can generate handlers, such as `FileServer`, `RedirectHandler`, and `NotFoundHandler`.

Interceptors

There are cases, such as request logging, error handling, or authentication handling, where we need an action invoked by the framework BEFORE or AFTER a specific event, and those sorts of invocations will happen through a Revel function called **interceptors**. In other words, interceptors are a function that gets invoked by the framework. Revel supports three forms of interceptors—function interceptor, method interceptor, and controller interceptor.

Filters

Revel has independent functions called **filters**. Filters help to implement horizontal concerns, such as request-logging, cookie policies, and authorization. Filters are middleware, and most of Revel's built-in functionalities and request-processing functionalities are filters. They are interfaces that allow them to be nested.

Cache

Revel comes with a library that facilitates server-side, low-latency, and temporary storage to act as a cache. If you need to take advantage of, and minimize access to, the database, cache is a good choice. Another example is implementing cache for user sessions where cookie-based sessions aren't preferred or are insufficient.

Other noteworthy features

Here are some other noteworthy features of Revel:

- **Websockets**: Revel supports full-duplex communication over a single TCP connection with WS methods or with the server `WebSocket` parameter as an action.

- **Database**: DB support through app conf (application configuration) database section configuration. Note that DB isn't preconfigured and it's up to the developers to use modules, such as GORM.

- **Testing**: Revel comes with pre-built modules that make it easy to write and run functional test cases.

Benefits of Revel

Now we are ready to look at the pros of the Revel framework:

- Hot-code reload
- Comprehensive libraries
- High performance
- Modular, it's built around composable middleware, called filters, which implement most of the request-processing functionality
- Built-in test modules facilitate functional test-case execution
- Well-documented

Drawbacks of Revel

The factors that may make Revel less appealing are as follows:

- Comprehensive libraries are Revel's advantage in most cases; there are situations that it makes the code base hefty and generates a large footprint (in contradiction to Go's lean principle)
- May incur a steep learning curve
- No community standard for managing package versions and it's up to the developers to manage and release with the necessary latest dependencies (no backward-compatibility)

Python RESTful API frameworks

Python is one of the top-rated programming languages. It's also known for its less-complex syntax, and its high-level, object-oriented, robust, and general-purpose programming. Python is the top choice for any first-time programmer.

Overview of Python

Since its release in 1991, Python has evolved and powered by several frameworks for web application development, scientific and mathematical computing, and graphical user interfaces to the latest REST API frameworks. In this section, we'll explore two comprehensive frameworks, Django and Flask, so that you can choose the best one for developing your RESTful API.

Django

Django is a web framework also available as open source with the BSD license, designed to help developers create their web app very quickly as it takes care of additional web-development needs. It includes several packages (also known as **applications**) to handle typical web-development tasks, such as authentication, content administration, scaffolding, templates, caching, and syndication. Let's review the **Django REST Framework** (**DRF**) built with Python, and use the Django core framework for REST API development and deployment in the following section.

Django Rest Framework

DRF is an open source, well-matured Python and Django library intended to help APP developers build sophisticated web APIs. DRF's modular, flexible, and customizable architecture makes the development of both simple, turnkey API endpoints and complicated REST constructs possible. The goal of DRF is to divide a model, generalize the wire representation, such as JSON or XML, and customize a set of class-based views to satisfy the specific API endpoint using a serializer that describes the mapping between views and API endpoints.

Core features

Let's have a quick introduction on some of the core features of Django in the following paragraphs and then move on to its noteworthy features.

Web-browsable API

This feature enhances the REST API developed with DRF. It has a rich interface, and the web-browsable API supports multiple media types too. The browsable API does mean that the APIs we build will be self-describing and the API endpoints that we create as part of the REST services and return JSON or HTML representations. The interesting fact about the web-browsable API is that we can interact with it fully through the browser, and any endpoint that we interact with using a programmatic client will also be capable of responding with a browser-friendly view onto the web-browsable API.

Authentication

One of the DRF out-of-the-box capabilities is authentication; it supports broad categories of authentication schemes, from basic authentication, token authentication, session authentication, remote user authentication, to OAuth Authentication. It also supports custom authentication schemes if we wish to implement one. DRF runs the authentication scheme at the start of the view, that is, before any other code is allowed to proceed. DRF determines the incoming requests privileges from the permission and throttling policies, and then decides whether the incoming request can be allowed or disallowed with the matched credentials.

Serialization and deserialization

Serialization is the process of converting complex data, such as querysets and model instances, into native Python datatypes. Converting facilitates the rendering of native data types, such as JSON or XML. DRF supports serialization through serializers classes. The serializers of DRF are similar to Django's `Form` and `ModelForm` classes. It provides a serializer class, which helps to control the output of responses. The DRF `ModelSerializer` classes provide a simple mechanism with which we can create serializers that deal with model instances and querysets. Serializers also do deserialization, that is, serializers allow parsed data that needs to be converted back into complex types. Please note that the deserialization happens only after validating the incoming data.

Other noteworthy features

Here are some other noteworthy features of the DRF:

- **Routers**: The DRF supports automatic URL routing to Django and provides a consistent and straightforward way to wire the view logic to a set of URLs
- **Class-based views**: A dominant pattern that enables the reusability of common functionalities
- **Hyperlinking APIs**: The DRF supports various styles (using primary keys, hyperlinking between entities, and so on) to represent the relationship between entities
- **Generic views**: Allows us to build API views that map to the database models

There are many more features, such as caching, throttling, and testing, that the DRF supports which we won't cover.

Benefits of the DRF

Here are some of the benefits of the DRF:

- Web-browsable API
- Authentication policies
- Powerful serialization
- Extensive documentation and excellent community support
- Simple yet powerful
- Test coverage of source code
- Secure and scalable
- Customizable

Drawbacks of the DRF

Here are some facts that may disappoint some Python app developers who intend to use the DRF:

- Monolithic and components get deployed together
- Based on Django ORM
- Steep learning curve
- Slow response time

Flask

Flask is a microframework for Python developers based on Werkzeug (WSGI toolkit) and Jinja 2 (template engine). It comes under BSD licensing. **Flask** is very easy to set up and simple to use. Like other frameworks, Flask comes with several out-of-the-box capabilities, such as a built-in development server, debugger, unit test support, templating, secure cookies, and RESTful request dispatching. Let's have a look at one more powerful RESTful API framework, called **Flask-RESTful**, in the following section.

Flask-RESTful

Flask-RESTful is an extension for Flask that provides additional support for building REST APIs. You will never be disappointed with the time it takes to develop an API. Flask-Restful is a lightweight abstraction that works with the existing ORM/libraries. Flask-RESTful encourages best practices with minimal setup. Now let's get a glimpse of the core features that Flask-RESTful offers.

Core features of Flask-RESTful

Flask-RESTful comes with several built-in features; this section covers a few unique RESTful features since we've covered the most common RESTful framework features with Django, and there isn't much difference between their supporting core features.

Resourceful routing

The design goal of Flask-RESTful is to provide resources built on top of Flask pluggable views. The pluggable views provide a simple way (defining a resource method) to access the HTTP methods. Consider the following example code:

```
class Todo(Resource):
  def get(self, user_id):
     ....
  def delete(self, user_id):
     ....
  def put(self, user_id):
     args = parser.parse_args()
     ....
```

Restful request parsing

Request parsing refers to an interface, modeled after the Python parser *interface* for command-line arguments, called `argparser`. The RESTful request parser is designed to provide uniform and straightforward access to any variable that comes within the `(flask.request)` request object.

Output fields

In most cases, app developers prefer to control rendering response data, and Flask-RESTful provides a mechanism where you can use ORM models or even custom classes as an object to render. Another interesting fact about this framework is that app developers don't need to worry about exposing any internal data structures as its let one format and filter the response objects. So, when we look at the code, it'll be evident which data would go for rendering and how it'll be formatted.

Other noteworthy features

As we've covered a few unique features in the previous section, here are some other noteworthy features of Flask-RESTful:

- **API**: This is the main entry point for the restful API, which we'll initialize with the Flask application.
- **ReqParse**: This enables us to add and parse multiple arguments in the context of the single request.
- **Input**: A useful functionality, it parses the input string and returns true or false depending on the Input. If the input is from the JSON body, the type is already native Boolean and passed through without further parsing.

Benefits of the Flask framework

Let's look at some of the advantages of Flask and the Flask-Restful framework:

- Built-in development server and debugger
- Out-of-the-box RESTful request dispatching
- Support for secure cookies
- Integrated unit-test support
- Lightweight
- Very minimal setup
- Faster (performance)
- Easy NoSQL integration
- Extensive documentation

Drawbacks of Flask

Here are some of Flask and Flask-RESTful's disadvantages:

- Version management (managed by developers)
- No brownie points as it doesn't have browsable APIs
- May incur a steep learning curve

Frameworks – a table of reference

The following table provides a quick reference of a few other prominent micro-frameworks, their features, and supported programming languages:

Language	Framework	Short description	Prominent features
Java	Blade	Fast and elegant MVC framework for Java8	Lightweight High performance Based on the MVC pattern RESTful-style router interface Built-in security
Java/Scala	Play Framework	High-velocity Reactive web framework for Java and Scala	Lightweight, stateless, and web-friendly architecture Built on Akka Supports predictable and minimal resource-consumption for highly-scalable applications Developer-friendly
Java	Ninja Web Framework	Full-stack web framework	Fast Developer-friendly Rapid prototyping Plain vanilla Java, dependency injection, first-class IDE integration Simple and fast to test (mocked tests/integration tests) Excellent build and CI support Clean codebase – easy to extend
Java	RESTEASY	JBoss-based implementation that integrates several frameworks to help to build RESTful Web and Java applications	Fast and reliable Large community Enterprise-ready Security support
Java	RESTLET	A lightweight and comprehensive framework based on Java, suitable for both server and client applications.	Lightweight Large community Native REST support Connectors set

JavaScript	Express.js	Minimal and flexible Node.js-based JavaScript framework for mobile and web applications	HTTP utility methods Security updates Templating engine
PHP	Laravel	An open source web-app builder based on PHP and the MVC architecture pattern	Intuitive interface Blade template engine Eloquent ORM as default
Elixir	Phoenix (Elixir)	Powered with the Elixir functional language, a reliable and faster micro-framework	MVC-based High application performance Erlong virtual machine enables better use of resources
Python	Pyramid	Python-based micro-framework	Lightweight Function decorators Events and subscribers support Easy implementations and high productivity

Summary

We are about to conclude another exciting chapter that dealt with unique, high-productive, lightweight, developer friendly, quick-time-to-market, highly-scalable frameworks from three major programming languages—Java, Go (Golang), and Python. You might have observed that this chapter covered the most popular frameworks and their core functionality and touched on a few noteworthy features along the way. This chapter gave readers a few ideas about the frameworks' advantages and disadvantages. We discussed *Spring-Boot, Light 4j, Spark Framework, Dropwizard, Gin-gonic, Revel, Django,* and *Flask*. It's evident that there are several excellent frameworks you can use to jump-start your RESTful API development using your programming language of choice. But one chapter, and only a few pages of information, doesn't begin to cover the greatness of these frameworks and what they bring to the table. We hope this chapter gave you a fair idea of the popular frameworks so that you can kick-start not only your prototyping but also production-grade RESTful applications. In the next chapter, we'll explore best practices for migrating legacy applications to capable microservices.

Further reading

- *Building RESTful Python Web Services* by Gastón C. Hillar, `https://www.packtpub.com/application-development/building-restful-python-web-services` October 2016
- *Building RESTful Web services with Go* by Naren Yellavula, `https://www.packtpub.com/application-development/building-restful-web-services-go`

11
Legacy Modernization to Microservices-Centric Apps

Legacy applications are typically monolithic, massive, and inflexible, comprising millions of lines of code. They are neither modular nor modern. It's very difficult to bring in any changes on particular portions of them. However, they have been contributing immensely in successfully running a majority of the business behemoths across the globe. Mainframe servers are the most powerful and high-performance IT infrastructures hosting and running a variety of complex legacy applications. Though mission-critical applications are being run on mainframes, modern-day computing mandates for a kind of marriage between mainframe computing and web-scale computing. That is, we need easily-manageable and -maintainable applications. On the infrastructure side, we need open, highly compartmentalized, programmable, optimized, and organized IT infrastructures.

Thus, there is a push for legacy applications to embrace the newly-introduced innovations in software engineering. There are many noteworthy architectural styles, process optimization techniques, and tools to speed up the transformation process. Digital transformation forces us to deliver faster. Every organization's priority is to have well-designed
applications, the ability to deploy to on-premise and cloud environments as well as deploy independently, update services, and deploy defect fixes and new features in hours or days, not months.

In this chapter, we'll discuss how the **microservices architecture (MSA)** is the way forward for modern applications that are highly nimble, versatile, and resilient.

The chapter objectives include the following:

- Describing the needs for legacy application modernization
- Delineating why applications have to be modernized to be migrated and run in cloud environments
- Depicting how the combination of microservices and containers is the preferred one for legacy modernization
- Detailing the legacy modernization methodology

Technical requirements

Readers should be comfortable with the following popular technologies and tools:

- Docker-enabled containerization platforms
- The microservices architecture
- API gateways and management suites
- Microservices design principles and patterns
- Microservices composition (orchestration and choreography)
- Cloud operations

A preview of containers and microservices

With the surging popularity of the open source Docker containerization platform, the domain of containerization has accelerated in an unprecedented manner. Today, use of containerization has become widespread among IT professionals. Any kind of software can be easily containerized through automated tools. Thus, there are container-ready images in standardized format made available in public and private repositories. To modernize legacy applications, the use of containers as the most efficient wrapping mechanism is emerging and evolving.

The use of containers to modernize legacy applications brings forth a few advantages. The main point of containerization is to remove the infrastructure dependency from legacy applications. That is, containerized applications can run on any platform and infrastructure without any tweaking. Any of the infrastructure's complexities are instantly eliminated with this containerization paradigm. Thus, legacy applications become portable and can be integrated with other applications easily.

Once containerized, any legacy application can interact with third-party applications. Enabling compatibility with web, cloud, and mobile platforms becomes easier and faster. With the aid of various platform solutions for delivering multi-container applications, legacy applications can be blended to become more relevant for their owners and end users. Migrating containerized legacy applications from a local cloud to remote clouds, or from one public cloud to another public cloud, becomes simple. The security, stability, and scalability of legacy applications can be strengthened by attaching additional capabilities from outside.

Thus, the noteworthy advancements being brought into the containerization phenomenon directly and indirectly impact legacy modernization. There are several crucial advantages of the containerization movement, especially for the strategic and tough goal of legacy modernization. Legacy software can be subdivided into many different domains, and each of those modules is being deployed in different containers. Now, to guarantee higher performance and throughput, different containers can be run on different infrastructures. An I/O-intensive application module can be made to run on physical/**bare-metal (BM)** servers. Some containerized application services can be deployed in public clouds to take advantage of their availability, scalability, and security capabilities. Thus, legacy applications that are modernized through the use of containers are typically empowered to be modern, agile, and adaptive.

Modernizing legacy applications is accomplished through the following methods:

- **Rearchitecting the application**: A new appropriate and modern architecture is being produced and, accordingly, architectural decisions, components, connectivity, and capabilities are designed and implemented.
- **Replatforming the application**: The legacy application can be deployed in newer platforms in order to be categorized as a modern application.
- **Refactoring the application**: Applications are partitioned into many components, which target a specific business functionality. The identified business functionality is rewritten with microservices, which are then fused with one another to produce the desired application.

Introducing the microservices architecture

As mentioned several times in this book, MSA is being positioned as the next-generation application architectural pattern. Microservices are constructed, compiled, and deployed as a separate project. Containers are the most optimal unit of microservices development and deployment. Every microservice is blessed with its own data store. They aren't compiled into software solutions. Instead, they're implemented as standalone services to be integrated and orchestrated via standards-based and communication protocols.

Every service is being given an interface using the simple-to-use RESTful APIs. Microservices are carefully versioned not to adversely affect any other user microservices and applications. For example, for a **business-to-consumer (B2C)** e-commerce application, a microservice may be developed to provide a products catalog. Another microservice takes care of procurement, another is for payment, and so on. Thus, microservices are independently developed by distributed teams and then deployed.

Complicated and sophisticated applications are being constructed through the leverage of microservices. On the other side, massive applications are being dismantled into a collection of microservices.

Microservices are typically small and independent processes that communicate with one other using well-defined and language-agnostic APIs. They are usable, reusable, interoperable, dynamically-composable, and self-defined. Microservices expose their unique and business-centric capabilities through well-intended interfaces to the outside world. Thus software integration gets simplified and sped up in a formalized manner. There are cross-cutting concerns and horizontal (business-agnostic) functions that usually get replicated across the source code for any enterprise-grade software system. They can be centralized using microservices. Some functions have to be frequently updated and upgraded using advanced technologies. Thus, not only application development, but also the maintenance aspect are both worrisome factors for worldwide enterprises. These specialized functionalities can be built as microservices and then exposed so they can be easily found and bound in software applications.

Why legacy modernization?

Legacy software applications were written decades ago using outdated programming languages and are usually run on mainframe servers. They are massive in size, and hence, the goals of modification and maneuverability are very tough to implement. Third-party integration is another difficult assignment. To incorporate changes (induced by business, technology, and user) is time-consuming and error-prone. They're tightly coupled and usually run in a single process. All these properties make them unamendable and unapproachable for any kind of crucial advancements. They are not modern in the sense that they are not generally web and mobile-enabled. Precisely speaking, they aren't agile or adaptive. They're resisting technology upgrades, which makes them very expensive to maintain. Thus, moving from legacy applications to modern applications by leveraging a bevy of pioneering technologies, programming languages, and development frameworks and platforms has gained a lot of attention. With newer architectural patterns and styles emerging and evolving, software architects and developers are keen to embrace them to bring forth competitive applications that can easily fulfil the varying expectations of businesses and people.

The concept of DevOps is sweeping across IT organizations in order to eliminate any kind of friction between development teams and operation teams. Greenfield projects and cloud-native applications are being deployed and operated using this new concept. There are write-ups in this chapter about DevOps, which is being positioned as a must for the digital era. As there is constant chopping and changing being demanded in software solutions from various sources, the significance of DevOps is garnering more support.

For monolithic applications, functionalities are duplicated in the source code. Several units across the enterprise bring forth their functionalities, which have to be integrated with the core application. When a company buys another company, their source code has to be integrated. Such integrations ultimately lead to the duplication of the same functionality. If there's any modification to be incorporated in to a single functionality, the whole monolithic application has to be recompiled and redeployed. There are definitely some deficiencies as far as legacy applications are concerned. That's why modernization has started to gain attention.

Legacy-to-digital application modernization

Application modernization is all about empowering currently-running applications to meet business goals and customer expectations, which are constantly evolving. There are a number of digital technologies and **artificial intelligence** (**AI**) algorithms emerging, which are evolving quickly. We have scores of edge/digitization technologies, such as sensors, actuators, implants, wearables, stickers, tags, codes, chips, controllers, smart dust, specks, beacons, and LED elements, for creating digitized entities out of physical, mechanical, and electrical systems. That is, our ground-level physical systems become digitized, joining mainstream computing.

A bevy of digital technologies (cloud, mobility, social, IoT, and analytics) are gathering a lot of attention because they're capable of bringing in a dazzling array of digital innovations, disruptions, and transformations. With the maturity of AI algorithms, the domain of digital intelligence is gaining prominence in making sense of digital data. Thus, the real digital transformation involves digital and digital-intelligence technologies. Also, there are outdated and old-fashioned applications and technologies aplenty. To attain a real digital transformation, these old, yet currently-running, applications have to be modified using modernization and migration tools. The hugely popular digital technologies that we've mentioned have to be leveraged to bring advancement to legacy applications.

Accomplishing modernization

Many modernization and migration experts have spoken on how to accomplish modernization without bringing down existing business workloads and IT services. To perform modernization, whether to go for re-engineering, re-architecting, re-platforming, and so on, is the moot question to be answered. Other considerations include whether modernization helps applications maintain their original performance level and capabilities, such as scalability, availability, reliability, and security. The following diagram shows how a litany of application modernization and migration technologies come in handy for elevating legacy applications to newer applications that fulfill business needs, market demands, customer satisfaction, and higher productivity:

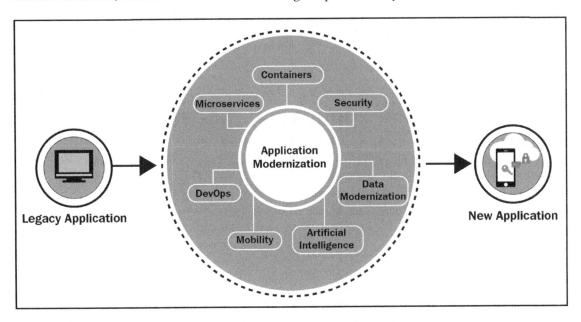

Source: https://www.winwire.com/wp-content/uploads/2018/07/Application-Modernization-Assess-Strategize-Modernize.png

Path-breaking technologies and breakthrough tools enable the smooth transition toward newer applications that are knowledge-filled, event-driven, service-oriented, cloud-hosted, process-aware, and people-centric.

Approaching legacy application modernization

Having realized the need to modernize legacy software packages in order to be relevant to their stakeholders, partners, employees, and consumers, business organizations are asking their IT teams to come with viable techniques to speed up and simplify the aspects of modernizing legacy applications. There are a few strategically-sound application architectures, scores of methodologies, and best practices toward application modernization. Modernized applications are being readied to work on cloud environments, which are generally consolidated, centralized, shared, virtualized and containerized, and automated ones. In short, cloud environments are highly optimized and organized in order to be extremely and elegantly agile and adaptive. Applications have to be readied to run in clouds without any problem and to reap all the originally envisaged benefits of the cloud. The emergence of MSA can help to accelerate legacy modernization.

Microservices-centric legacy application modernization

Microservices are fine-grained, self-defined, and autonomous services that produce and sustain next-generation, enterprise-grade applications. With MSA, every application is structured as a collection of microservices. In other words, when appropriately combining multiple microservices, we arrive at competent applications, which are cloud-hosted, service-oriented, event-driven, insight-filled, enterprise-grade, and people-centric. Software architects are very excited about the futuristic and artistic role of the MSA pattern in architecting production-ready software solutions. The design of complicated and sophisticated applications that leverage hundreds of different and distributed microservices as application modules is attracting a lot of attention. The MSA paradigm is being positioned as an agile application design methodology. This is being seen as a positive development in **software engineering (SE)**, as there are many agile development techniques and frameworks. Also, the solidity of the DevOps culture in large-sized business enterprises is speeding up the rollout of applications into production environments. That is, issues and friction between development and deployment teams are being surmounted and this empowerment leads to speedier application deployment in various environments (development, testing, staging, and production). Thus, development and deployment are being augmented through a host of advancements in the IT field.

The flourishing MSA style significantly simplified designing and architecting applications. If our business workloads and IT services are made out of microservices, they become extremely flexible, scalable, customizable, and configurable. We've seen why worldwide enterprises are very serious in embracing the MSA pattern in order to be competitive in their day-to-day activities.

Architects and experts have come out with a few achievable mechanisms for smoothly transitioning from monolithic to microservices-based applications. The modernization steps are being accomplished through multiple phases. The first phase is illustrated in the following diagram (source: `https://dzone.com/articles/choosing-a-legacy-software-modernization-strategy`). This talks about identifying the distinct business functionalities of the legacy application and separating them out to implement them as microservices by giving the underlying service implements, which are typically polyglot, a RESTful API. In the *Service composition* section, we talked about phase two of the following diagram:

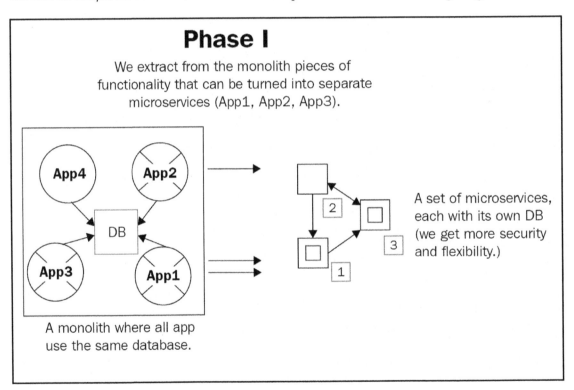

Service extraction

At the end of the first phase, we get a number of microservices with their own data-storage facilities. These microservices are modular in nature and interoperable, and they are intrinsically capable of interacting with one another through the APIs. The widely-recommended design approach is to design and develop microservices for different domains. The widely-used aspect is **domain-driven design** (**DDD**). For example, take an e-commerce application. The domains include the shopping cart, payment, shipping, notifications, credit verification, and analytics. Every domain is looked at as a business functionality and hence implemented as a microservice. There can be multiple methods within a microservice. There can be intra- as well as inter-microservice communication and collaboration.

The microservices within a domain are supposed to interact frequently. There are situations where microservices in a domain have to connect and correspond with microservices in other domains in order to fulfill different business processes and activities. Thus, an e-business and e-commerce application is bound to have several domains and hundreds of microservices. With containers emerging as the best fit for hosting and running microservices in a fault-tolerant manner, there can be thousands of containers to run microservices-centric applications.

Service composition

The second phase (`https://dzone.com/articles/choosing-a-legacy-software-modernization-strategy`) is to go for service composition. In the other chapters, we discussed various composition techniques and tools; there are two approaches—orchestration and choreography.

The following diagram conveys how a centralized broker/hub/bus comes in handy when establishing connectivity and accomplishing data processing:

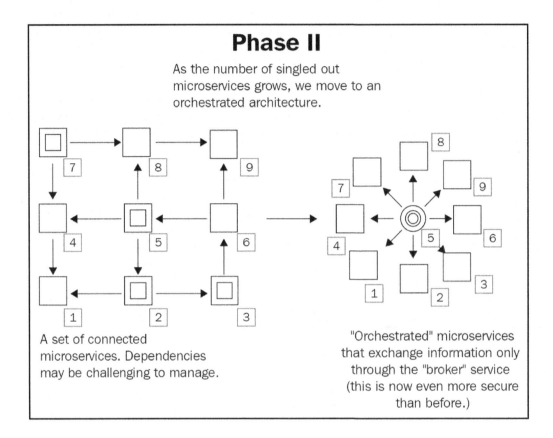

Service migration

The third phase is all about migrating microservices to cloud environments (private, public, and hybrid). There are several public cloud environments across the globe and they offer a number of benefits, such as affordability, scalability, availability, and security. Microservices can accommodate all kinds of changes induced by business needs, end users, expectations, and technology advancements. The scale and simplicity, along with frequent changes, make microservices the perfect tool for enterprise IT in fulfilling the various functional and non-functional requirements. Also, microservices enable the smooth transition from monolithic to microservices applications.

Not all applications are fit for modernization and migration to cloud environments. Applications have to be continuously subjected to a variety of investigations in order to double-check their value and validity. Application rationalization, optimization, and modernization are vital for applications to be continuously relevant for their administrators and users. With the arrival of highly-optimized and -organized IT infrastructures, applications need to be be able to work in newer environments while guaranteeing all the performance requirements. Some applications have to be meticulously refactored to be taken to the cloud. Experts prescribe a series of best practices for legacy modernization and migration. We'll look at one such approach in the following section; more details can be found at `https://dzone.com/articles/choosing-a-legacy-software-modernization-strategy`.

Container-centric legacy application modernization

Legacy applications can be directly containerized to be presented as modernized applications for cloud environments. The other prominent option is to subdivide the legacy application into multiple components, where each component caters to a business functionality. Now every business functionality can be converted into a microservice. Thus, there are microservices-centric and container-centric methods for effecting legacy modernization and migration to cloud environments.

Any application can be directly containerized, but this transition may not work in the long run. Hence, applications have to be segmented into smaller, more easily-manageable pieces. Then those segments have to be service-enabled and then containerized. There are best practices, enabling patterns, knowledge guides, success stories, case studies, optimized processes, integrated and insightful platforms, and proven procedures for smoothening this sort of legacy remediation. Best-in-class frameworks and automated tools are flourishing to tackle the complexities that are associated with legacy transformations. Here's a list expressed by one modernization expert.

The first step is to break the monolithic application into a group of distinguishable components. These components can be easily and elegantly service-enabled and containerized. Those containerized images are stocked in publicly-available image repositories. These components have to be extremely modular (loosely or lightly coupled and highly cohesive) in order to contribute to the goals of modernization and migration. These are the business functionalities, the typical middle-tier components in any three-tiered application.

Having created a collection of microservices that together make up the business logic of the application, the second step is to build data access as a service. That is, develop data services and expose them so that any application can use them to get the right data to complete business tasks. This setup decouples business and data logic so that there's no possibility for any kind of dependency-initiated issues. This data-logic layer is the final one, as per the specifications of three-tier applications. In the first step, we focused on creating application containers. In the second step, we talked about volume containers in order to store data to empower applications accordingly.

The last step is all about testing. For an enterprise-scale application, we can have several microservices and their instances. Also, containers as the service runtime are now manifold. Microservices and their many instances can be run in separate containers and hence there will be many containers in a typical IT environment; that is, for an application, there can be multiple interactive and collaborative microservices. Each microservice can be run in multiple containers in order to support redundancy. Widely-demanded high availability can be achieved through multiple containers for a single microservice. Due to the fickle nature of containers, architects recommend many containers for hosting one microservice. To ensure high availability, there can be many instances of microservices. This way, if one service or container goes down, its service instances deployed in other containers come to the rescue. However, the real difficulty lies in testing such an intertwined environment. Precisely speaking, monolithic applications need to be tuned to become distributed and complicated applications. Though modern applications are agile, affordable, and adaptive, the management and operational complexities of microservices-centric applications are bound to escalate. Further on, detecting errors and debugging them to make applications error-free is a tedious job indeed. There are a few automated testing tools emerging for testing microservices. Experts are unearthing various ways of testing distributed microservices. Also, the testing procedure is being illustrated for composite microservices.

Refactoring and rewriting

We've been writing about how the powerful emergence of microservices architecture is instigating the need for legacy modernization in order to embrace modernity. As we all know, the key mitigation technique has been *divide and conquer*. This mantra has been shining not only to engineer fresh systems but also to disintegrate legacy systems. As legacy applications are hugely complicated, partitioning them into a number of smaller pieces is also being accomplished through segmentation approaches. Functionality-based segregation is one way of implementing disintegration. Once a legacy application is subdivided into a number of application modules, the real modernization begins; that is, there are many application services to be extricated out of archaic and massive applications.

As mentioned previously, the extracted application components are made into microservices in order to easily migrate them to cloud environments. There is a big gap between application components and microservices. Functionally, they are almost the same. But the structure of application components is hugely different from microservices. Therefore, it's paramount to devise a viable mechanism to close the gulf between application components and microservices. Refactoring or rewriting is the recommended approach to achieve modern legacy applications. Refactoring legacy software into a suite of microservices and enabling them to talk to one another on a per-need basis is being promoted as one of the surest ways to achieve modernization. With the faster maturity and stability of the microservices architectural style and containerization-enabled platforms, refactoring large-scale applications into fine-grained and well-designed microservices is gaining prominence.

Modernization technique terms

Legacy modernization is being accomplished in several ways. Applications can be subdivided into a number of smaller service components and each service is being rewritten using a modern programming language while guaranteeing the legacy application's functionality. Even the original architecture of the legacy application can be changed using the latest architectural styles, such as SOA, EDA, or a combination of both. The legacy applications currently running on centralized and mainframe servers can be modernized to run on completely new platforms and infrastructures, such as cloud environments. Thus, the modernization strategy development and planning are done by taking several principles, goals, technologies, and tools into account. At different layers and levels, the required modernization gets done in a risk-free and strategically sound manner:

- **Refactoring** typically refers to reorganizing an application's source code in order to bring some clarity and changes. Suppose the code written isn't modular, or the code has a lot of duplicated code as it's been written by different teams over the years of its development and maintenance. The integration with newly-acquired company software may also bring in some complexities. There are several other reasons to modernize. So, factoring out the code in order to fulfill some new requirements (business, technology, and users) is being touted as code refactoring.

- **Rearchitecting and redesigning** both mean the same thing. Legacy applications can be modernized by rearchitecting the application using newer technologies, such as middleware solutions, database systems, execution platforms, visualization toolkits, and software infrastructure solutions. Also, with newer patterns for designing application components, redesigning is gaining prominence. With these architectural and design changes, new applications can have higher performance, scalability, security, availability, resilience, and sustainability. With powerful message-oriented middleware platforms and newer databases, such as NoSQL and NewSQL, modernization is a continuous affair to satisfy evolving business needs and to ensure the delight of customers.

- **Replatforming** involves taking the legacy application to be deployed and running it on newer platforms and infrastructures in order to accrue the platform's and infrastructure's benefits.

- **Rewriting** the application source code using modern programming languages is done in order to experience the distinct advantages of the new programming language. For example, **Ballerina** is a new programming language and is considered by some as the best-in-class language for coding microservices. This language simplifies service, data, and application integration.

Here's a list of a few best practices while performing modernization:

- We must be sure that the refactoring technique works. After taking an easy-to-do application component out of the legacy application under transformation, then we must embark on refactoring or rewriting; that is, we can refactor the source code of the application component to convert it into a microservice. Otherwise, we can rewrite the code to craft a microservice without changing the functionality of the original application component. Then, the idea is to take the version that's very close to the final implementation.

- There's no need to refactor or rewrite the other components of the legacy application. Use the stub mechanism to check whether the refurbished or rewritten component mimics the old behavior; that is, it's mandatory to establish a seamless and spontaneous connectivity for the existing application components (not yet refactored or rewritten) with the newly-formulated service to understand whether there's any deviation or deficiency. This way, little wastage of time is guaranteed for legacy modernization, which happens to be a time-consuming job.

- Once a microservice is readied, it has to be taken to one or more software repositories (public and/or private) to enable access and usage by software developers and testers. This kind of centralized storage also contributes for source-code version control. There are **continuous integration** (**CI**) solutions to integrate, build, and test software services. With the overwhelming adoption of the enterprise DevOps concept, business applications get continuous and consistent integration, delivery, and deployment in order to take applications and services to their end users quickly, without any risk.

- With the unprecedented popularity of the containerization movement, containerizing software applications has been getting more attention. Containerizing microservices brings a number of technical advantages to the table. There are write-ups and articles detailing how to quickly deliver and deploy microservices individually and collectively. With container clustering, orchestration, and management platform solutions emerging, the containerization paradigm is becoming penetrative, participative, and pervasive. There are a litany of automated tools to augment the various activities associated with cloud orchestration, realizing multi-cloud container applications, and infrastructure as code. The convergence of containers and microservices opens up a growing array of innovations, disruptions, and transformations. There are integrated platforms that enable the dream service era.

- Application components have to be chosen for refactoring or rewriting using some priority factors. Not all components are suitable for modernization. There are a few important parameters required to do the prioritization properly. The key parameters to be considered include the ease of extraction, the roadmap, and possible risks. Some of the components may become obsolete. Thus, prioritization plays an important role in accomplishing the modernization job in an affordable, risk-free, and strategically-sound manner.

- Data virtualization is the way forward for application modules to correspond realistically with the data sources of the legacy application. It's therefore recommended that instead of focusing on data-structure transformation, focus on creating and using appropriate proxies that can transform data from different databases into a standardized format. This standardization helps the newly-created microservices (whether through refactoring or rewriting) to connect and interact with the data without any major hitch.

Microservices are small and accommodative. Fixing defects, security holes, and vulnerabilities is quite easy with microservices. Performance increments, root cause analysis, and unified threat management form composite applications that are business-critical, process-aware, and cloud-enabled. The faster deployment of microservices in production environments is another positive factor. Specific microservices in microservices-centric applications can be replaced with newer ones, whereas this sort of facility isn't available in monolithic applications. Adding features is therefore a smooth affair.

Legacy modernization through microservices

There are many real-world reasons why the industry is very optimistic about MSA for modernizing legacy applications. There are several valid differences between monolithic and microservices-centric applications, as represented in the following diagram:

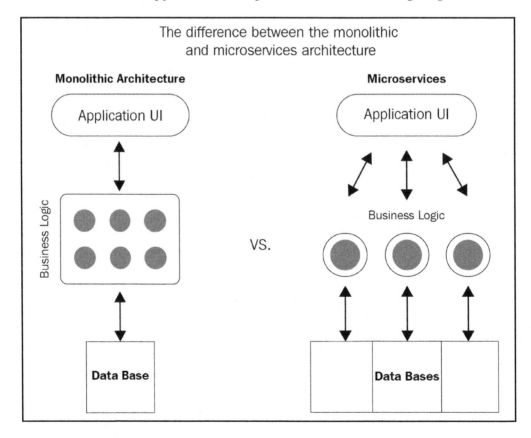

Monolithic applications follow a heavily-centralized architecture, whereas **Microservices** go for a distributed architecture. Due to the exponential increase in data size and the usage of commodity servers, the IT world is leaning toward distributed computing. Also, services are being developed and deployed by worldwide software developers to geographically-distributed servers. Thus, distributed computing can't be taken lightly anymore. MSA intrinsically supports the distributed computing characteristics and hence, is flourishing.

As previously explained, each microservice fulfills one or more business functionalities. That is, different business capabilities are implemented through separate microservices running on different processes. For an e-commerce application, we can have microservices for various modules, such as the shopping cart, customer analytics, the payment gateway, warehousing, shipping, replenishment, inventory management, and email notifications. Web-scale applications are embracing the MSA in order to be business-friendly.

For applications with frequently varying loads (where the number of users changes quickly and there can be sudden spikes in the number of messages with different data sizes), there is an insistence for mechanisms that innately support dynamic, horizontal, and real-time scalability. Through containerized microservices, we can achieve that kind of scalability, as containers are lightweight and can boot up in a matter of seconds.

Microservices eliminate the problems associated with the tightly-coupled application components of monolithic applications. Microservices can be integrated through various middleware products (synchronous and asynchronous communication). Due to the decoupling nature of microservices, microservices can be independently designed, developed, and deployed in production environments. That is, updating and upgrading microservices dooesn't affect other components of a microservices-centric application. There are a few novel testing and deployment methods emerging and evolving in order to bring the utmost dynamism to microservices environments.

The distinctions of microservices

Microservices are technology-agnostic, which means the technology lock-in problem gets resolved through the MSA style. Therefore, it's being touted as a solution that fully complies with the polyglot architecture pattern. And microservices can be coded using any programming language. There are several microservice development frameworks for speedy implementation and installation. MSA supports a number of the latest communication and data-transmission protocols. The service adapter ecosystem is continuously growing in order to integrate with disparate application services. The interfaces of microservices are very formalized and hence dependency issues don't rear their ugly heads.

Composite applications are quickly realized through static as well as dynamic service-composition methods. There are script languages for writing configuration and composition files. There are data representation, exchange, and persistence mechanisms. The closer association with the containerization movement has come at the right time for microservices to speed up software engineering tasks. On the other side, microservices emerge as the best at partitioning legacy and old-fashioned applications into multiple interactive and autonomous microservices. Thus, legacy modernization is being spruced up by business enterprises due to advancements in the MSA space.

The code samples

In the GitHub repository, readers can find some examples for developing microservices using the Java language. Then, there are some examples of how to compose multiple microservices to produce process-aware and multi-container composite applications. Legacy refactoring is all about making changes in the code segments of a legacy function to present it as a microservice. The combination of such microservices results in microservices-centric modern applications. Microservices can be built from the ground up. Or, using automated tools, legacy application code snippets can be converted into microservices.

The major hurdles to overcome

However, there are certain hurdles to overcome. This section lists them out. Though the MSA style is being proclaimed as the most optimized and organized approach for legacy modernization, there are a few tricky issues confronting business and IT teams:

- Microservices, as previously indicated, result in distributed systems and hence, developers have to explore how to extract the various business functions from the tightly-integrated monolithic applications, refactor or rewrite the chosen ones as microservices, and keep the newly-formed microservices linked to the remainder of the legacy application in order to verify whether everything works as wanted. This isn't an easy task and hence it's a definite obstacle on the modernization journey.

- Previously, any monolithic application ran inside a single process. The participating application components talked to one another using the language feature. There are **remote procedure calls (RPCs)** and **remote method invocations (RMIs)**; in-process communication is risk-free and fast. However, microservices' calls go over a network. RESTful interfaces are the dominant way of approaching distant microservices. Network latency and other network-related problems can damage the resilience of microservices. That is, inter-service communication can cause some network-associated issues. Microservices are being stuffed with APIs. APIs are the first point of contact for any microservice to interact with other microservices, which can be running in the same machine, rack, floor, or even in geographically-distributed cloud environments. API versions can differ, the data formats of messages getting exchanged between microservices APIs can create mismatch problems, network congestions can occur, and the varying loads on microservices may contribute for the slowdown and even failure of microservices.
- Testing microservices brings its own problems. Monolithic applications can be easily tested because they have a combined, single code base. That isn't the case with microservices. In the case of microservices, every microservice has to be individually tested. Further on, microservices also have to be tested collectively. There are newer approaches that simplify testing microservices.

Microservices acquire special consideration because of the widespread adoption of DevOps tools. The aim of DevOps is to speed up service deployment. That is, specific services can be chosen and deployed. Thus, to avail of all the benefits of the MSA, business enterprises have to embrace DevOps.

Without an ounce of doubt, microservices open up fresh possibilities and opportunities. Though there are a few options for legacy modernization, modernizing microservices-centric legacy applications is being pronounced as the best way forward. The microservices approach is the best way for enterprises to be digitally disrupted and transformed.

Modernizing and migrating legacy applications – the role of cloud environments

The technology space is continuously evolving, and is being strengthened with the adoption of newer technologies and tools. For example, the cloud paradigm has redefined the IT domain completely. Cloud technologies have made it possible to have highly optimized and organized IT to host any kind of business application. Hitherto unknown IT services are being formulated and delivered, and newer business models are emerging to cater to different sections and segments of the market, which is extremely knowledge-driven these days.

In the recent past, we've heard about containers and microservices more often. They are showing a lot of promise in bringing advancements in software engineering. The cloud journey is also progressing speedily. This progress means old applications need to be refurbished using the latest technologies, so they can be hosted and managed in cloud environments. That is, massive applications are partitioned into a pool of microservices, then they are containerized, and stocked in container-image directories. Container orchestration platforms then provision container resources, fetch container images, and deploy them.

The extensive use of DevOps concepts has accelerated IT operations. A kind of DevOps pipeline (the end-to-end workflow) gets created to sequence the actions to be taken to take the code to production environments. When the source code of any freshly-baked or changed microservice is committed into code repositories, typically a signal is sent to the chosen CI tool (such as Jenkins). CI tools are for building, testing, and integrating software applications. Then, continuous delivery and deployment tools take the application to production environments. In this chapter, we've talked extensively about how legacy applications are being modernized into a spectrum of microservices and then migrated to cloud environments.

The need for cloud environments

The cloud idea has brought a paradigm shift into the IT space. Businesses are consciously embracing this technology in order to be relevant to their customers and consumers. Cloud environments are software-defined and hence cloud infrastructures (server machines, storage appliances, and networking components) are programmable, network-accessible, remotely monitorable and manageable, and customizable. All kinds of infrastructures can be virtualized and containerizable. Thus, clouds are consolidated, centralized, and shareable. Increasingly, cloud environments are being integrated, allowing us to have hybrid and multi-cloud environments. Further on, with the steady growth of the device ecosystem, there's a rush toward setting up and sustaining fog or edge clouds in order to accomplish real-time data capture, processing, knowledge discovery, and dissemination and actuation. That is, our everyday environments (homes, hotels, hospitals, and so on) are being stuffed with a variety of heterogeneous devices. These devices are mainly resource-constrained and some are resource-intensive. These devices are deeply connected and embedded systems. There are solutions and approaches to dynamically create device clouds. Thus, edge clouds are expanding the cloud landscape. There are a litany of communication and data-transmission protocols for enabling **device-to-device** (D2D) integration.

There are IoT gateway solutions and brokers for mediating between devices at the ground level and software applications getting hosted in faraway cloud environments; that is, device-to-cloud.

Device-to-cloud (D2C) integration is gaining prominence these days with the increased availability and adoption of device middleware solutions. In short, there are new cloud environments emerging and evolving in order to cater to varying demands. That is, there are public, private, hybrid, and edge clouds. Multi-cloud environments are also being considered by enterprises to escape the vendor lock-in problem.

With enabling technologies being unearthed and supported, federated cloud environments may soon emerge to meet some special requirements. Clouds are highly optimized and organized IT infrastructures. Resource utilization has gone up significantly with cloudification. Appropriate cloud locations are chosen to guarantee higher performance. Clouds are intrinsically meeting various non-functional requirements, such as scalability, availability, security, and flexibility. Web-scale and customer-facing applications are already deployed in public cloud environments. Through extra security measures, such as **virtual private networks (VPNs)**, firewall and load-balancing appliances, and intrusion-detection and prevention systems, public cloud environments are secured and made safe in order to boost the confidence of users and enterprises alike. Workloads are subjected to a variety of investigations and deployed in the most appropriate physical machines/BM servers, **virtual machines (VMs)**, and containers. There are pioneering scheduling solutions and algorithms for tasks and resources; that is, scheduling resources for all kinds of incoming jobs is fully automated. Then, there are energy-efficiency methods being applied in order to ensure power conservation and reduce heat dissipation. There are cost efficiencies being accrued out of the cloudification movement.

Thus, IT infrastructures are set to become agile, adaptive, and affordable in their offerings. These are the reasons why the cloud paradigm is becoming an important ingredient in the IT journey. Businesses are being automated and augmented through IT disruptions and transformations. People-empowerment through scores of innovations in the IT space is the next realistic target. Thus, we have clouds being formed out of commodity servers, appliances, and high-end server machines. There are converged and hyper-converged infrastructures to serve as cloud environments. In the recent past, it was forecast that the future belongs to networked and embedded devices that form ad hoc and purpose-specific clouds quickly to achieve specific data-processing requirements. Thus, applications are being modernized as pools of services, and these services are being taken to cloud environments (public, private, hybrid, and edge/fog). Due to the surging popularity of the cloud as the one-stop IT solution for all kinds of business needs, legacy modernization and migration is seeing heightened attention.

A case study for legacy modernization and migration

Having understood the strategic significance of integrated and insightful applications, enterprises are strategizing and planning modernization and migration plans. As reported earlier, most of the enterprise, cloud, web, and embedded applications are being built as containerized and microservices-centric applications; legacy applications should be modified with a variety of automation processes and products.

Blu Age Velocity (`https://www.bluage.com/products/blu-age-velocity`) is famous for automated modernization. This offering automates and accelerates modernizing legacy applications. It can do both reverse and forward engineering. That is, it can translate legacy applications into microservices-centric applications. Readers can find many case studies and references for automated application modernization at `https://www.bluage.com/references`.

We all know that there are two key data-processing methods. Batch or bulk processing is all about batching or accumulating data to initiate the processing at scheduled hours. However, with the availability of real-time data-processing technologies and platforms, real-time data processing is picking up. Also, data starts to lose its value as time passes, and hence it should be collected, cleansed, and crunched immediately in order to extricate timely insights. In the mainframe era, batch processing was the main method for data processing due to inherent IT resource constraints. Legacy applications are predominantly single-threaded and hence parallel execution isn't possible at the language level. With multi-threaded languages and applications, parallel execution gains immense prominence. With multi-core and multi-processor computers becoming affordable, parallel processing at the infrastructure level is being achieved. With the emergence of virtual machines and containers, having multiple instances of these server resources leads us to fast-track the application's execution. Newer programming languages intrinsically support multi-threading and hence concurrent processing is prominent these days. With cloud infrastructures increasingly being compartmentalized, the goal of doing tasks in parallel has gained momentum. Now, with the surge of edge, local, and remote cloud environments, these restrictions are slowly fading away and real-time analytics is booming. That is, legacy applications that previously did batch processing are modernized to do real-time processing using cloud-based platforms.

The combination of microservices and serverless computing speeds up legacy modernization

As mentioned previously, microservices can be orchestrated to craft bigger and better applications. For legacy modernization, business capabilities are subdivided into discrete microservices. On the reverse side, these easily-manageable, independently-deployable, and autonomous services can be composed into process-aware, business-critical, and composite services. Microservices are operating in their own environments and interact with other services in a loosely-coupled manner. Thus, microservices are isolated and hence if there's a problem with one microservice, it doesn't affect other microservices. Because of this independence, microservices can be replaced and substituted by advanced services, replicated across, updated, and upgraded without impacting others.

Serverless computing is a recent phenomenon unleashed by various public **cloud service providers (CSPs)**, such as AWS, Azure, IBM, and Google. The server infrastructure is being readied and taken care of by CSPs for smoothly-running functions. That's why the buzzword **function as a service (FaaS)** is being widely reported. The idea is as follows. We started with bare-metal servers. Then virtual machines and containers came into the picture as the optimized resource and runtime for applications. Now, we are heading toward functions. Many developers started to create modular systems using code-level components (functions). These code-level components are attached to current applications on a per-need basis in order to enable applications to be relevant to their constituents. A library is a collection of functions. Then the empowered applications are compiled and deployed to be subscribed to and used for a small fee. This arrangement can guarantee high performance. But the reusability of functions is not up to the level of microservices.

Primarily, the configuration management challenges of functions cause a lot of trouble. That is, different application projects may mandate different versions of the function. If a library of functions gets updated, all the applications that depend on the library have to go through a series of updates, recompiles, and redeployments. On the other hand, as repeatedly written in this book, microservices are self-contained and the goal of reusability is easily accomplished.

Serverless computing is emerging as an ideal underpinning for hosting and running microservices. Thus, it's clear that the MSA and serverless computing will provide an extensible and scalable environment. With the automation level rising continuously in cloud environments, service developers and assemblers won't need to bother setting up infrastructural components in order to run, verify, and showcase their services. Through containers, functions are deployed as an accessible entity. Containers can be quickly created to run functions and microservices. Containers are famous for real-time horizontal scalability. When the number of users goes up, new instances get provisioned immediately in order to tackle the extra load.

Summary

Microservices enabled with RESTful APIs are the hot commodity these days. Microservices have emerged as the optimal unit of application development and deployment, not only for building and running enterprise-grade and production-ready applications, but also for modernizing currently-running applications. That is, legacy applications are being dismantled as a collection of microservices. Because of their unique features, microservices are becoming established as the most appropriate unit for migrating applications to cloud environments; that is, microservices contribute immensely to crafting and running cloud-enabled applications. Fresh applications are being directly developed in cloud environments, called cloud-native applications. This chapter discussed legacy modernization, why it's becoming essential, and how the MSA pattern assists in creating modern applications from outdated applications.

With the unprecedented adoption of the microservices architecture as the most beneficial architectural style for designing and developing next-generation business-critical and IoT applications, the RESTful paradigm has earned a new lease of life. That is, due to the simplicity and sustainability of RESTful APIs, microservices are increasingly stuffed with RESTful APIs. This book covered the practical and theoretical information aspects of how RESTful services and APIs contribute to futuristic and flexible web/cloud, mobile, and IoT applications.

Other Books You May Enjoy

If you enjoyed this book, you may be interested in these other books by Packt:

Building RESTful Web Services with Java EE 8
Mario-Leander Reimer

ISBN: 9781789532883

- Dive into the latest Java EE 8 APIs relevant for developing web services
- Use the new JSON-B APIs for easy data binding
- Understand how JSON-P API can be used for flexible processing
- Implement synchronous and asynchronous JAX-RS clients
- Use server-sent events to implement server-side code
- Secure Java EE 8 web services with JSON Web Tokens

Hands-On RESTful Python Web Services - Second Edition
Gaston C. Hillar

ISBN: 9781789532227

- Select the most appropriate framework based on requirements
- Develop complex RESTful APIs from scratch using Python
- Use requests handlers, URL patterns, serialization, and validations
- Add authentication, authorization, and interaction with ORMs and databases
- Debug, test, and improve RESTful APIs with four frameworks
- Design RESTful APIs with frameworks and create automated tests

Leave a review - let other readers know what you think

Please share your thoughts on this book with others by leaving a review on the site that you bought it from. If you purchased the book from Amazon, please leave us an honest review on this book's Amazon page. This is vital so that other potential readers can see and use your unbiased opinion to make purchasing decisions, we can understand what our customers think about our products, and our authors can see your feedback on the title that they have worked with Packt to create. It will only take a few minutes of your time, but is valuable to other potential customers, our authors, and Packt. Thank you!

Index

Made in the USA
Columbia, SC
24 November 2022

72008181R00207